TEACH YOURSELF BOOKS

# UNDERSTANDING SOCIAL ANTHROPOLOGY

David Pocock, after graduating from Pembroke College, Cambridge, was lecturer in Indian Sociology at Oxford from 1954–66. Initially a Reader, and now Professor, of Social Anthropology at the University of Sussex, he was Dean at the School of African and Asian Studies from 1969–74. In 1973 he was awarded the Rivers Memorial Medal by the Royal Anthropological Institute. Professor Pocock's first field research was amongst the Asians in East Africa, followed by a study of the Gujarat in western India where most of the immigrants came from. He is now engaged on research on the Asians' adaption to life in Britain since their expulsion from Uganda. As a general anthropologist, he is particularly interested in epistemology and what he defines as the 'ethics' of the subject, in particular the belief that unless social anthropology can continue to justify itself as an education for living it should have no claim on the attention of either teachers or students.

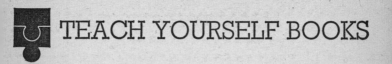
TEACH YOURSELF BOOKS

# UNDERSTANDING SOCIAL ANTHROPOLOGY

David Pocock

TEACH YOURSELF BOOKS

HODDER & STOUGHTON

ST PAUL'S HOUSE    WARWICK LANE    LONDON EC4P 4AH

*First printed 1975*

ISBN 0 340 20376 5

*Printed and bound in Great Britain for Teach Yourself Books, Hodder & Stoughton, by Cox & Wyman Ltd., London, Reading and Fakenham*

# Contents

# Foreword

When J. Manchip White published his *Teach Yourself Anthropology* in 1952 it was the first attempt by a British anthropologist to produce a systematic account of the subject for the non-specialist reader. Certainly textbooks by American scholars were available at the time, but the differences between the British and the American were so marked in those days that these accounts did not accurately reflect what was going on at British universities.

One important work preceded Manchip White's and that was Evans-Pritchard's *Social Anthropology* published in 1951. The introduction of the word 'Social' is highly significant because it points to the marked change that had been taking place in the early decades of this century not in the lecture rooms but in the research field of anthropology. This was a change which, like many intellectual changes, was slow in affecting university teaching at the undergraduate level. When Manchip White studied Social Anthropology at Cambridge he was required to read archaeology, physical anthropology and cultural or social anthropology; this syllabus is reflected in his book. Later students were able to specialise in cultural or social anthropology.

Despite this development in the universities, it is still the case that to a large extent the general reader retains ideas about anthropology which derive from an earlier period. In my experience quite a few of the people who have heard of the discipline assume that it has something to do with measuring heads and studying the differences between the various races of mankind. Others conceive that it has to do with collecting and describing the strange customs of alien peoples and to a certain extent the quaint customs which have disappeared from our own social scene, or survive only in remote rural areas.

My purpose in writing this book is twofold: first, it aims to introduce the reader to social anthropology as it is now taught in British universities; secondly, I hope to give the reader an idea of the moral and intellectual relevance of social anthropology to living in the increasingly complex society of the twentieth century. It is not possible in this field to separate moral from intellectual judgments. All our moral choices and decisions about what to do for the best, both for ourselves and for other people, rest upon our understanding of what man *is*—his nature, needs and desires. The social anthropologist, for all that he will not pretend to have a total understanding, will be alert to dimensions of human situations and problems which do not occur to other people or which they perhaps wantonly ignore. For example, when the social anthropologist hears in political or social debate the phrase 'it's only natural'—that people should act, think or feel in a certain way—he will be much more disposed to question this alleged 'naturalness' than someone who accepts it as an irrefutable proof. Much damage is done in the world simply by the abuse of the words 'nature' or 'natural'.

This book is to *introduce* the reader to social anthropology. Since 1952 there has been a steady flow of general introductions both to social anthropology as a whole and to specialised areas within the discipline. Since 1965 the Association of Social Anthropologists of the Commonwealth (founded in 1946) has produced a series of collected essays on politics, myths, economics, religion, the study of complex societies and on other themes. There are also many reliable and readable paperback books on a host of particular institutions, as well as 'readers' which bring together the writings of various hands on universal themes or theoretical issues.

The time is then past when it was sensible to try to include in a book of this nature an account of all the branches of the modern discipline of social anthropology. What I have tried to do is to teach the reader how to *think* anthropologically, to develop, that is, an anthropological sensibility. The development of such a sensibility is a prerequisite without which all the knowledge of the facts and of the theories is sterile. It is all too easy to turn the world and the diversity in human culture into a sort of museum of curiosities, interesting enough but irrelevant to our day-to-day concerns. The reader who is willing to *work* with this book, rather than simply *read* it, should find himself in the privileged position of one who is able to open up the show-cases, so to speak, handle the objects and know *why* they are interesting.

The emphasis must be upon working with this book and not simply reading it through in a few hours. If the reader wants to progress with any real profit to more specialised and detailed works, he or she will take seriously the invitation to think about and write essays on the various topics discussed. I stress the importance of this because it is the only way in the circumstances in which something like a conversation can develop not just between the reader and myself but, more important, between the reader and himself. By setting down in writing what he or she thinks to be the nature of the family or the nation, or the function of economic systems, the reader will be able to confront the facts and views which I adduce with his own experience and reflections. He will be able to assess precisely the extent to which his views have changed and the points on which he is unconvinced or with which he firmly disagrees; he will certainly know what questions he now wants to ask and therefore to which of the books listed in the reading notes at the end of each chapter he should turn. Disagreement with the views I express or the way in which I represent facts is as important as agreement. The reader who is using this book as a general introduction before going on to read social anthropology at university must not expect to find that all professional social anthropologists agree with my approach or my interpretations. The social sciences are *social*, and therefore debate and the systematic confrontation of varying points of view and sometimes of radically opposed positions is the life of these disciplines. What is important is that the reader end up with a point of view which is *personally* held, a view of what social anthropology is and what it should be about. Whether later studies are carried out in the library or the university the reader should have a position from which he or she can interact with those of others and modify or elaborate that position through interaction.

A final word on ethnography, by which is meant the detailed descriptions and analyses of whole cultures or aspects of them: nothing could be more important for the would-be social anthropologist. In this book I have tried as much as possible to limit myself to a few cultures and to refer whenever feasible to available works. I did not want to bewilder the reader with bits and pieces from all parts of the world. There is, however, a vast literature and I hope that the reader's appetite will be stimulated to explore it. In conclusion, let the reader keep eyes and ears open to the world around him. Radio discussion programmes, especially those that involve the public, are especially interesting, the correspondence columns of all newspapers, many television films and radio dramatic series—all these are full of judgments about the nature of man and woman in society, human rights and obligations, views of the state or nation, judgments about generations, social change and the causes of change. In the streets, in pubs, restaurants and cafés, at work and in public transport, all behaviour is significant—the way people dress and walk or sit, smoke or handle money. The social anthropologist does not need to travel to the Amazon or the Highlands of New Guinea in order to observe mankind systematically.

# I

# Introductory

'Live and learn' is an apt saying for anyone who picks up this book with the serious intention of studying social anthropology. This is because the subject is integral to the life of the student. It is not in any sense a part-time occupation. Whether you are an accountant or a chemist, whether you spend your working day in school, office or factory, these are activities which are part-time because you can and do switch off from them and turn your energies and attention to other things. Social anthropology is concerned with the whole of life, and not just something you do until six o'clock. The study of social anthropology encourages you to have a new kind of consciousness of life; it is a way of looking at the world, and in that sense it is a way of living.

What I have just said may seem strange to a reader who already knows, or thinks he knows, what social anthropology is all about. This is because there is always a time-lag in the history of ideas. The people in any field of inquiry who are making advances and discoveries are usually preoccupied with their own researches. If they write about them it is for the benefit of their own colleagues. It takes time for these new ideas to be tested by experience, and more time before they become part of the stock in trade of schools, colleges, newspapers and television. By the time that has happened, of course, new ideas are already being generated at the centre which will in time replace those already in currency.

The process which I have just sketched out explains why readers of different ages will have different expectations of this book. I suspect that the older you are, the less likely it is that you will think of *social* anthropology as distinct from anthropology in general. The younger you are, the more likely is it that you will expect social anthropology to be a kind of sociology, a discipline that studies culture. Whatever age you are, you are likely to think of social anthropology as being concerned with primitive society, or at least non-European societies. And the reason for all this is that the sort of proposition that I advanced in my first paragraph is only now beginning to be generally accepted.

This book is meant to be a book to work with, not a history of social anthropology. But for two reasons a certain amount of history is inevitable. First, I want to explain why different generations may have different expectations of the subject; second, I want to lay a base for future chapters. Some of the problems which we will discuss later are problems only because the history of the subject has made them so.

A good dictionary is often the best starting point for any inquiry and the three definitions of anthropology in the *Oxford English Dictionary* are particularly useful. They give us a brief history of the subject as it was in the 1880s. The definitions are listed as follows:

(*a*) The science of man, or of mankind, in the widest sense.

(*b*) The science of the nature of man, embracing Human Physiology and Psychology and their mutual bearing.

(*c*) The 'study of man as an animal' (Latham). The branch of the science which studies man zoologically, his 'evolution' and history as a race of animated beings.

The lexicographers insert the following note under definition (*a*): 'this seems to have been the original application of the word in English, but for two and a half centuries, to *circa* 1860, the term was commonly confined to the restricted sense (*b*). Since that date, it has sometimes been limited by reaction to (*c*).'

All three definitions are combined in a book, published in 1881, by a great pioneer of the subject, Edward Burnett Tylor.

In his classic work *Anthropology—an introduction to the study of man and civilisation* Tylor handles the physical characteristics of the races, language, writing and the 'arts of life'—neolithic flints, agricultural machinery, weapons, transport, housing, weaving and sewing, navigation, cooking, metalwork and commerce. He deals with the development of artistic forms of all sorts, with the history of science and logic, of religion, of myth, even the history of history itself. In the very last chapter, 'Society', Tylor discusses the developments of human institutions—marriage and the family, justice and law, property and government.

Presiding over all these detailed discussions is the author's concern to show that the history of civilisation is the history of moral progress; in that sense Tylor, like many of his contemporaries, believed in social evolution. It would take me far off course to discuss here the various theories of social evolution current in the nineteenth century, but if this potted history is to be adequate to my purpose I must at least point to the fact that, long before Darwin, beliefs and theories about the evolution of human society from inferior to superior forms were often the unexamined bases for historical studies. Darwin's fame no doubt gave such theories renewed energy, and even encouraged some scholars to discuss whole societies as though they were natural organisms. Although scholars had abandoned simple theories of social evolution by the 1920s, we can still hear evolutionistic views about other races and other cultures expressed in our own society today; this is a good example of time-lag in the spread of ideas.

Theories about social evolution did not stand unchallenged, but even those who opposed them worked within the tripart definition of anthropology given by the *Oxford Dictionary*. It was assumed by all that anthropology was to be the scientific history of mankind, embracing man's physical and moral being, his social institutions and his artefacts. Although different scholars specialised in particular studies, anthropology remained undivided well into the twentieth century.

How then did *social* anthropology come into being? The split with the older tradition is associated with two scholars, B. Malinowski (1884–1942) and R. Radcliffe-Brown (1881–1955). These two men, who dominated what is now the most senior generation of British anthropologists, differed in many ways, but they shared two emphases. For them the study of man was essentially the study of man as a *social* being, and this study, this *social* anthropology, was to be an *empirical science*. It was not to deal in conjecture, it was not to reconstruct history, it was not concerned with the evolution of institutions or with the diffusion of beliefs and artefacts. The social anthropologist was to take living societies as his objects, he was to treat them as natural phenomena to be studied with all the rigour of the natural sciences and to be studied at first hand. The aim was to discover the laws governing the operation of these natural phenomena, to predict and control their motions.

This change in Great Britain followed upon an earlier development in France. Through the latter decades of the nineteenth century and the early decades of the twentieth century, Emile Durkheim (1858–1917) and his colleagues founded the famous school of French sociology. These French scholars extended their inquiries well beyond the confines of modern Western society and to a great extent anticipated the theoretical interests of Malinowski and Radcliffe-Brown. For them also the important thing about man was his social nature, and social facts were to be studied as natural phenomena.

Social anthropology in Great Britain derives from the tradition established by Durkheim, via Malinowski and Radcliffe-Brown, and to Malinowski in particular it owes a strong insistence upon fieldwork; that is, the method of inquiry which requires the researcher to live with the people he is studying, to share their life as fully as possible and to speak their language.

The British social anthropologists who carried out their fieldwork under the influence of Malinowski and Radcliffe-Brown are known collectively as the British functionalist school. The name is derived from one of Malinowski's injunctions to his students: they were to study societies as functioning wholes. Everything that they observed in a society was assumed to have a function in maintaining that society, and their business was to discover that function. They were not to talk of mere survivals from earlier ages, nor of items borrowed from other societies. Everything that existed in a society existed for some purpose; it must have a function.

The achievements of the British functionalists were considerable. Working for the most part in Africa and New Guinea they produced a considerable number of monographs on tribal and peasant societies, each one of which modified existing theory and raised new problems for research. They were not a dogmatic group of zealots, they differed freely amongst themselves. Collectively their contribution to social anthropology has been the insistence upon detailed fieldwork conducted through the language of the people studied, and the appreciation that societies are coherent wholes. However irrational, or even contradictory, any idea, belief or practice may appear to be, the social anthropologist assumes that it makes sense at some level, and he makes it his business to see and to demonstrate how it makes sense, and to whom.

British functionalism had its heyday in the period between the two wars. After the last war it increasingly came in for critical inspection. The criticisms centred upon the functionalist rejection of history and upon the inadequacy of functionalist theory for the explanation of social change. The post-war generation was also disposed to question the scientific pretensions of the inter-war years. A leading and influential critic, E. Evans-Pritchard, wrote in 1950, 'It is easy to define the aim of social anthropology to be the establishment of sociological laws, but nothing even remotely resembling a law of the natural sciences has yet been adduced.' Hand in hand with this criticism went the questioning of other assumptions about the nature of society and about the functionalist approach to the study of it. Could the social anthropologist be objective in the way that a natural scientist was supposed to be objective? If a social anthropologist assumed that the behaviour he observed was socially determined, then were not his own observations equally determined by his own society? What was the relation of a functionalist explanation to the views which people themselves held? Ought there not to be some sort of relation between a people's own theory of life on the one hand and the theory of the social anthropologist on the other? Had not Radcliffe-Brown's insistence upon empirical studies tended to reduce society to the interaction of groups and thus turned attention away from those things which often mean most to the people studied—religion, myth, art?

As members of the younger generation began to formulate their doubts into questions, they began also to formulate alternative approaches to society and to move towards the study of neglected areas. The shift can be characterised as a turning away from an interest in *function* to an interest in *meaning*. The notion that societies are natural organisms, or that it is useful so to regard them, has gone; the contemporary tendency is to think of them as structured complexes of meaning much more resembling languages. With this goes the appreciation that in order to understand human phenomena one has first of all to understand what they mean to the people concerned.

I seem to have come a long way from my opening remarks and I have inevitably anticipated on future discussions. Nevertheless I have reached the point at which I can expand on the remarks in my opening paragraph.

Social anthropology has, in our own times, returned to the broader perspectives of people like Edward Burnett Tylor to the extent that it excludes nothing human from the range of its interests. It has, however, been at once disciplined by the functionalistic period and, by reaction, been led to inquire more deeply into its philosophical, methodological and even moral assumptions.

Probably the most important product of these speculations has been the still continuing growth of a relative theory of knowledge. This rather portentous phrase can be defused by one final look at the history of the work 'anthropology'. There is a very important sense in which we can use the word not to designate a particular area of study but in a more general and personal way, as we commonly use the words 'psychology' or 'philosophy'. There is a psychology studied by professional psychologists, and there is a philosophy studied by professional philosophers; but we can also speak of Shakespeare's psychology or Dickens' philosophy. When we use these words in this way we do not mean that Shakespeare had a psychological theory of his own or that Dickens had an explicit philosophy. What we are pointing to are certain, often implicit, assumptions of a psychological or philosophical order respectively in the works of these two men. With equal good sense we can speak of the anthropologies of particular authors.

In this older and deeper sense of the word, what does anthropology mean? It means the whole mass of assumptions and evaluations which a person makes about human nature and, because to be human is to be social, about society. This is by no means a simple matter and it is something on which we shall have to work.

One could point to certain key areas for a start. What beliefs does one hold about authority? What are one's attitudes towards money? How does one define friendship? What are the respective roles of men and women? The list of such questions is almost infinitely extendable and to it must be added a complementary set: what is the relation between one's notions of how things are or should be and what one actually does? The point to be made, however, is that each man and woman, each reader of this book, has his or her personal anthropology which is an individual construct derived from the common stock. The ways in which beliefs about justice, for example, are (or are not) modified by beliefs about class or race, or the relative values attached to social stability, technological change, moral reform and the like all go together to make up for each individual an unique complex, unique because he or she is unique.

As a complex this personal anthropology is unique, but the bits of which it is composed are social, they are shared with others. Even particular areas of one's personal anthropology are shared by people of one's own family, class, generation, and by even wider groupings on occasion. Because of this we can talk of the anthropologies of groups, the shared assumptions in a group about, say, the place of man in the universe, and the nature of his rights and duties.

I hope that it is now clear why I suggested at the outset that social anthropology has as much to do with living as with learning, if not more. It can produce an alteration in one's consciousness of society, and this is achieved by the constant interaction of one's personal anthropology with the anthropologies of others, whether these others are professional anthropologists, or the people about whom social anthropologists write, or colleagues at work.

## Myself and My Society

It is at this point that I would ask the reader of this book to write something. It is essential to get something down on paper now if you are going to use this book as something to work with. Some people may understandably encounter an initial resistance to this suggestion, a sort of embarrassment perhaps, not unlike the feeling one has at performing the first of a set of slimming exercises or trying to adopt the first position in a *yoga* course. Nevertheless the exercise which I propose is necessary.

I want you to write as fully as you can on the theme *Myself and My Society*. I will give very little guidance on how the theme should be tackled because it is essential that you find out what *you* think, and you can only do this by setting it down on paper. How, given this challenge, do you understand 'Myself' and the word 'Society'; and how do you think and feel that they are related? Perhaps you may think that there is no real distinction between the two terms. Whatever your reaction, explore it and write it down.

When the essay has been written, and not before, set it aside and turn to the Appendix. I have reprinted there a random collection of essays by university students in the age range of nineteen to thirty. The essays were all written before the writers had embarked upon any formal course of social anthropology. I have printed them in the Appendix so that we can use them as an alternative to the tutorial discussion of your own essay which would now follow were you at university.

The essays vary in quality. Some read more easily than others it is true, but I myself do not regard one as being *better* than another. Their value to their writers and to me is that they are relatively spontaneous reactions to the title given, *Myself and My Society*. I hope by a critical examination of them to suggest ways in which you might be able to look at your own work with a view, if you so wish, to a rewriting when the whole of this book has been read. But for the present I suggest you close the book at this point and write your own essay.

Now that your essay has been written, turn to the Appendix and read the essays through. Do not content yourself with one reading only. It is, I'm afraid, a tedious task, but I must ask you to read them several times if the operation is going to be of any use at all. Your aim should not be to judge them in any sense. You may find some of the views expressed attractive and some repulsive; you may agree or disagree with the writers on various points; aim, however, to get past these initial reactions in order to go deeper. Through successive readings, try to discover what general propositions about the relation between self and society seem to underlie each particular essay. Then try to compare the essays on different points. When two writers speak of education, what do they mean, what do they expect, how do they think education works in their society? When social class is discussed, how does the handling of the various writers differ?

In the pages that follow I shall be trying to do what I have asked you to do in the preceding paragraph. I hope that I shall be able to draw your attention to some interesting points of comparison. Certainly you will find others that do not occur to me. My purpose is simply to get you started so that when the operation is complete you should be able to turn back to your own essay and look at it with a new consciousness. You will by then, I hope, be able to question some of your own assumptions and perhaps note some questions on which you will reserve your judgment until you have read and thought more.

One of the most general comparative assessments that can be made of these essays concerns the balance between 'objectivity' and 'subjectivity'. What I mean by this in this context is that in some essays there is more 'self' than 'society', and in others more 'society' than 'self'. In some essays one feels that one gets to know the person writing and his or her views on marriage, education, the 'generation gap' and so on; but one learns very little about the milieu in which the writer was brought up or lives in now. One hears little about the society that exists outside and beyond the immediate experience of the writer. On the other hand, there are those who generalise about class and other institutions at great length, and may indeed include jargon borrowed from professional sociologists or economists: and yet one can discover nothing, or very little, about the person writing. Sometimes it is only a word or two that reveals the sex or age of the writer. When you re-read your own essay, try to assess the extent to which you fall into one class or the other, or have arrived at a satisfactory balance between the two.

Turning now to the particular essays, we see that essay A starts with a view of society as a complex of interdependences. Interdependence is not apparently general in the sense that each one of us is dependent upon everyone else. For this writer 'the education of most people in the society does not include the learning of these (necessary) skills, but a bond of dependence is created between those who do not have them and those that do'. Incidentally, this writer tends to identify with the specialists who pass on new information, the teachers. The teachers exemplify those people in society who have again apparently freed themselves from dependence by the acquisition of 'skills'.

This view of functional interdependence makes social life a contractual affair; people have bonds derived from dependence. Let us note that the lack of instruction in domestic skills (paragraph A2) is congruent with the denial of filial obligation to elderly parents (paragraph A7). We observe that friendships are also determined by the acquisition of functional specialisation (paragraph A4).

Society is in general represented as a powerful external force over which the author's self appears to have no control; and this extends to other selves. Observe that legislative and judicial specialists are also represented as ciphers, in a sense, which act in the name of 'the impersonal body' (paragraphs A10 and 11).

Over against the view summarised in the preceding paragraphs, there is in addition a thin line of criticism. This emerges in the discussion of the school (paragraph A3); at the end of the discussion of large industrial and business organisations (paragraph A8); and at the end of the discussion of economic growth (paragraph A9). I say that this line of criticism is thin because the writer does not allow the critical observations to modify the view of the social machine. For the lack of this we can only assume that the school, 'an institution for conserving middle-class culture', is inevitably part of the irreversible specialising process. The 'self' presented in this essay certainly has values, but they can only be gleaned by inference; they appear to be opposed to the values of society, but there is no indication that the self derives either strength or the capacity for action from them.

In essay B the relation of self and society is represented as an opposition between the real self and a social performance (paragraphs B1 and 10). There is some suggestion that this opposition of reality and unreality is a relative one, in the sense that the team is viewed as real in itself but capable of presenting an 'unreal image for visitors and outsiders' (paragraphs B5 and 7). The team stands in the same relation to the outside society as does the role-playing self.

However, we note that this 'real self' depends upon this role playing: 'disruptions ... anger or embarrassment can occur if the situation ceases to be clearly defined' (paragraph B9). At the same time the 'real self' can experience a sense of bad fit between self and role and do something to change the situation (paragraph B3).

Despite the reference in paragraph B6 to consciousness, it is not clear how far this writer distinguishes between the two different ways in which the word 'role' can be used. First, we can speak of a role as in a film or play, where there are limits within which the individual actor can vary his performance but which he may not overstep; in this sense we can speak of the role of Hamlet or the role of the Prime Minister in the Cabinet system of government. A role in this sense must be consciously adopted; the actor or politician consciously steps out of his role when he acts as a father and he must not confuse his professional role with, for example, his friendships. When, however, we speak of the role of the father or mother in the family we have in mind a state of affairs in which the role player need not be conscious. A father or a mother could not describe their role in such a way that every father and mother would recognise themselves. The self presented in essay B is sometimes cast in a role simply by virtue of being social (paragraph B6), while at other times the self is conscious of role playing, artificiality and the power to manipulate situations (paragraph B5).

The writer of B depends heavily upon one author, Irving Goffman, and is apparently content to fall in with Goffman's views and, in a sense, to play the role which Goffman has written. From this point of view it seems that the 'true self' never really emerges. It is interesting in this connection to note that we can identify the author of essay B by only one remark, 'myself, a student' (paragraph B8); we learn nothing of his or her sex, age, social background or values. The final sentence of the essay effectively sums up the balance between self and society in the eyes of author B.

The self in essay C is not subdued as it is in A or absent as it is in B. Here the self is seen as reflecting certain conditions in the society, and the society is represented as more complex and more mobile than appears in A or B. The general theme is that of uniformity and diversity. Note how in paragraph C2 this theme is initiated: the writer's experience of cultural diversity is partially equated with and made a reflection of the working-class child's experience of school values. In paragraph C3 the general increase in social mobility is reflected in the writer's account of present friendships. This compares markedly with the view of friendship as expressed in essay A.

In C, as in A, social forces are represented at work, making for diversification of communities and for the diversification of the life of individuals; retraining, we note, will be necessary (end of paragraph C7); human inertia is contrasted with the need to uproot oneself and to move (paragraph C8). This increasing diversification is seen as increasing the richness of social life (paragraph C5). At the same time I am disposed to attach some importance to phrases such as 'frightening powerful forces' at the close of paragraph C8 and 'this potent force that uproots' at the opening of paragraph C9; social change is accompanied by human suffering.

However, social forces also have their benign aspect for this writer. We note that diversification and change make for a greater consciousness of difference, which in turn assists the process of humanisation (paragraph C3) and can break down the barriers of fear and ignorance (paragraph C5). Also, 'pop' culture provides a sort of alternative cultural home for the younger generation, although this is not unaccompanied by friction (paragraph C6), and the retraining of workers could compensate for earlier educational deprivation (paragraph C7).

In general, in essay C there is more interaction between the self and the society than in the preceding essays. The self perceives the effect of social forces upon it, for all that these social forces are also regarded as still mysterious and not fully understood. At the same time the self here feels it necessary to assert values and to evaluate social processes; the individual is not impotent.

More specifically than A, B or C, D lays an emphasis upon the historical approach (paragraph D2). It is not only that the past is thought of as essential to an understanding of the present; the future as seen by D shapes the view of the present relation between the self and society. The force of this observation comes out if D is compared with A and B, where in different ways a fixed relation with little sign of change or development is presented.

In D's essay there are two societies and the self has different relationships with each of them. On the one hand there is the society of childhood, understandably characterised by the word 'security'. The adult world of the council estate is governed by norms, it could be relied upon (paragraph D3). Compare with this the absence of any such security in A.

Encompassed by the adult world is the generation group, the gang. Here again, the emphasis is upon norms and security; even the predictable recurrence of the 'seasons' is noted with satisfaction (paragraph D4). It is striking at this point in our review that, although D's 'gang' engaged in activities of which the adults would have disapproved, there is no hint of 'generation gap' or generation conflict such as was found in the earlier essays.

The expectations of D's peer group, which appears to replace the 'gang', are also as predictable as the conker season and extend the sense of security into the future (paragraph D6).

The contrast between this secure society and society as represented in the latter part of the essay is marked. Whereas the writer had earlier a precise and well-known localised scene in mind, now the most immediate society is 'Western Civilisation'. One has no impression that in this 'Western Civilisation' anything like the world of D's childhood could exist; indeed, we are told that 'our society is becoming less and less integrated' (paragraph D10).

In fact, we observe that, once D has broken with the expectations of the old peer group (paragraph D7), society as a world of face-to-face relationships ceases apparently to exist. The relative optimism that we noted in C here gives way to pessimism: 'I see a society doomed to conflict because of the contradictions within it, contradictions which are exacerbated by the lack of shared expectations, and conflicting belief systems' (paragraph C9).

The contrast of the two worlds is so striking that one would be tempted to ask D whether the practices and attitudes castigated in paragraphs D10 and 11 are, or were, absent in the world of the council estate.

Finally, we note that the early self in D's essay interacts with society and sees itself as a social product; the later self is identified with the thinker or intellectual, to the exclusion it seems of all else; with this change society also changes—it becomes a dangerous force, driving mankind on to a suicidal course. The self can diagnose and judge, but it can do nothing. The lack of security described in paragraph D13 when compared with the security referred to in paragraph D3 sums up the contrast.

By this point you may well be wondering why you have been asked to engage in a process of introspection which you may have found extremely tedious and not at all what you had expected of this book. It is because, in my view, it is necessary before all else that you fully appreciate that you have an anthropology of your own.

By this I mean that you have a set of notions about human nature, about the relations between the sexes, about the family, the neighbourhood and the state. You have ideals about these and a host of other things, and in the light of these ideals you make judgments about how things are and about how they should be. If, for example, your occupation requires you to be rather mobile and you therefore have friends scattered up and down the country, it is possible that it may not occur to you to consider whether your immediate neighbourhood is friendly or unfriendly. Someone living near you, on the other hand, who works locally may be concerned with just such judgments.

This is only a simple example because your personal anthropology is not simply determined by present circumstances, job, locality and the like. People create expectations from one situation and carry them to the next, and judge the latter accordingly. No doubt some fundamental expectations, for example of authority, marriage, possessions, etc., are carried on from the earliest experience of life as a child. Someone who has not had a family might attach a high value to family life, but equally they might not. Someone who comes from a large family might expect all his or her relationships to approximate to the familial; equally, such a person might come to lay great value on individualism and on privacy, and prefer to keep relationships on a rather formal or contractual basis.

It might now seem that I am really talking about personal psychology and not personal anthropology. It is very important, however, that we distinguish between the two. Looking back at some of the essays in the Appendix, some readers may have thought that there was an 'obvious' connection between the childhood experience of the writers and their views of society at large. Quite frankly, I would be surprised if there were not such a connection; but although the formation of one's basic personality is achieved in a social setting, and is likely to be continuous with one's social expectations and judgments, the personality is not the same as the personal anthropology. I can put the matter most simply by saying that, whereas we can and do think of a personality in isolation from its social or historical context, we cannot separate the personal anthropology from its social milieu: the personal anthropology expresses the *relation* between the person and the society. I should add what is again obvious that, whereas someone's personality is by no means easily available for the inspection of others, the personal anthropology can, admittedly with some effort, be brought into the light of consciousness, there to be examined with some detachment. In conclusion, the whole purpose of this exercise will, I hope, become clear in the section that follows.

## Models

The readers who have worked carefully through the preceding pages will, I hope, have already derived some benefit from the exercise, even if so far they have taken on trust the fundamental importance which I attach to it. In this section I shall explain myself more fully; the value of the operation will emerge still more as we proceed with the work.

I want to start from my personal experience of teaching social anthropology, which began in the Institute of Social Anthropology, Oxford. There we were teaching postgraduates at a time when the majority of young men in this country were still required to serve a period in the armed forces before beginning or resuming their higher education. I discovered from these men that they had already had, as a result of national service, what I used to call the anthropological experience.

By this I do not mean that travel and residence in different parts had shown them the enormous variety of social systems in the world, let alone that it had given them any deeper understanding of these societies. Travel does not necessarily broaden the mind unless one is disposed to make it do so.

The anthropological experience was worked through nearer home when young men of very different backgrounds were thrown together in the alien world of the armed forces and required to go through a period of very intensive training. They lived together as equals and were obliged to come to terms with members of their own nation who represented, nevertheless, societies in that nation, or sub-societies if you like, which they had never encountered before.

Few had previously had occasion to move out of their own social environment; for the majority their social experience had been homogeneous in the sense that parents, family, friends and school teachers had all shared certain values, all shared, by and large, a common view of the world. I don't believe that anyone was ignorant of the fact that there *are* differences within one and the same society; but very few indeed had ever come to intimate terms with such differences: now they experienced the distinction between knowing about something and living it.

In these circumstances a host of concepts, judgments and expectations of life, hitherto taken for granted and perhaps even given the status of absolute truths, were now suddenly questioned. Attitudes towards sexual relations, to money, ideas about the family, about government, definitions of such terms as friendship were all, sometimes slightly but always significantly, jolted. The easy-going attitude towards 'borrowing a quid' of the young man from a relatively affluent family came up against an attitude based on a tighter budget in a world where the notion 'friendship' did not connote casual borrowing. Even in the uniformity and relative confinement of the barracks some people experienced privacy and a kind of autonomy for the first time; others who had all their lives enjoyed a room, and a bed, of their own now had to learn to live, as it seemed, in public.

I do not need to elaborate with further examples. The point that I am trying to make is that each of us has, through his or her socialisation, a host of conceptions that gives shape to our worlds, and that these conceptions are so firmly internalised that they are often taken for granted as self-evident, natural truths.

But this host of conceptions is not made up of natural, universal truths; it is composed rather of theories, or hypotheses, about the world, which work so long as they remain unchallenged by contrary experience. And for the vast majority of people in any total society their theories about the world are *not* challenged. And further, not only is there no reason why they should be challenged but also it is difficult to imagine social life going on if, at any given time, the vast mass of assumptions was not taken for granted.

Nevertheless they can be challenged and they can be changed, however slowly and with reluctance. Human beings the world over act like scientists with cherished theories: they will ignore contrary evidence for as long as possible; they will try to accommodate it within the existing theory; they will even build up special little sub-theories to account for variations from their expectations, rather than relinquish the security of their established view of the world. The business of the social anthropologist is to become conscious of this in himself and in others.

The point of writing the essay, and of comparing it with the other essays, was to get you to explore more consciously and systematically than you would normally have done your own theory of society, which must include *your* social expectations and judgments; you have begun, in short, to define what you mean by, say, 'marriage' or 'friendship', 'the place of the individual in society', 'politics', etc.

All these theories, expectations, judgments and the definitions I

now propose to call *models*. The term is one that you will encounter in later reading, and it is a very important one because it
is through the use of models that we understand. For the moment,
however, I am concerned with your personal models because
they are necessarily the only starting point that any of us have
when we set out to understand others.

First, let us examine the suitability of the word 'model' to
carry so large a load. A model is always related to something else
as smaller, simpler, as temporary and as typical. A model has
ideal, or essential, qualities in so far as we expect to find in it
basic or required characteristics, principles or arrangements that
are fundamental to the thing of which it is a model. Nevertheless
as a model it is less 'real' than that to which it relates.

Thus it is quite correct to say that you have a model of
'friendship' and that you could very easily build into this model
beliefs about financial relations derived from your model of the
economic system, for example friends lend each other money or,
equally, friends do not lend each other money. Whatever the
proposition, it is a model.

Imagine that, having been governed by this model for most of
your life, you establish a relationship that corresponds to all the
other characteristics of your model of friendship, namely affection, confidence, informality and so on. Imagine that you need
to borrow some money in a hurry, that your friend can afford to
lend it and that you can guarantee to repay. Imagine that this
friend agrees to the loan and says that, because you are such good
friends, he will not charge interest. It may well not have occurred
to you that there would be any question of interest. Whatever
your reaction to his remark, you will appreciate that his model
of 'friendship' is different from yours because the place of the
financial component in it is different.

If you are now concerned to *understand* this friend of yours,
you must modify your own model of 'friendship' in the light of
your experience of him. Quite simply, you must learn to speak
his language.

The example I have given probably strikes the average reader
of this book as an unlikely one. However, the process of the

adaptation of models is going on all the time wherever people are interacting. When the interaction is intense and over a period, the adjustment of models is more marked. Buying a ticket on a bus is an interaction resting on a simple shared view, or model, of a situation—you will not pass the time of day, you will probably not proffer a £1 note for a 4p fare (although you would not hesitate to give a £1 note in a greengrocer for a pound of onions), you proffer as near to your fare as you can, you receive your ticket and that's about all.

At the other extreme, I suggest, a couple in love who go on to marry and raise a family are perpetually modifying their models of each other and of the world in the light of their experience of each other and the children. He or she, the other says, is like this or like that. A new discovery is made, perhaps a distasteful one, and it is argued away as a temporary departure, the result of a cold, worries or 'something one has said'. If the relationship survives, the initially distasteful bit is incorporated into a new understanding, and so it goes on.

People speak different 'languages' in one and the same language; the social anthropologist tries to learn other languages and to translate them back into his own as faithfully as possible. If there are such differences in one and the same society, the British, we must expect to grapple with more considerable differences when we turn to societies that differ considerably from our own. In Indian society, for example a man may well describe someone who is not related to him by blood or by marriage as a 'brother'. He is saying 'we are such good friends that we are (like) brothers'. This is in striking contrast to our own society, where a man may say of his male sibling 'we are (not only brothers but) friends'. An analysis of this contrast would bring to light much about our own and Indian society.

Let me now return to this question of models. I have suggested to you that you already have a set of home-made models, so to speak, with which you shape and understand the worlds in which you live. Some people who don't like the particular models you operate with may call them prejudices; other people, perhaps you yourself, may think that you must rid your mind of all such preconceptions if you are going to try to understand other societies. I want to stress that these home-made models, prejudices or preconceptions, are valuable to you as the base, the only base, from which you can begin.

However, they are home-made, and that term is usefully ambiguous in contemporary usage. On the one hand it connotes intimacy and wholesomeness, on the other it suggests a certain rough and ready quality: your home-made cake doesn't always have that symmetry, the equal consistency and the perfect distribution of raisins, or whatever, that you get in a 'bought' or 'shop' cake.

The models that you will use as a social anthropologist are all tidier versions of your home-made model. They are consciously constructed out of your home-made models, which are, for the most part, unconsciously constructed out of experience. Whereas your home-made models serve in your day-to-day coping, your consciously constructed models serve in your deliberate task of setting out to understand.

On p. 5 I raised the matter of 'objectivity' in social anthropology. The problem is easily stated: how can we be objective about human society when we are so much part of it that it is like the air we breathe? One might as well expect a fish to study the ocean.

The great pioneer who helps us to tackle this was a German historical economist, Max Weber (1864–1920). His life coincides roughly with that of Emile Durkheim (see p. 4) and his thought has posthumously been fully as influential as Durkheim's. I shall have to spend some time setting the scene before the value of Weber's contribution can be appreciated. The reader must be patient.

Durkheim and his school derived great strength from what we might call a down-to-earth approach to social facts, a kind of 'facts are facts' attitude. He tried to devise a method for social scientists which would guarantee the objectivity of their observations and save them from the preconceptions that, as members of society themselves, they were bound to have. For him intro-spection was not merely useless, it was dangerously non-scientific. Durkheim's method was intended to establish social facts 'out there', as solid, measurable, ponderable and predic-table as rocks.

Durkheim, and those who followed him, hoped that by estab-lishing this method they would discover once and for all the true nature of social facts, their essential characteristics. What would happen after that he never explained. There is some suggestion in his work that the sociologist could then take over the job of government, or that the politician would simply be a social scientist. All that is important for us at this stage is that a Durk-heimian approach leads us to expect that ideally we can *know* the objects of our study through and through, exhaustively, to the point where there is nothing more to be known about them. Weber's thought leads us to have rather different expectations.

Weber was as much concerned as Durkheim to establish a science of society. The difference between the two men comes out clearly in the opening pages of one of Weber's most impor-tant works: 'Sociology ... is a science which attempts the interpretative understanding of social action ... action is social in so far as, by virtue of the subjective meaning attached to it by the acting individual or individuals, it takes account of the behaviour of others and is thereby oriented in its course.'

This tight-packed definition is worth pondering and it deserves a great deal more consideration than I can give it here. For our present purpose let us note two features only: sociology aims at an interpretative understanding; and action is social when the meaning that it has for the people concerned is affected by others.

First of all, social scientists aim at an *interpretative under-standing*. What does this mean? Weber recognises that we can understand a fellow human being's behaviour directly; we observe from his facial muscles that he is happy or angry, for example. We understand and we act accordingly, we run away or we laugh. By *interpretative* understanding Weber means an understanding of the system *within which* people behave, and that means going beyond the particular action or the look on a man's face; this is an understanding which can explain. Weber is not concerned with the pursuit of the eternal laws governing human phenomena.

Let us split the second proposition into two bits: first, actions have subjective meaning for the actors. In the original Weber uses the German word *Handeln*, which we translate 'action'. It's important to note that this word connotes rather more than action, if you think of *action* as opposed to words or thoughts. *Handeln* connotes *action-with*, 'trafficking', as in Shakespeare's 'the two hours traffic our stage' in *Romeo and Juliet*, and 'commerce', as in Goldsmith's 'friendship is a disinterested commerce between equals'. *Handeln* might, then, be better translated 'dealing', because when you have 'dealings' with someone these involve thought, speech, motives, feelings and actions. I must, however, stick to the word 'action' because this is the word chosen by Weber's major translator and commentator. Actions, for Weber, are not, then, mere behaviours such as we might observe in animals; they are *human actions* which *mean* something to the people who perform them.

But Weber is not talking about such actions to the extent that they may be individual acts, having only private meaning for the actor. He is concerned with those human actions, or dealings, which are governed and influenced by the existence of others, i.e. social actions. For example, I am writing this book now, and as I write I often use shortened forms of words, initials instead of names, and pepper the page with arrows, question marks and the like to remind me to expand on certain points and to reserve others for later. Clearly all this is meaningful to me; the writing is a subjectively meaningful human act. When the text is prepared for typing I shall have to translate my private shorthand so that the typist understands, and so that you will understand also: my actions will be orientated by your existence.

So much for social action; but how do we understand interpretatively? I can return now to Weber's contribution and to our home-made models. It's very helpful, Weber says, when we can by empathy and imagination 'enter into' someone else's frame of mind, but this is not enough, and it is not always possible. The ultimate aims and values which govern other people's actions and dealings with each other often differ from our own. The more radically they differ, he says, 'the more difficult it is for us to make them understandable by imaginatively participating in them'. What, then, can we do?

Weber advises us to construct rational models of the human performance that we are trying to understand. He calls these models rational because they are systematic, coherent, they make sense to us, and we can communicate them to others. To take one of his own examples, 'in analysing a political or military campaign it is convenient to determine in the first place what would have been the rational course, given the ends of the participants, and adequate knowledge of all the circumstances. Only in this way is it possible to assess the causal significance of irrational factors as accounting for the deviations of this type.'

The constructed model is a sort of definition devised for a special purpose. Most definitions, like our day-to-day home-made models, are used as boxes; we arrange things and classify them. We are not concerned with things that don't fit in, only with those that do. These constructed models are used much more like frames which we set upon or against things in order to see where the discrepancy is between our model or definition and the thing we are trying to understand. Consider the following model, or expanded definition. The family is a group consisting of a legally married man and a woman and their children, whether they are living together or not. It is normally the basic unit of social structure within which the two primary links of kinship are formed, i.e. those of parenthood and siblingship.

If we treat this definition as a box into which the facts must fit or be discarded, then we shall behave as some eighteenth- and nineteenth-century scholars behaved who denied the existence of the family in 'Savage Society'. We should have to discard as not families polygamous households where a man has more than one wife and polyandrous households where a wife has more than one husband. We should not, without modification, be able to include either grandparents, adopted children or young couples living in parental homes. We should incontinently dismiss unmarried couples with children.

However, we are not interested in boxes. Our aim is not to reduce outside things to our own preconceptions, whether conscious or unconscious; it is rather to use our own preconceptions as the primary material for the construction of conscious models with which we intend to understand situations outside our own. That model of the family, or anything at all, can be used as a tool in understanding, provided that you set it up with the intention of modifying or even discarding it. In his example Weber, equally, defines a course of action which would have been rational given the aims of the participants, precisely so that he can focus his attention upon factors that do not fit into the model he has constructed. So also by the use of your own models you proceed outwards, perpetually modifying in the light of your experience.

Your models must always link your experience and your mind; that linking is what we call understanding. Every model that you encounter (and I include, remember, definitions, theories, general propositions about society, human nature, etc.) must make sense to you. If it does not make sense it is not necessarily *wrong*, but it does mean that the author is writing in the light of experience which either you have not had or he has not communicated to you. Consider the model of the family given on p. 24. Is it true of your family, and the families of friends and relations? What would you add to it or subtract from it which would make it relate to your own experience?

As you read the next chapter you will come upon examples of groupings which correspond, some more, some less, to your models. Contrast and compare each new example.

## Summary

In the nineteenth century anthropologists shared the common view that the variety of human cultures reflected the different steps of social evolution from 'savagery' to modern 'civilised man'. In the early decades of the twentieth century there was a break with these evolutionist theories and the emphasis fell upon the study of societies in their own right. The influence of French sociology turned British anthropology into social anthropology and gave it discipline. This advance was achieved at the cost of a certain narrowing of focus and a preoccupation with institutions, making for the organic solidarity of society. The social anthropologists called themselves functionalists and hoped that, like the natural scientists, they could discover the laws governing the formation and functioning of society.

After World War II these pretensions were increasingly called in question and social anthropologists, without losing what they had learned from French sociology, began to widen the scope of their inquiries. The modern emphasis falls upon the ways in which man shapes his universe and makes sense of it. This can be represented as a return to an older meaning of the word 'anthropology'—all the assumptions and evaluations which a person makes about human nature and society.

In order to embark upon such a study we have to recognise that each one of us has a personal anthropology in this sense, and our first business is to try to become as conscious of it as possible. From this consciousness we derive our basic analytic tools, or 'models'. Models are not simply the assumptions that we have about the nature of 'marriage' or 'friendship'; they are rather intellectual constructs which we make up out of these assumptions once we are conscious of them, and the process of *understanding* requires the perpetual modification of one's own models by interacting them with the models of others. It is important to remember that the formal understanding of a quite alien situation is not essentially different from our day-to-day understanding of the world around us. In our dealings with other people we are constantly interacting in terms of shared and differing models and we are often modifying our models, or should be. The only difference between this and the attempt to understand a very different social scene is that in the latter case the process of interaction is slower and much more conscious.

## Reading notes

Aron, Raymond, *German Sociology*, English translation, New York, 1964. This work by a distinguished French sociologist, originally published in 1936, concludes with a chapter on Max Weber, which is a useful commentary on Weber's thought.

Aron, Raymond, *Main Currents in Sociological Thought*, 2 volumes, Pelican, 1971. See Volume 2, the chapters on Durkheim and Weber.

Anon., *Notes and Queries on Anthropology*, 6th edition 1951. This work was sponsored by the Royal Anthropological Institute. It is mentioned here because it provides a succinct survey of the various branches of anthropology as they have traditionally emerged. The lengthy section on Social Anthropology provides a variety of models in the form of definitions which the reader should not take as authoritative.

Banton, Michael (ed.), *The Relevance of Models for Social Anthropology*, ASA Monographs, London and New York, 1965. This work is mentioned here to introduce the reader to this important series published by the Association of Social Anthropologists of the Commonwealth. Apart from the Introduction which can be read now, the reader should note the contents for later reading, especially the contributions of I. M. Lewis and Marshall D. Sahlins.

Beattie, J., *Other Cultures*, London, 1964.

Burrow, J. W., *Evolution and Society—a study in Victorian social theory*, Cambridge University Press, 1966. Chapters 7 and 8.

Evans-Pritchard, E. E., *Social Anthropology*, London, 1951. This brief book is based on six broadcast lectures and the whole of it can be profitably read at this stage.

Evans-Pritchard, E. E., *Essays in Social Anthropology*, London, 1962. A collection of essays on social anthropology in general and on particular subjects. The first essay 'Social Anthropology: Past and Present' should be read at this stage.

Hocart, A., *The Life-Giving Myth and Other Essays*, London, 1952. This is not an introductory work in the usual sense; it is a collection of essays on a wide range of topics by the one British anthropologist in this century to whom we can attribute genius.

Lienhardt, G., *Social Anthropology*, Oxford, 1964.

Mair, L., *An Introduction to Social Anthropology*, Oxford, 1965. Probably the best general introduction to British social anthropology.

Pocock, D., *Social Anthropology*, London, 1961. A condensed and perhaps idiosyncratic account.

Shapiro, H. (ed.), *Man, Culture and Society*, New York and Oxford, 1960. Essays by various hands on physical anthropology, archaeology, primitive technology, as well as on the family, social groups, religion and economics. The work represents the breadth of the American tradition and is a wholesome corrective.

Tylor, Edward B., *Anthropology: an introduction to the study of man and civilisation*. First published in 1881, this is a comprehensive attempt to survey mankind as a whole. It is marked by the theories current in the nineteenth century but remains valuable for the mass of detailed information it contains, for the highly intelligent perceptions of the author and, not least, because it reminds us that social anthropology is more than the sociology of primitive peoples.

Weber, Max, *The Theory of Social and Economic Organisation*, English translation, London 1947. Chapter I, 'The Fundamental Concepts of Sociology', should be read, perhaps with the assistance of Aron's works. Many people find Weber very tough going: for the present a careful reading of pp. 79–86 is sufficient. If the reader finds Weber's argument too condensed or abstract, he could look at Chapter III, where Weber more concretely discusses ideal types of authority. If Weber's way of expressing himself seems intractable this reading can be deferred.

**2**

# The Family

I am requesting the reader to reverse the 'normal' procedure to be found in most textbooks, and to write out his or her own position on the various matters discussed *before* reading the relevant chapter. Some readers may well find this difficult, but if they persevere they will find that by setting about the work in this way they will be in a better position to react with the facts and ideas expressed than if they merely responded passively after doing the reading.

So before reading this chapter, write an essay on 'The Family in Modern Society'. In your essay, think about your own family and consider to what extent you think it is typical; then examine your notions about the typical family. Try to imagine what society would be like if there were no families, and from this exercise in imagination try to spell out the function of the family in your own society. Try also to reflect upon the relation of the family to other institutions—educational, economic and political. Is, for example, the school taking over some of the functions of the family; how is the family affected by the employment or non-employment of the young, of women and of the old?

\*     \*     \*

Polygamy is marriage with several, or more than one, at once. This word is carelessly used to refer to the case of a man with several wives which, strictly speaking, is polygyny. We have to make this distinction because there is another kind of polygamy, not so common, whereby a woman has several husbands; this we call polyandry.

Let us take the commoner form, polygyny, first. What does the word summon to your mind? There is, of course, the cartoon maharajah or sheikh surrounded by his harem. Try to stretch your imagination. What in the family as you have experienced it and conceptualised it would have to be adjusted if you had several co-wives, or indeed only two; or several half-brothers and half-sisters; or had to maintain three or four wives and their children; or had to share one husband with several co-wives and so on? You must imagine that you have money and space at your disposal. Which interests would you want to keep separate, which would you wish to defend? What conflicts would you seek to avoid, and how would you do it? How does the following arrangement suit?

You have unlimited space and money at your disposal, so you construct first of all a large single-room hall, a very big living room. This you construct in the centre of your garden or estate; it is to be the social centre of your family where you keep your television, record player, books, table tennis, etc. Around this focus you then build several bungalows with two or three bedrooms apiece, kitchen, bathroom and lavatory; each with its own garden.

You can now arrange your family. The wives and their children will live in the bungalows, and the husband will circulate between them. He will not have a private sleeping place of his own.

The evenings will usually be spent in the central living room and the evening meal will be eaten there. The women will collaborate in cooking the supper. Each wife will be independent when it comes to preparing the midday meal, which she prepares for her own children.

What do you think of this as one of various possible arrangements? We are, of course, assuming the impossible, namely that the general values of our own society survive unchanged. It seems a good idea to give the women their independent households; at the same time it makes sense to bring the whole family together in the evening. There might be difficulties here, especially as the children grow up, but we shall need to counter a tendency towards fission of the whole family into its separate 'motherhoods'. Equally, the women should have opportunities to develop their own interpersonal relationships, and have more in common than an interest in the husband's sexual 'favours'.

What other advantages or disadvantages occur to you? How would you budget? Do you think that the commensal living room is sufficient to hold the family together? How would you hope to prevent quarrels between wives, and between the children of co-wives? What if one wife reprimands or slaps another's child? Don't you think that the husband is bound to prefer one wife to another? And what about the woman who cannot bear children?

Materially and morally, what would you add to the basic arrangements that I have sketched out? Might it not be a good idea to provide separate accommodation for the adolescents, domestic youth clubs of some sort? The communal living room could be hell on earth without some such provision. At the same time you must think about adolescent sexual experimentation; are you happy if this occurs between half-brothers and half-sisters? Would you hope to establish some kind of etiquette governing the relations between co-wives, and between their children, for example that young children should be subject to a common discipline as regards manners, bed time, etc.

If you have pondered these problems, let me add one final set. What happens when the children marry? Conventionally in our society the bride is married out of her parental home and leaves it to live with her husband. When the sons of this imaginary family marry, do you propose to accommodate them and their wives? You might consider giving house room to your first son and his first wife, until he is in a position to set up his own homestead. And when he does so, his mother might very well like him to set it up near the parental estate. Or perhaps you might think of reserving a place for your youngest son and his wives. The advantage of that arrangement would be that there would be people to care for you and your wives in your old age, and there would be a young, growing polygynous family to take over the estate. This touches on the complicated business of inheritance. Had you thought about it before?

By this point we have probably gone as far as our imaginations can stretch. Let us return to social reality; a social reality other than our own.

The polygynous arrangements that I have suggested might in their general outlines have been based on one of many societies that exist and have existed in different parts of the world. The particular society that I had in mind is one made famous in the discipline by Professor E. E. Evans-Pritchard, the Nuer of the Southern Sudan. Evans-Pritchard's accounts of these people became classic in his lifetime, and I shall use them a good deal in this book.

The Nuer polygynous household is arranged along the lines sketched out above (p. 31). It has also distinctive differences quite apart from the obvious ones. The Nuer are a cattle-keeping, cattle-loving people; the language and imagery of cattle-keeping imbue every aspect of their life. The homestead itself is called the *gol*, and when a Nuer speaks of his home he refers to his *gol*. The primary meaning of *gol* is, in fact, the cattle-dung fire and its surrounding hearth which smoulders continuously in the centre of the byre (*luak*). The byre is the equivalent of our central living room, the moral and material centre of the homestead. The byre is the centre of social life, the family 'clubroom' and the guest house for visitors. It is also a sacred centre where the ancestral shrine is kept. Around the byre is the stockade for the cattle, and in the rainy season the cattle sleep in the byre also.

In a Nuer polygynous homestead, the wives' huts and gardens surround the byre. Each hut has its own outside kitchen, a hearth protected by a windscreen. The wife and her children sleep in the hut; the husband has no one sleeping place, he sleeps in his wives' huts in turn. In large homesteads there may also be sleeping huts for the youths, and separate sleeping huts for the older girls.

The Nuer are fully conscious of the problems to which polygyny can give rise. The very word for co-wife, *nyak*, has a verbal form which means both 'to be a co-wife' and 'to be jealous'. They insist upon an etiquette that emphasises the solidarity of the whole homestead rather than that of the constituent group of families. The co-wives are expected to cook for each other on occasion; the children address their father's wives as 'mother'. When boys go hunting or fishing they are brought up to take the meat or fish not to their own mothers but to one of the co-wives. This etiquette goes a good way towards countering fissive tendencies in the homestead. The polygynous homestead is more than a matter of sexual and marital relations. We shall see, a little later, that the Nuer boy is not, however, unconscious of the difference between full brothers and sisters on the one hand and half-brothers and sisters on the other. At a certain level of activity the distinction is important.

Finally, as regards the regulatory customs of the homestead, there remains the matter of sexual interest. In fact, Nuer children are instructed early in sexual matters, and with this instruction goes social training about the people one may have sexual relations with and those with whom one may not. The Nuer concept of incest extends across a far wider range than it covers in our society and is related to marriage prohibitions; a person may not have sexual relations with someone whom they could not marry. Here I touch upon the complicated matter of kinship, which I shall deal with later. For the present it is sufficient to say that the Nuer are in contemporary jargon 'permissive' in that brides are not expected to be virgins. At the same time Nuer behaviour is governed by a stricter code than prevails in our society.

I have so far minimised, as far as possible, the differences between the Nuer family and our own. My intention has been to turn your imagination upon the facts of our own society and to play at polygyny. There are, as you might expect, important differences, and one of the most important is the emphasis that the Nuer lay upon descent.

I have described the Nuer byre as a sort of club or living room for the homestead. In fact, it is a place for the men. Nuer boys are encouraged to move away from their mothers' huts at an early age. From the age of eight or so they sleep and eat in the byre, and the women take it in turns to provide the food for all the boys, youths and men who centre their life there.

This separation, the men in the byre, the women and the girls with the small boys in the huts, expresses an important principle of Nuer society, what we call the *agnatic* principle. '*Agnatic*, of or pertaining to agnates; related on the father's side. *Agnatic*, a relation by descent from a common male ancestor.' (*OED.*) Nuer society provides a good example of what we call *unilineal descent*; that is to say, a society in which the emphasis is upon one line of descent rather than another. This does not mean that a given people is ignorant of the alternative line or attaches no significance to it. It means simply that one line receives the major emphasis, and the agnatic principle determines such matters as inheritance, rights and duties, political solidarity, etc. Because the agnatic principle is embodied in groups that are based upon descent lines, or lineages, we most commonly refer to them as patrilineal societies as opposed to matrilineal societies. In these latter the descent line that receives moral and political emphasis is the female one.

A patrilineal society is not merely one in which the wife takes the husband's surname and the children are known by the name of the father. If you want to gauge the force of the agnatic principle you should think of the comparable effect of social economic class divisions upon yourself. Wealth, or the lack of it; attitudes based on wealth, whether supported or not; still-surviving beliefs in upper, middle and lower classes, whether endorsed or rebelled against—all these and more determined where and how you spent your childhood, if not indeed your later years. They determined the locality of your home, the kind of education you received, the circle of your friends and, for the majority of those who are married, the choice of your partner. The agnatic principle in a patrilineal society is fully as powerful as social class still is in our own.

The world of a Nuer person is divided very broadly into two: there are other Nuer, and there are inferior foreigners. Among the Nuer there are 'bulls', people who are connected to a man through a male ancestor, agnates; and there are the cognates who are not agnates, what the Nuer call 'children of girls'. A man identifies himself with his father's byre and it is his ambition to build, one day, a byre of his own. He identifies also with the ancestral shrine of the byre, and this links him with the byres of other homesteads which share the same ancestors. Step by step as we proceed back in time new links emerge which wield together larger and larger groups. The largest group bound in this way that a Nuer knows is the clan; the clan is 'the largest group of agnates who trace their descent from a common ancestor and between whom marriage is forbidden and sexual relations considered incestuous'. At the time of Evans-Pritchard's investigations there were about twenty such clans among the Nuer.

Were you to devote a certain amount of money and a great deal of time to the task you could find your *biological* equivalent of the Nuer clan. It must occur to some of us some time or other to wonder where the other descendants of our grandparents or great-grandparents are and what they are like. Imagine that you had done the job and that you had traced back, through precise genealogical links, the ancestors of your father and the lines descended from them through males. The task is not impossible; a relative of mine has traced our particular lot of Pococks back through ten inclusive generations from the youngest member to a Charles Pocock who was born in Berkshire in about 1673. You would find your clan scattered up and down the country, and not a few might be in other countries. At the same time, I don't doubt, you might well discover pockets where your family had concentrated.

Imagine now that all the descendants of one man, some six generations back, knew about this kinship, exchanged Christmas cards and felt an obligation to call on you when they were in your area. You have to stretch your imagination a little further to conceive that all the younger members of the group would not 'date' each other and would no more think of marrying than they would contemplate marriage with a brother or a sister. Such a situation would basically be that of the Nuer clan. If a young man met a girl of the same name he would check—and he would be able to check—whether or not the girl was of his clan. In other societies, let us note, the distant genealogical links are lost, and in such societies an identical clan name alone suffices to bar the couple from sexual relationships and from marriage. The equivalent situation to this in our society would be that in which all Pococks were forbidden to marry whether they knew of a relationship or not.

To return, however, to your reality. You probably do not know where your second cousin on your father's side is. You may not be able to distinguish between a second cousin and a first cousin once removed. In fact, second cousins are the children of first cousins, whereas your first cousin once removed is your first cousin's son or daughter, and you are, reciprocally, first cousin once removed to him or her.

Your own group of kin is probably smaller, smaller even than the area of kinship that you know about or recognise. I mean by this that you have your immediate family, your parents and siblings and perhaps children; there may be others with whom you interact in all sorts of ways, and then there are also kin that you know about, uncles in Australia for example, with whom you have no contact. There may be a sort of intermediate category with whom you have, or have had, formal interaction. I mean someone like Auntie X who must be invited to the wedding because she was always so good to you when you were a child. This intermediate category of kin is only apparent, if at all, on such occasions as weddings and funerals.

See now how vague the word 'interact' in that last paragraph was. I used the jargon term 'interact', and I could not confidently affirm that you feel any sense of having rights or duties of any specific kind in relation to any particular member of your kin, with the exception of your children if you have them. But even in this case, could you say what obligations they have, or will have, to you? It's quite likely that you may be particularly 'close' to an aunt, uncle, grandparents or even to a first cousin, but reflect on the historical and personal circumstances that have made this relationship 'close'; by the very 'closeness' of it you will be able to gauge the distance between yourself and other aunts, uncles, etc. In other words, outside a very small group, and sometimes only for the relatively short period of childhood, the criteria that give kinship strength are the same as those by which you select and maintain friendship.

It is likely that you have more friends or neighbours than you have recognised kin. In the course of your life you may accumulate several sets of friends and neighbours. According to the nature of these relationships and the sort of person you are, you may accumulate these as the years go by, you may retain some and drop others, or you may allow one set to wither away after the first Christmas cards have been exchanged, and take up a new set. Whether you have one or many of such sets will depend on your mobility. Very few people in British society today live out their years and die in the neighbourhood in which they were born.

In some other societies your neighbours *are* your kin. The equivalent of this would be that all, or the majority, of the members of your imaginary clan lived in the same place. Such a situation appears to have been achieved by the Archers in the BBC series. I myself worked among people collectively known as Patidar, a commercial and agricultural caste in Gujarat, western India. There all the known male descendants of one man lived in one village, but even they had members of other castes as their neighbours in the village.

A particular Nuer lives in his homestead with his kin, and the homesteads of his father's brothers may well be nearby. But he also has a neighbourhood because the homestead is part of a village. The size of the village will depend upon the lie of the ground. It may consist of a few homesteads, or stretch over a wide area and have a population of several hundreds.

In British society we still sometimes speak of kith and kin, and these two terms correspond to the more modern 'friends and relations'. Kith are literally people one knows and kin are, of course, relations. In the Nuer village Evans-Pritchard tells us 'Whoever is kith must also be kin.' The Nuer certainly have words for stranger and for foreigner, but the people amongst whom they live are all kin. In order to make this clear I shall have to say more about lineages and clans.

I have pointed out (see p. 36) that the Nuer clan is not a localised group, its members are found throughout Nuer territory. The clan is built up by a demonstrable genealogical structure such that any two members of a clan know, or can find out, at what point in the genealogy they have a common ancestor. Some are united at the fifth ascending generation, more still at the sixth and so forth. Clan membership has to do with marriage and with cattle; it is also a religious connection because clansmen share certain sacred symbols. But the clan is not the same as the tribe, which *is* a territorial division in Nuer society.

A tribe is a defined area within which members of different clans live. Some tribes are small and comprise only a few villages, others are large and have subdivisions within them. Tribes and sub-tribes have distinctive names and evoke strong loyalties. The traditional loyalty to his county of the Yorkshireman in Britain is a pale shadow of the feelings that a Nuer has for his immediate neighbourhood, his village, and the wider territory of which it is a part, his tribe.

We can use the reference to the Yorkshireman to show how clan and tribe are related on the ground. Not only in Yorkshire but also in other parts of the British Isles we hear of local distinctions between the 'real' or 'genuine' members of that society and 'foreigners' or 'others'. This feature of some areas has been much publicised in recent years with the growth of the 'country cottage' class. On television, radio and in the Sunday newspapers one can hear or read people reporting with delight that the inhabitants of their adopted village regard them as 'foreigners'. I presume that this authenticates to them the genuinely rustic quality of their particular converted cowshed.

Among the Nuer also, but much more formally and with much greater significance, we find the distinction between the real members of a territory, small or large, and the later settlers; the former are *dil* or *diel*, the latter *rul*. Going back to our imaginary clan (see p. 36), let us suppose that your 'clan' was believed to have originated in Hertfordshire. You could point, perhaps, to graves in a local churchyard or to some similarity between your own surname, Hemstead, for example, or Ware or Alban; or family history might supply records that that's where your family originated. Imagine now that those members of your 'clan' who still live in Hertfordshire were universally accorded there a special status. They need not be in a majority by any means, but all the other inhabitants would seek to establish their Hertford-shireness by association with your clansmen. In the same way, were you living in Sussex, shall we say, you would associate yourself with the members of the Hailsham, Chichester or Petworth clans resident in that county, because in Sussex *you* would be the stranger, or late-comer.

Among the Nuer each tribal area is associated with a particular clan. Where the tribal area is divided into named sections, each section is associated with a division of the clan, right the way down to the smallest political unit, the village. Remember, however, that when I say associated I am not talking about numbers. People in Nuer society are not as mobile as they are in our society; nevertheless they travel freely, and whole groups migrate from time to time. The *diel*, true, original, first settlers who constitute a focus for tribe, sub-tribe and village, may still be in a minority all the way down the line. It is perfectly possible for the majority population of the same clan to be *rul*, strangers, late-comers, in various other tribal areas.

How then do the people of a tribe or a village associate themselves with their local *diel*? The answer is through women and by marriage. The clan is exogamous and so, it follows, is the lineage. The members of different clans living in a particular territory must therefore intermarry. I mentioned earlier (p. 36) the distinction between agnates and the children of girls. Any

Nuer man has, then, two kinds of relatives, those with whom he is connected by men, and those with whom he is connected by women. And these latter fall into two categories, those with whom he is connected by his mother, and those with whom he is connected by his paternal aunts, his sisters and daughters; the difference is between women who have come in and women who have gone out.

Nuer villages have grown up through the progressive accumulation of marriage ties. Evans-Pritchard gives an account of this as it was described to him by a Nuer: 'Members of a lineage beget children and they become numerous and spread over the countryside, wandering here and there, and everywhere. Then their close relationship ends and they go to live in the midst of other clans who are distantly related to them. Here they dwell as friends and slowly develop new cognatic relationships by intermarriage. Hence lineages are much mixed in all local communities.'

Relations by marriage are for the Nuer, as for the great majority of societies that exist and have ever existed in the world, far more important than they are in our own society. Marriage may well be based on courtship and on love, but although a Nuer couple choose each other, whole groups of kin are involved and are welded together by the act of marriage.

To give a bride is to give a gift. In a society where exogamy prevails over a wide range of relations, a society which, moreover, attaches importance to perpetuating one's line, the gift of a woman from one line to another ensures that the line of the receiver will go on. A Nuer feels a permanent sense of obligation to the family that has given him his bride; his lineage is grateful to her lineage. In return for this gift his kinsmen give cattle.

This compensation by cattle is appropriate. I cannot here go into the rich symbolism that the Nuer have derived from their cattle and the affection they feel for them. We saw on p. 36 that a man's agnates are 'bulls'; let me add only that when a boy achieves manhood the greatest gift that he receives is an ox, and from that ox he takes his 'ox name'. The cattle are known as individuals, and the genealogies of cattle are known. A man knows which cattle came into the herd when his mother was married and which went out when his sister was married. The ox is, above all, the supreme object of sacrifice. In a sense a man knows that he has come into the world through cattle and can only have legitimate progeny by giving cattle.

Women and cattle are then gained and lost as they are exchanged. Both belong to the lineage. It follows in Nuer thought that a group must be compensated for the loss of the girl that is given. The cattle are then distributed among the bride's relatives according to definite rules. The cattle that come into the byre in this way help to provide wives for the bride's brothers and half-brothers. Cattle not only go to the agnatic relatives of the bride; her maternal kin, her mother's brothers etc., also receive their shares. The girl is, after all, the daughter of their daughter, they have contributed to her being and an additional compensation of cattle is proper when she is married.

The network of relationships which comes into being after a marriage extends the ban on marriage. A Nuer may not marry anyone connected to him by male or female links up to about six generations. It is clear then that, as strangers link themselves by marriage to the *diel* in any particular locality, each marriage generates affinal relationships, which themselves prevent further intermarriage. According to this rule you could not marry your great-great-great-grandmother's daughter's daughter's daughter's daughter's son or daughter. It is easy to see then how in the Nuer village all kith are kin.

I have given a very simplified sketch of the relation between descent and neighbourhood, or clan and tribe, among the Nuer. The division into tribal areas is a sort of trellis upon which the clans grow like vines. Some spread across the whole trellis and develop vigorous offshoots, others are quite small and may only cover a portion of it. But each vine intertwines with the others as it grows.

Evans-Pritchard has described the Nuer nation as an 'anarchic state'. It has no chiefs, no central courts, no police, and yet a population of some 200 000 spread over an area of about 30 000 square miles orders its affairs, arranges its marriages, controls warfare and feud, and organises cattle raids on neighbours. It is the system of clans and lineages interlocking with the neighbourhood by marriage that gives the organisation on which the coherence of Nuer life is based.

The interplay of these principles is there in miniature in the homestead with which we began. Nuer children play at 'mothers and fathers': 'they make cattle byres and huts of sand, and mud oxen and cows, and with these conduct bride wealth negotiations and perform marriage ceremonies, and they play at domestic and conjugal life'. Very soon they come to recognise that all the children of one father are children of the byre. Nevertheless they know full well that there are potential divisions between the children of different mothers. Even if they do not address their half-brothers as half-brothers, they have all the same different words to mark the distinctions. If we try to imagine such a situation, we might tend to exaggerate the tension and perhaps be disposed to think that a man's 'real' feelings are for his full brothers. This, I think, would be wrong; nevertheless some tension does exist. Various lineages, which in their divisions and subdivisions make up the clan, are conceived by the Nuer as existing in embryo in the polygynous homestead; it is a paradigm of the whole: the Nuer are united by their fathers but separated through their mothers. Significantly, the name for a lineage is *thok dwiel*, which also means the entrance of a mother's hut.

Let us turn now to consider situations yet more remote—societies where matrilineal succession is the rule and societies where polyandry is the custom of marriage. But first a word on matriarchy. We know what a patriarch is, an elderly, lordly man who rules over his family—by extension, any venerable old man. A matriarch is the female equivalent. Nowadays perhaps, if we use either term, matriarch is the more common to refer to a dominating old lady. Be that as it may, we think of the terms as being equivalent.

Now for patriarchy and matriarchy. Here again the terms are equivalent as far as meaning is concerned. They both suggest forms of social organisation in which the head of the family is the father or mother respectively. The *Oxford English Dictionary* goes on, reasonably enough at first sight, to link patriarchy with patrilineal descent and matriarchy with matrilineal descent.

In reality, however, we know of no truly matriarchial society, namely a society in which women occupy the positions and have the responsibilities, privileges and authority that men have elsewhere. Some nineteenth-century evolutionists seem to have believed that such societies once existed, and that the matrilineal societies which *did* exist were the vestiges of defunct matriarchies. As we shall see, however, matriarchy—rule by women—is quite different from matriliny—the reckoning of descent through women.

Similarly, polyandry—one wife with several husbands—appears at first sight to be a simple reversal of polygyny—one husband with several wives. Think now how polyandry could be possible in our own society. What basic conditions would have to be met? It is not difficult to imagine the situation because our divorce laws make a kind of serial polyandry possible, and one can read reports of wealthy women who have families fathered by several men. (Equally, of course, serial polygyny is possible in our society.) But apart from economic independence, what other conditions would have to be met? Would you think male jealousy inevitable, and would you seek to regulate the visits of the husbands? Would you think it wise to provide for 'natural feelings' in the father, so that each would be allowed to know his own offspring and to have some sort of special relationship with them? Would the fathers individually or collectively have financial or other responsibilities? Could you devise an appropriate form of household such as I invited you to think of on p. 31?

The task is difficult because where we find polyandry it is

not a simple reversal of polygyny. Whatever the word polyandry *means*, it *amounts* not to one wife *having* several husbands but to several husbands having one wife; this puts a different complexion on the matter.

First, however, let us look at matriliny. It is not simply a matter of reckoning descent through the mother. If this were all, do you think that it would make a great deal of difference if the husband took the wife's surname at marriage and the children were known by that name? The roles of father and mother, husband and wife would be unchanged. What's in a name? We have, however, to think also of the rules of residence, inheritance and authority.

In some matrilineal societies the married couple spend some or all of their married life in the homestead or village of the bride. Such marriages are called uxorilocal, from the Latin *uxor*, a wife. We distinguish such marriages from virilocal marriages, from *vir*, husband. In our society most marriages are virilocal, in that the husband's place of work determines where his wife shall live. In most societies where we speak of virilocal marriage, this usually means residence with the groom's father's people, as among the Nuer.

Inheritance does not count for much in our society, at least for the majority of us. What difference would it then make to your own relationships if, according to your age, you either expected to inherit from your maternal uncle or proposed to make your sister's children, more particularly your sister's sons, your heirs? What difference *would* it make, especially if your own sons inherited from their maternal uncle and your own father's property passed to your maternal cousins?

If you have been thinking about the last question raised, you may have touched on the question of paternal *feelings*, and perhaps authority. Let us look at the latter first. Paternal authority has decreased in this country and it is probably safe to say that a father cannot any longer expect to lay down the law to his children, especially once they are in mid-adolescence. We cannot imagine calling our fathers 'Sir', let alone the authority, backed by power to bless and curse, which prevails in most other parts of the world. In India I have seen a man in his forties stand up when his father came into the room and stay deferentially silent until spoken to. There is no question of fear here, it is a way of expressing affection through deference. Nevertheless, whether you are parent or child, the child–parent relationship in our society is still one of dependence so long as the child is not a wage earner. What authority, explicit or implicit, does this give to the parent?

You may say that it has, or should have, nothing to do with authority; it's a matter of natural feelings, parental love and the like. Nevertheless, try to imagine for a start that the main provider in your own family was another man, not the father: imagine that it was your mother's brother, or wife's brother, who bought such major items as clothing, paid the rent, paid for holidays and was responsible for the expenses of Christmas and the like. Would it not make a difference?

Before giving examples from life, let us go one step further. It is not uncommon in our society where there has been a divorce for a baby to be born after its mother has remarried. The child grows up to think and feel for the stepfather as a father. And there are, of course, people who are adopted at a very early age. In such cases the *genitor*, i.e. the begetter or natural father, is not the same as the *pater*, the social father. Unless some special provision is made, do you think that natural feelings will give the *genitor* a special interest in his own children, or his own children a special interest in him? If, to take an extreme case, you had been brought up in the house of your maternal uncle, a house that your own father only visited at night to see your mother, can you conceive that you would have developed any feelings for him comparable with those you feel for your own father now?

The problems raised in the preceding paragraphs are not easily solved in societies where matriliny prevails. Dr Audrey Richards rightly refers to 'the matrilineal puzzle' and describes the various ways in which such societies arrange their affairs as 'solutions'.

Let us have a look at the Bemba of Zambia, with whom Dr Richards herself worked in the 1930s.

The Bemba at the time of the study were a poor people practising shifting agriculture; that is to say, they would seek fresh agricultural land every four to seven years. This was made possible by a low population density—as low as 3·65 people per square mile. As in other parts of Africa, tsetse fly, which is a carrier of fatal disease for man and beast, makes it impossible for the Bemba to rear cattle. As they have no cash, permanent sites or stock, the Bemba have little to inherit.

There is an important distinction in Bemba society between the royal clan and the commoners. We need not be concerned with this for the moment, except to mention a detail concerning Bemba theories of procreation. According to them blood is passed on from generation to generation by women and the male semen only activates the foetus. Without the semen the foetus would not grow and the child would not be born. The male act is essential, but the semen contributes nothing to the child. Equally or more important are the ancestral spirits, which also enter the womb to become the guardian spirits of children. Among commoners this guardian spirit may be of the father's line or of the mother's; in the royal clan they are exclusively of the mother's line. Even so we have a hint of difficulty, for the spirits of the father's line can trouble the living whether these are aristocrats or commoners.

The Bemba male will probably contract to marry his bride before she has achieved puberty. This contract was traditionally made between him and his proposed bride's father and her maternal uncle. Even in Bemba eyes the gifts given at marriage were small. Dr Richards tells us that traditionally the gifts comprised one or two cloths and some hoes. At the time of her study some young men had begun to work in the Rhodesian mines and gave from 5 to 10 shillings. Note here a significant difference from Nuer custom: the gift is small, but it appears to be solely the responsibility of the young man; he is not dependent, as among the Nuer he would be, upon kinsmen to provide him with substantial numbers of cattle.

More important than the gift was the service that the groom would provide for his bride's family. He would build a hut in their village and assist in the agricultural work. Before the bride achieved puberty she would sleep in the groom's hut and keep it clean for him. Even after puberty and when the marriage had been consummated, she would still not be allowed her own kitchen. For a few years the couple would eat from her mother's hearth.

This sort of marriage has the appearance of a trial marriage. The young man gets to know his proposed affines, and they him, before he has sexual intercourse with his wife. If he pleases he can cut his losses and leave, or his proposed affines can make it clear in all sorts of ways that they have come to regret the contract. The marriage is only stabilised when the relations between husband and wife, and between husband and affines are so good that a final ceremony can be performed, called 'the entering in of the son-in-law', whereby the man is fully accepted as a member of the family. Only then can he move his wife away, if he chooses, to set up his own house, but even this is dependent upon the goodwill of her own male relatives.

Let us now imagine the history of a young man who has quite amicably effected such a separation. Because land is plentiful he can move where he pleases, provided that he stays within the area of his chief. He must, however, attach himself to some existing group because he is dependent upon others in a variety of co-operative enterprises. Finally, he would be foolish to settle among people whom he does not know, and it is likely therefore that he will go back to his father's people.

I say 'father's people', but in Bemba society this means either mother's people, on the assumption that the father has stayed put in his own wife's village, or grandmother's people, on the assumption that his father has also, like himself, moved. In effect, then, our young man moves within the jurisdiction of his maternal uncle or maternal grandfather.

In the course of time the man's daughters are contracted to their grooms, who then come to live in the same homestead. If our man has several daughters and can attract a good work team of grooms, if he himself is industrious and in addition wise, generous and amiable, he may well so attract his sons-in-law that they will stay with him. As word of his thriving household spreads around, he may be joined by a widowed sister, and perhaps by her daughter and sons-in-law. Later his sister's sons may choose to bring their wives and children to settle with him. In time he becomes the head of a substantial group.

Dr Richards emphasises the importance of personality in such a development. A man 'gains as a grandfather what he loses as a father'. 'The position of a Bemba grandfather is one that gives great power and authority and is in some respects more enviable than that of the grandfather in a typical patrilineal ... society, since the head of a Bemba grand-family has established his rule by individual efforts and not through the help of his brothers of his patrilineage.' You will recall that the sons of one mother had a sense of close identity among the Nuer (see p. 34). Among the Bemba they set out to pursue their individual destinies relatively early in life. Later they may happen to settle in the homestead of the same maternal uncle, but even if this does occur they will have arrived there by independent routes. The individuality of achievement is only underlined when we remember that the village changes its site every so often. It is at this time, Dr Richards tells us, that loosely attached segments are likely to hive off elsewhere. A man who can in these circumstances maintain and expand his following is inevitably a man of considerable character.

This simplified account of the Bemba family and matriliny does not impose a great strain on our imagination. It must often have happened in some of our own farming families that a farmer who had no son has been pleased to take his able son-in-law into his house and make him his heir. If the young man was not a local boy he might still take root in the neighbourhood of his affines, or he might be able to persuade his wife to sell up and move. We can easily imagine that if there were a large group of the girl's kin in the area considerable pressure might be brought to bear upon her to make her husband stay in the neighbourhood.

Such a situation in our own society is probably exceptional; among the Bemba the rules require uxorilocal residence and authority is derived through matrilineal descent. Nevertheless the families are mobile and relatively small. Membership of the matrilineal clan does not appear either to alter the status of women or significantly to affect the man's freedom of choice. Among the Ashanti, whom we shall look at next, we shall see an all-round tightening up of the matrilineal principle.

Ashanti society was a powerful confederacy in what used to be called the Gold Coast (now Ghana), and it is quite proper to refer to this confederacy as a state. Taking into account obvious differences, the situation was not unlike that which we find in the historical plays of Shakespeare. There was a king, but each of the five chiefs of the confederation was jealous of his own rights and relative autonomy. Chiefs could and did rebel, and the king was dependent upon the loyalty of other chiefs in putting down the rebel.

The Ashanti were finally defeated and annexed by the British after the Sixth Ashanti war in 1901. Their confederation was originally formed in the eighteenth century for the purpose of overthrowing the dominance of Denkyera, a neighbouring state to which the Ashanti were subject. Through the years the confederacy became extremely powerful. Once liberation was achieved it turned to trading wars, both for slaves and for the important trade routes.

There were only eight clans (all founded by women, personalities of mythology) among the Ashanti. These clans were scattered across the confederation, but each was represented in every chiefdom. Each clan had within it noble lineages, in the sense that chieftainship and sub-chieftainship were vested in different clans. Unlike the clans of the Nuer, the Ashanti clans were not genealogically demonstrable; beyond a certain point membership of the clan was simply a political fact, an act of faith. For all that, the membership of the clan was numerous, the law of exogamy applied; a clansman could expect hospitality from fellow members even though they had been hitherto strangers to him; if some office could not be filled by a member of the immediate lineage, the elders of that lineage would call in any suitable man of the same clan to fill it.

Matriliny was not, however, a simple ordering principle, the way in which, so to speak, one got one's surname. The principle of matrilineal descent affected profoundly where, with whom and how one lived. Among the Nuer, clans were only some ten to twelve generations deep. For them the effective lineage was formed by the descendants of a male ancestor some five or six generations back. Among the Ashanti we find that both clans and lineages thrust back far deeper in time, the origins of the former are lost in mythical antiquity and the latter derive from ancestors ten to twelve generations back.

This is important for the Ashanti because the lineage is a local group, occupying a defined territory. So strong is this principle that even in modern times the descendants of a woman who long ago was captured in war could return to the natal lineage of their ancestress and claim rights in its land.

Each such territorial lineage had, moreover, its own head, chosen by the senior men and women of the lineage, who would also be one of the chief's counsellors. The powers and duties of this lineage head included the settling of internal disputes, dealings with other lineage heads, approving the marriage arrangements of lineage members, approving divorce, and in general seeing to the political, moral and economic stability of the community.

I said that the senior women joined with the men in the choice of the lineage head. Ashanti society is marked both by the equality of women in such matters and by the recognition of maternal authority. Whereas among the Bemba one has the impression that women were the channels of a matrilineal society but no more, among the Ashanti the matrilineal organisation is matched by a greater equality of the sexes. Each chief has, for example, a senior woman counsellor who is chosen for him by the elders. In the same way in each chiefdom the senior woman of the royal lineage is the Queen Mother of that chiefdom. You will note that this woman is not, and could not be, the Chief's wife.

Despite the clarity with which the matrilineal principle is spelled out in their social organisation, the Ashanti are not free of the 'puzzle'. They are aware of a conflict between the ties which bind a father to his children and those which bind a man to his matrilineage.

It is possible that the very strength of the matrilineal principle makes this conflict more acute. Custom demands that a mother bear her child in her natal home, and women often spend the early years of married life there. Because the mother has her own agricultural work, the grandmother is often largely responsible for the child's upbringing. In this way the child's legal rights in the matrilineage are affirmed, and the affective ties with his or her maternal kin are established in early infancy. When I say 'affective ties' I refer to something more than the natural love between mother and child which is found the world over. Among the Ashanti, motherhood and the mother–child relationship have very high moral value. Fecundity is a virtue, and a mother who has borne ten children is congratulated in a public ceremony. A barren woman, on the other hand, is an object of 'pity not unmixed with scorn'.

A mother is also the immediate guardian of her children's rights. She keeps her eye on her own brother, the legal guardian of her children, and her husband. Her brother may be tempted to favour his own children, but equally her own husband may be disposed to favour his nephews or nieces. Professor Meyer Fortes points to the dilemma of the Ashanti family. 'To show disrespect towards one's mother is tantamount to sacrilege . . . throughout her life a woman's foremost attachment is to her mother . . . for a man, his mother is his most trusted confidante, especially in intimate personal matters. A man's first ambition is to gain enough money to be able to build a house for his mother if she does not own one.'

It is difficult for us to enter imaginatively into this situation. We can, by referring back to our constructed plan (pp. 44–6), understand the *facts* of the situation, but it is difficult to find an analogous situation which could give us sympathetic entry to that of the Ashanti. This tells us something about our own society.

We accept the cliché about the complexity of life in modern industrial society, and yet I dare to say that very few readers of this book face, or will ever face, moral problems as complex as those of an Ashanti. No doubt there are comparable problems in our own families. A fairly recent feature in some of our newspapers deals with men's wages and women's housekeeping money. These, incidentally, make very interesting reading for the social anthropologist because they bring out the variety in the ways in which people look at marriage and money in our society; we discover a range from the young professional couple with a joint bank account to the couple that positively endorses the view that the man should earn and keep, but give money to his wife when she asks for it. Another notorious problem centres on the generations, notably the older, when the elderly are neither economically or physically independent. Again there are the problems of the professional couple where his professional interests clash with hers, or where the professional interests of both clash with the desire to raise a family. There are also problems of a deeper nature, the tendency to favour one child rather than another, problems of sexual compatibility, mutual boredom and so on.

All these are no doubt problems to which our society gives rise, but they are not directly imposed by our institutions. Indeed, most notions of liberal reform tend to have at their base a notion that improvement means the removing of problems by institutional means; by the provision of creches and 'old folks' homes', by providing contraception, abortion and divorce. An Indian friend of mine who found the treatment of the dependent elderly in our society most repulsive likened 'old folks' homes' to *gaushala*, charitable institutions where aged cows, which being sacred cannot be killed, are kept often in wretched conditions. The nearest moral equivalent to those of the Ashanti that I can think of in our society are the problems of the practising Catholic facing up to his or her own desires, the ban on artificial contraception, and the emotional and economic welfare of the family. Another equivalent might be that of a dedicated member of one of the poorer trade unions called out on strike, who faces the conflict between socialist values and his family's well-being.

The point that I am stressing here is that Ashanti *society* makes for a life more morally complex than our own. In the preceding paragraph I have preferred to speak of 'facing up' and being 'faced with' problems rather than to stress the conflict of values. The word conflict suggests the victory of one side over another or a resolution, a dissolution of conflict by agreement or by the intervention of a third party. The Ashanti know that to try to be a good father or mother, a good brother or sister, or a good son or daughter is to be perpetually balancing values, striving in each circumstance to arrive at a fair distribution of loyalty, affection, care and assistance. They appreciate that this is by no means always possible, that grandmothers can become autocrats, that men can succumb to the temptation to prefer their own children and that the marital union calls for attention if it is not to break up as a result of one partner's failure, however innocent, to preserve this reasonable balance.

If our society is more complex, it is complex in a different way. None of us would give an outsider an account of it as reliable as an average Ashanti adult could give of Ashanti society. Our society is institutionally complex, but morally it is less so. It is interesting to wonder whether the problems to which our society gives rise do not in part relate to our lack of moral complexity, our tendency to translate moral problems into conflicts and our hope or belief that these conflicts can be institutionally solved.

I am going to conclude this particular discussion of family

matters with an example of a society that practises polyandry. Matrilineal societies can perfectly well contain polygyny, and patrilineal societies can have polyandrous marriage. Among the Jaunsari of Northern Uttar Pradesh in India, we find families that are formed from both polygynous and polyandrous unions, together with those that are based purely on one or the other form. There are also families based on monogamous marriages.

The society to which I now want to draw your attention is in south India, in the state of Kerala. Here we are dealing with the Indian caste system, in which we cannot separate one people from another in the way that we could speak of the Nuer or the Ashanti and discuss them in isolation. This is peculiarly true in this case because I have to talk about a matrilineal caste intermarrying with a patrilineal one.

The peoples in question are the Nambudiri Brahmins and the Nayar. Both of these large castes have played an important part in the history of Kerala State. Traditionally they were respectively landlords and warriors. The Nambudiri had, as Brahmans, the highest status, whereas the Nayar belonged to what is classically referred to as the Sudra class, the lowest. The Nambudiri were patrilineal, the Nayar matrilineal. Despite these marked differences the relation between the two castes presents a remarkable instance of social symbiosis, as we shall see.

The Nambudiri Brahmins have a custom which is, I believe, unique; they allow only the eldest son to have a proper marriage, and he also succeeds to the management of the family household and land. The household comprises the man, his wife, sons, unmarried daughters and sons' unmarried daughters. The Nambudiri see in this arrangement an excellent device for limiting the population of any particular family and also for ensuring that the family property is not, as it is elsewhere in India, diminished by division among the sons after the father's death. For the same reasons, although polygyny is not unknown amongst them, the Nambudiri do not encourage the practice.

What about the large number of unmarried women which such a system must create? We know very little about them.

Certainly there was no question of their marrying men of other castes. They were not allowed to go out unattended, and only when they were dead or dying was some form of the marriage ceremony performed to ensure that they did not die as spinsters. I am very struck by the fact that one of the older authorities on south India gives in great detail the procedures, rituals and penalties in cases of adultery by Nambudiri women. It is possible that he is describing the procedures employed for guarding the chastity of all women, married or not. He and other authorities agree that an adulteress, or a woman who had sexual relations with a man of inferior caste, was driven away and treated as socially dead.

The Nambudiri young men, as one might expect, were not so confined and might enter into liaison with women of inferior castes, and it is here that the Nayar become significant.

The Nayar matrilineal family is composed of sisters and brothers, the sons and daughters of the sisters, and the children of their daughters. The children of male members of the family are excluded. The husbands of the women belong to other households and only visit their wives. Similarly, the men of the household visit their wives in other households. It was not, however, the case that a Nayar woman could entertain as many husbands as she pleased from within the Nayar caste; she had to take husbands from families having the same social standing as her own, or a superior standing.

Here I must introduce a new term—*hypergamy*. This word is used by social anthropologists to refer to marriages in which the woman is regarded as marrying a superior, a custom that is commonly associated with a severe ban on marriage of a woman to an inferior. Hypergamy may be formally instituted in society or it may be informal; readers of nineteenth-century novels may have noted that hypergamous notions governed marriage in British society when the two partners were of different rank—a man could marry 'down', but a woman who did not marry into an 'equal' family or a 'superior' one disgraced herself by marrying 'down'. In the twentieth century we can observe the same theme in such works as D. H. Lawrence's *Lady Chatterley's Lover* and, later, John Osborne's *Look Back in Anger*. In the classical law books of ancient India the Sanskrit word for hypergamy is *anuloma*, which means literally to go with the hair. The opposite would be *pratiloma*, against the hair. Among the Nayar *anuloma*, or hypergamy, was not simply permitted to women who could find no husband of equal rank; it was regarded as a higher form of marriage because it brought into the family the superior blood of the husband.

The traditional relationship between the Nayar and the Nambudiri was that the women of royal or princely families among the Nayar were permitted to find partners among the unmarried younger brothers of the Nambudiri family.

This relationship between the two castes was not informal and ungoverned by custom. We saw that the Nambudiri performed token marriages to prevent their women dying as spinsters. The Nayar also had a marriage ceremony which was not necessarily associated with cohabitation. Whether or not a Nayar girl of high rank actually cohabited with a Nambudiri Brahman she was required to go through a marriage ritual with him before having sexual relationships with other men. This Nambudiri 'husband' would be a kind of spiritual father to the children that she would in future bear by other men. These children would, for example, at his death observe certain mourning customs just as though they were his progeny. By this device the Nayar matrilineal family could enjoy the superiority that a hypergamous marriage brings even in circumstances in which there were no Nambudiri men available as regular lovers.

The word 'lovers' must be understood in its most general sense because, to the extent that it suggests a degree of casual liaison, it would misrepresent what, by and large, was the situation among the Nayar. Certainly occasional visitors to a woman were not unknown, but they had to be of suitable status and were expected to make a gift to the family on their departure. A more common situation was one in which a group of Nayar men shared what we would call a 'common law wife'. The largest number of such 'visiting husbands' recorded dates from the early eighteenth century, when we are told a woman might have 'twelve but no more at one time'. In more recent times it would appear to have been somewhere in the range of four to six and, as we might expect, these were men from the same neighbourhood as the woman.

It was customary for a husband to visit his wife after the evening meal and to leave early in the morning. The first-comer would leave his weapons outside his wife's room to signify his presence to any later-comer. Individual husbands were expected to make some gift, such as a cloth, at the beginning of the relationship and to maintain it by regular gifts at the main festivals of the year. If these gifts were not given it was taken as a sure sign that the man wished to end the relationship. More important than these gifts was the collective responsibility of the group of husbands to acknowledge paternity when the woman became pregnant. This one or more of them would do by paying the expenses of the delivery and by giving a gift to the low-caste woman who acted as midwife. A modern authority, Dr Kathleen Gough, tells us that even in the late 1940s 'a Nayar girl who became pregnant before the modern marriage ceremony was regarded as acting within the canons of traditional religious law if she could simply find a Nayar of suitable sub-caste to pay her delivery expenses'. For lack of this it was still possible for her and her child to be totally ostracised. In such circumstances, Dr Gough tells us, her kinsmen would perform her funeral rites as if she were dead and she herself would become a refugee in some distant town. Finally, we should note that all the people, both men and women, who were currently engaged in this sort of relationship with the members of a particular Nayar family were referred to collectively as *bandhukkal*—'joined ones'—were given appropriate kinship terms and were invited to household feasts.

Despite all this the visiting husbands had no economic obligations to their shared wife or her children, and no customary obligation apart from the matter of childbirth expenses. Even the gifts that they gave her were 'personal luxuries', such as 'extra clothing, articles of toilet, betel and areca-nut the giving of which is associated with courtship ... not, be it noted, [with] the maintenance of either mother or child'. Even when the biological fatherhood was known, the father was not expected to show any particular interest in his children and certainly had no obligations to them. *All* the children of one woman would address *all* her visiting husbands as 'lord' without discrimination; they looked to their maternal kin, headed by their mother's eldest brother, for all the emotional, moral and material care which any family provides. Dr Gough tells us that a man who developed a particularly loving relationship with his wife might be suspected by his matrilineal kin of giving her more in the way of gifts and money than custom required.

The polyandrous marriages of the Nayar are now a thing of the past. The institution was well suited to the professional militarism of the Nayar caste and the days when able-bodied men would spend a large part of the year in military exercises of various sorts. After the establishment of British rule Nayar men returned to their estates and, inevitably, as the sex ratio of the neighbourhood was restored to normal, monogamous relationships began to emerge. This tendency was strengthened by the barrage of European criticism of the earlier customs. Dr Gough tells us that many modern Nayar are ashamed of the old custom and some go so far as to deny that it ever occurred.

## Summary

We have distinguished two kinds of polygamy: polygyny which means one man with several wives, and polyandry which *appears* to mean that one wife has several husbands. We looked at the way in which the Nuer of the Southern Sudan arranged their polygynous homesteads and we attempted to compare this with our own notions of the family by imagining what problems such an arrangement would give rise to in our own society. From this we were led to consider the importance of descent in Nuer society and we spoke of unilineal descent, a way of reckoning descent which emphasises either the male or the female line as the important one. Unilineal descent among the Nuer is governed by what we call the *agnatic* principle, according to which men and women who share a common male ancestor feel themselves to be bound together politically and spiritually in a very special way. We saw how, step by step, as we go back in time, the links of agnatic descent spread out across the whole of Nuerland. The largest unit of people united in this way we call the clan, and we saw that the clan is not the only important unifying factor among the Nuer. From a consideration of our own ideas about kith and kin, neighbours and relatives, we went on to look at the Nuer tribe, which is a territorial unit inhabited by people from a variety of clans. This in turn brought out an important distinction in Nuer thinking about the world— the distinction between *diel* and *rul*, the first-comers and the second-comers. Because the members of one clan are scattered all over the Nuerland it followed that members of one and the same clan could be first-comers in one tribal territory and second-comers in another. We saw how the second-comers in any particular tribe identified themselves with the first-comers and linked themselves with them by marriage, and this gave us some insight into the role of marriage as a political institution weaving together people from different clans in one tribal territory and thus converting neighbours into kinsmen.

We turned from the Nuer to look at another form of unilineal descent, matriliny, and had another look at the word polyandry. We saw that matriliny and polyandry are not simply the reverse of patriliny and polygyny; this was because, first, we do not know of societies in which women wield power as men do in others and, second, because polyandry in effect amounts not so much to one woman having several husbands as to several husbands having one wife. This discussion led us to introduce two new terms—virilocal and uxorilocal marriage—which distinguished kinds of marriage according to whether the married couple lived in the homeplace of the husband or of the wife.

As an example of a matrilineal society we looked at the

Bemba. We saw how young Bemba men enter into trial marriages which are uxorilocal and we noted that the man is less dependent upon his kin in the matter of bridewealth than among the Nuer. If the marriage proved a success the young man could move off with his bride to associate himself with some successful male relative in his matrilineage. We saw how a Bemba man can become successful and attract others to join him, and also how the perpetual need to move and found new settlements was a constant test of this ability.

Matriliny among the Bemba did not seem to affect the status of women or the relative freedom of men. We looked, for contrast, at the matrilineal Ashanti. Here we were dealing with a powerful confederation of five chiefdoms. We noted that the eight clans founded by female figures of Ashanti myth were scattered across the whole federation and that the Ashanti were not unlike the Nuer in that respect. The big difference lay in the fact that Ashanti lineages had a much greater time depth and were much more closely associated with particular territories. Unlike the Bemba women, the Ashanti women commanded much greater respect and appeared to have more voice in the political and domestic affairs of the lineage. Even so, we saw that the Ashanti were not free of the conflict between the formal principles of a matrilineal organisation and the ties of affection between a man and his own children. This gave us the opportunity to appreciate the considerable moral complexity of Ashanti society and to compare it, from this point of view, with our own.

We concluded with a brief look at the relation between the patrilineal Nambudiri and the matrilineal Nayar of south India and introduced the term *hypergamy*—a rule which requires a woman to marry a superior if she does not marry an equal and which severely condemns the marriage of a woman to an inferior. The Nambudiri had a rule which allowed only the eldest son to marry a Nambudiri girl and the younger brothers could only have inferior liaisons with Nayar girls. But from the Nayar point of view these 'inferior liaisons' were hypergamous marriages, which they valued highly even when these marriages were only token affairs. We saw also that the Nayar practised polyandry and we looked at the rules and etiquette governing these 'visiting husbands'. Finally, we saw that, suited as this polyandry was to the old days of Nayar militancy, it declined with the advent of British rule and the spread of Western notions of marriage.

## Reading notes

Arensberg, C. M., and Kimball, S. T., *The Irish Countryman—an anthropological study*, New York, 1939.

Bohannan, P., and Middleton, J., *Kinship and Social Organisation*, New York, 1968. See Part II—'Unilineal Descent'.

Bott, E., *Family and Social Network*, London, 1957. This study should be read together with Willmott and Young (see below).

Evans-Pritchard, E. E., *The Nuer*, Oxford, 1940. See particularly Chapters IV and V. A simpler and more general account of the political and lineage systems will be found in Fortes and Evans-Pritchard (see below).

Evans-Pritchard, E. E., *Kinship and Marriage among the Nuer*, Oxford, 1951. Also useful background for Chapter 3.

Fortes, M., and Evans-Pritchard, E. E. (eds.), *African Political Systems*, Oxford, 1940. The whole of this could profitably be read in association with Chapter 5; for the present the articles by Evans-Pritchard 'The Nuer of the Southern Sudan' and by Richards 'The Political System of the Bemba Tribe' provide a useful background to the preceding discussion.

Frankenberg, R., *Village on the Border*, London, 1957. This is a study of a Welsh village which does not focus on problems of kinship; nevertheless it draws our attention to the importance of kinship in contemporary society.

Frankenberg, R., 'British community studies: problems of synthesis' in *The Social Anthropology of Complex Societies*, Association of Social Anthropologists (ASA) Monographs, London, 1966.

Frankenberg, R., *Communities in Britain—social life in town and country*, Pelican, 1966.

Gorer, G., 'The Perils of Hypergamy', *New Statesman and Nation*, Vol. 53, 4 May 1957. A brief article which highlights the theme of interclass marriage in some novels of the 1950s. It was reprinted in an edition by G. Feldman and M. Gartenberg, *Protest*, London, 1959.

Gough, E. K., 'The Nayars and the definition of Marriage', Journal of the Royal Anthropological Society, Vol. 89, 1959.

Lewis, I. M., 'Problems in the Comparative Study of Unilineal Descent' in *The Relevance of Models for Social Anthropology*, ASA Monographs, London, 1965.

Mair, L., *New Societies*, London, 1963. Chapters 3 and 5. The effects on the family of social and political change.

Majumdar, D. N., *Himalayan Polyandry*, London, 1962.

Malinowski, B., *Crime and Custom in Savage Society*, London, 1926. Part II, Chapter III, 'Systems of Law in Conflict', considers a situation where paternal love conflicts in a matrilineal society with the rights of the maternal kin. This book would also provide some useful background for Chapter 4.

Mayer, A. C., *Caste and Kinship in Central India*, London, 1960. This is very good study of kinship in an Indian context. In Chapter VIII the author makes a useful distinction between 'kindred of co-operation' and 'kindred of recognition' which can be compared with the British situation sketched out on pp. 36–40 of the preceding chapter.

Pocock, D., *Kanbi and Patidar*, Oxford, 1972. This is a study of a peasant community in western India where hypergamous marriage is highly valued for all that the problems which it poses are recognised. A general account will be found in Chapter 3.

Radcliffe-Brown, A. R., and Forde, D. (eds.), *African Systems of Kinship and Marriage*, Oxford, 1950. See in particular the articles by Fortes 'Kinship and Marriage among the Ashanti' and by Richards 'Some Types of Family Structure amongst the Central Bantu'; this latter article compares the Bemba with other matrilineal societies of Central Africa. As a whole the book will be useful in reading Chapter 3.

Schneider, D. M., and Gough, K., *Matrilineal Kinship*, California, 1961. This is the only substantial modern work that attempts to achieve an overall view of its subject.

# 3

# Marriage

Before reading this chapter, write an essay on marriage. How do marriages occur and how are they socially recognised? What is the purpose of religious and civil ceremonies connected with marriage, and are they necessary? Do other relationships come into being as a result of a marriage and, if they do, are they associated with certain rights and duties? Think about divorce, its effects and the circumstances which make it possible, and consider what light the possibility of divorce throws upon your understanding of the role of marriage in society. Finally, reflect upon the advantages or disadvantages of marriage between people of different social background; do your reflections tell you anything about your views of class, nationality or race?

\*     \*     \*

Human beings, like all mammals, mate, copulate and have issue. Like these other creatures, they rear families which survive until the young can be independent. Among most animals the extent to which the father is a member of this family varies. Humans, unlike animals, marry. Marriage is the basis of human society as we know it. Western society today can clearly tolerate a number of couples who mate without producing issue or who have issue, in both cases without marriage. However, the reader is invited to consider what other changes would be necessary in our society were the whole range of institutions relating to marriage, together with marriage itself, to be abolished.

Marriage produces society and daily our social forms are

reinforced by marriages. The reader may entertain ideals about the classless society, or the need to reduce discrimination between the races, or about romantic love. Nevertheless the overwhelming majority will marry, or have already married, into their own race, nation and class, having, I trust, fallen deeply in love, and enjoyed to the full the illusion that they have made an entirely free and individual choice. How could it be otherwise? Nevertheless distinctions between classes or races in any society can only be obliterated by obligatory miscegenation.

The conservative power of marriage is best illustrated by an anecdote from my own experience in East Africa. A young Hindu acquaintance of mine in Zanzibar had ruined every attempt his father had made to find him a wife. Zanzibar in those days, the 1950s, was a quiet friendly world in which the only segregated societies were the English club and the women folk of the older Arab families. Apart from these, social intercourse between races and religions was a good deal more free than on the main land. My young friend had plenty of girlfriends, an English girl working in the British Council, a Christian Goanese nurse, a Moslem girl who had been a class-mate at school. This degree of quite innocent intimacy was enough to damn him in the eyes of prospective fathers-in-law in his own community, the Bania, trader caste.

This young man, like many of his generation among the Asians of East Africa, was a great romantic and nourished his ideals on Western films and novels. However, a year or so before I met him, he had finally succumbed to his father's pressure and his mother's distress, and married a girl of their choosing. He had settled down happily and explained himself as follows: 'In my community when women are serving rice, if the rice sticks to the spoon they tap their wrists to shake it off. In other communities the women bang the spoon on the *tali* (metal eating dish). Imagine having to listen to that every day of my life!'

This story sums up the dependence of the marital relationship upon common culture and, as every married person will know, the example given is only apparently trivial. Had our young man married outside his community he would almost certainly have been obliged to live with his wife in isolation from the relatives on both sides. In other societies anomalous marriages have to bear a strain of a different order as relatives on each side make their presence felt all too much.

I would not wish to be misunderstood. I have no desire to perpetuate any form of discrimination. I am simply pointing to the fact that the vast majority of people in any society are governed by endogamy. Indeed, it is difficult to imagine our present society surviving were this not so. In most societies there are explicit rules. In our society such rules and ideals as we have blind us to the unconscious operation of racial, national and class endogamy, and we should make it our business to become conscious of these forces.

I said a little earlier that marriage produces society. To be more precise I should have said that exogamy produces society. Man separated himself from the higher primates when he began to exchange his womenfolk with men of other bands to create alliances. The so-called 'incest taboo' or prohibition of incest is simply the intensification of the exogamic injunction 'Thou shalt marry outside the band', and therefore 'Thou shalt not marry within it'.

In anthropological literature the incest taboo ranks high among the perennial problems, largely for historical reasons. First of all there was Freud's famous *Totem and Taboo*, in which Freud attempted to discover the origins of incest. This was first published in 1913 and was followed by an English translation in 1919. The significance of these dates is that the protagonist of psychoanalysis had made a great thrust into an area of anthropological discussion, just about the time that Malinowski, a mercurial character of great ambition, was about to claim the chieftaincy of that area! Malinowski inevitably clashed with Ernest Jones, Freud's apostle to the gentiles, and the debate which they began has, obeying the law of intellectual inertia, lingered on.

There is nothing surprising about the fact that the feelings appropriate to a rule governing a large collectivity are intensified in the smaller groups that compose it. Small wonder that dictators and totalitarian states direct a great deal of energy towards breaking up the sentiments that bind a family together. Consider loyalty, which at the level of the nation becomes patriotism. We all know very well that in the average family our loyalty to our parents and brothers and sisters is a more intense *feeling* than our loyalty to our employers or our country. Or perhaps we do not all know, simply because the majority of us are saved from the need to choose. Here, once more, I can only appeal to the reader's imagination. Could he or she report a criminal offence committed by a member of the immediate family as easily as an offence committed by a stranger? Or, to make the question more interesting, at what point in the reader's scale of values would he or she have no hesitation in breaking the disloyalty taboo?

There is no innate, in the sense of instinctive, horror of disloyalty and there is no innate horror of incest existing separately from the exogamous rule. The two constitute a solidary fact of human nature. To put the matter another way: you are only likely to give some credence to the existence of an instinctual 'horror of incest' if you also can think of human beings without culture. On a more factual level one has only to talk to people who have experienced real poverty in our own society and who remember the shared family bed to appreciate than an apparent 'horror of incest' is the product of favourable economic circumstances, public law and morality, and reasonable facilities for sexual experimentation and play with outsiders.

It may help if I give a brief example of incest as it is viewed by the Nuer and compare it with our own. We think of incest as a sexual relationship between any two members of a family composed of two parents and their children. (Interestingly, the Punishment of Incest Act, 1908, includes the grandparents in this category together with the presumption that the offender would be a male.) Are there any other category of kin that you would include yourself? Uncles and aunts perhaps, but would you have included cousins? If you are a married man, what about your wife's sister? If you are a married woman, what about your sister's husband? Would it be incestuous to have sexual intercourse with that person? You might think it traitorous and certainly adulterous, but I doubt that you would think it incestuous, let alone have any instinctive repulsion. Yet *marriage* with the deceased wife's sister was impossible in this country until 1907, when the Deceased Wife's Sister Marriage Act was passed. Even then, clergymen were still entitled to refuse to solemnise such marriages, and the Act still held that *adultery* with the wife's sister was *incestuous* adultery. To revert to the matter of cousins, what is your opinion about marriage between them? Is it or was it ever in this country regarded as incestuous?

It is in the nature of their social life that the Nuer recognise a wider range of kin, agnatic and affinal, than ourselves. We might expect that sexual congress and marriage are forbidden over as wide an area. Evans-Pritchard tells us, for example, that 'the thought of relations with (a full brother's) wife evokes the disgust Nuer feel at any association of sex with the mother'. The same goes for the wives of the father's own full brothers. But sexual relations with the wives of the father's half-brother, of a man's own half-brothers and of their sons is not incestuous at all. The Nuer do feel that it is disrespectful to commit adultery with the father's half-brother's wife; that is a different matter.

The Nuer word that is translated 'incest' is *rual*, and among them we observe, in the above example, an intensification of feeling in the smallest unity of their society, the mother's hut. As relationships become more distant and at the boundary of the exogamous area there are inevitably grey areas, and it is debatable whether marriage would be incestuous or not. Sometimes, Evans-Pritchard tells us, a fear of possible *rual* is advanced as a polite way of rejecting a suitor, when a desirable son-in-law of the same degree of kinship might have been accepted. Where real doubt exists the Nuer perform a special sacrifice as a precaution for fear that the possible *rual* might render the marriage barren.

In the example I have given from Evans-Pritchard's work I would like to draw attention to the word 'disgust' because of its emotional strength. Some of us would also use it, would we not, at the thought of sexual relations with siblings, but could scarcely feel disgust at the thought of sexual relations with a sibling's spouse. Or do you think that your own reaction is entirely normal, whereas the Nuer are a bit odd? In fact, your feelings are as imprinted by your culture as are those of the Nuer. To put it another way, one aspect of the Oedipus story that is not always emphasised is that Oedipus in ignorance did happily marry his mother and have issue by her; no natural instinct alerted him to his danger.

Man has, then, built into his nature the injunction to marry outside. If you consider the sexual life of all the higher primates you will appreciate the revolutionary character of this difference. Whatever similarities between man and the higher apes have been discovered, and there are increasingly many, human beings are alone in using women to create alliances with other bands. It is for this reason that we say marriage produces society. Whatever may be advanced against Freud's knowledge of the facts and his handling of them, his intuition was profound; when the young male primates no longer compete with each other and with their leader for the females of the band then, and only then, do we begin to speak of the human.

The emphasis falls then upon a positive injunction rather than upon a negative prohibition. When you turn to anthropological monographs you will find that the middle-class and twentieth-century preoccupation with incest leads many writers to describe and talk about 'marriage prohibitions'. Your thought and imagination will develop if, every time you find this phrase or its equivalent, you dismiss it and look for the categories or groups within which marriage is required or encouraged. Use the implicit rules of exogamy and endogamy in our own society. You do not feel *prohibited* from marrying your own siblings. Where you do feel prohibitions these will relate to the remoter areas of your experience (see p. 65). You would do well to probe your feelings in these areas because they indicate important contours of your present personal anthropology.

This realisation carries our argument a stage further. Man marries outwards, but not with infinite choice. If he is an exogamous animal, his exogamy is contained within a wider endogamy. This is not apparent if the injunction to marry out is specified, and a man is required to marry in this particular category or that particular clan. Where, however, his choice of marriage is not formally regulated, then the informal regulation of endogamy comes into play. As I have already indicated, it is here that the culture of his class, nation or race will work upon him. Man is at the stage in his evolution where he presents a paradox. His exogamous urge moves him towards the creation of unity, while his endogamous tendency perpetuates disunity.

The interplay of these two injunctions creates human society, and the way in which men in different times and places handle the situation accounts for the internal shape of a society at that time. The opposition of the two accounts for the thread of hostility which often interlaces the relationships between affines. Social anthropologists recognise the representative quality of the African aphorism 'We marry our enemies'. It is only an aphorism because the 'enemies', the outsiders, are chosen from within the infinitely wider circle of all possible outsiders. They are placed between two brackets, so to speak: (insiders [and affines) outsiders] = society. The shadowy vestiges of this situation are found in our own society in the perennial jokes about mothers-in-law. In these the tension is always supposed to be between the husband and his wife's mother, even though in fact the extent to which either mother-in-law can or does interfere with the life of the new family is equal. What these jokes express is the supposed hostility between those who give and those who receive the bride. The father who has given his daughter is the ally of the man to whom he has given her and cannot therefore be the butt of hostile jokes; it is his wife who must carry the invidious burden. Let us note, in passing, that what is said of the wife's mother is said 'in joke'. In our folk tales where tension is between the wife and her husband's mother this is not regarded as a laughing matter. In these tales the husband's mother is sometimes represented as a witch. This situation is a serious one because the groom's mother is represented as rejecting the new alliance.

Before we look at one particular case in some detail let me stress a fact that should ideally be printed in block capitals at the top of each of the following pages: MARRIAGE IS A SOCIAL FACT. Despite all illusion of freedom you will find, or have already found, your mate where society directed you to do so. Even if your marriage is statistically unusual it is within the tolerated area of deviation.

The case that I am going to examine in some detail is taken from my own fieldwork, and there are two advantages to this. First, there is the obvious benefit that I can from my own experience fill in aspects of reality that, when I am using someone else's material, I have to recreate imaginatively. The second advantage is that we can move straight into the consideration of traditional society in India, a country that those anthropologists who have worked in smaller collectivities quite unnecessarily regard as dauntingly complicated.

I shall discuss a caste in Gujarat, which is, roughly, the squarish peninsula that juts out of the west coast of India to the south of the border with Pakistan. The people in question are known as the Patidar, who inhabit an area of central Gujarat, approximately between Ahmedabad in the north and Cambay in the south. In the past the Patidar were farmers and the bulk of the population is still agricultural. However, in the nineteenth and twentieth centuries many of them have moved into commerce, industry and the professions, both in India and abroad. Whereas we can arrive at reasonable estimates of population in smaller societies, it is not possible when we speak of a large caste in India. The Patidar in India, in East and South Africa, in Fiji, in Canada, in America and in the United Kingdom would have to be counted in hundreds of thousands. To give you some idea of comparative scale: the village in which I lived

in India had a total population of about 2500 and was considered to be a small one. This is slightly more than the total
population of the Zulu at the time when we first hear of them
(see p. 133).

In the following pages I am going to isolate the Patidar from
the relations which they have with other castes in the caste
system and to concentrate on their internal organisation with
particular regard to their marriages.

Thus isolated, a large caste can very well be compared with
an endogamous clan as that institution is commonly described
in, say, literature on Africa. All the members of the caste are
regarded as having descended from, usually, a mythical ancestor:
the Patidar regard themselves as descended from a son of
Rama, the divine hero of Indian sacred literature and legend.
Marriage must take place within the caste and in principle,
therefore, any member of the caste can marry another.

Much like the African dominant clan, the Patidar caste is
dominant, if not quite in numbers, certainly in wealth and
power over a wide area, and its population is broken up into
villages, where its members live together with members of
several other castes. In his or her daily affairs a Patidar will have
as much to do with men and women of these other castes as
with other Patidar in other villages. He or she will certainly be
better acquainted with, and have more real friendships in, these
other castes than with Patidar in other villages where there are
no marriage ties.

The Patidar living in a village do not intermarry with each
other. In some villages the bulk of the Patidar population is
composed of the descendants of one man, in others the settlement is heterogeneous; in both cases, however, marriage within
the village is regarded not as incestuous or as a violation of a
strict exogamous rule, as marriage within a lineage (which is
unthinkable) certainly would be. A marriage within the village
could only take place between a family which had moved in
relatively recently and one of the poorest families in that village.
The fact that a family had had to leave its natal village and
settle elsewhere must imply that something was very wrong

with it, and the fact that people in the host village were willing so much as to contemplate marriage with such a family would suggest that they themselves were unable to find marriage partners for themselves anywhere else. Were such a marriage to occur it would then be contracted between the lowest of the low in that village; and so it would be regarded.

The vast majority of Patidar marriages are between groups in different villages. Marriage is an expensive affair and the one occasion on which the head of the Patidar household likes to be lavish. Not surprisingly, therefore, Patidar of relatively equal economic status tend to intermarry. Please note that we are dealing here with people who live in and operate a cash economy, and among whom there is considerable economic inequality. The total income of all Patidar resident in Gujarat alone is greater than the total income of any other caste in their area, but it is even less equally divided than income is equally divided in any category in our own society that we might call 'the middle class'. This is because the two concepts 'social class' and 'economic class' are closely related in our society, whereas in caste society they are less closely linked. As I have indicated there are some Patidar who are very poor despite the fact that, as members of this caste, they enjoy a relatively high status.

This tendency in the past to separate out into groups of intermarrying families allows us to make an interesting comparison with other societies. It must be the case that, in those cultures where a man must give cattle for his bride, a man with more cattle than another can have several wives, whereas a man with few cattle can have only one. Equally, a man who has many cattle, several wives and many sons and daughters must ask more cattle for his daughters in order to marry his sons than a man who has fewer of all these goods. The same goes for any society in which goods, however these are reckoned, can be accumulated. A man whose circumstances allow him to accumulate more grain, or human skulls, or pigs, or blankets—and all these have been reckoned as human goods somewhere—will, other things being equal, give his daughters to those who can reciprocate with gifts according to his own scale. The potential inequalities in such situations may be hidden by the social categories 'aristocrat', 'commoner' and the like, but they are nonetheless real. The situation is very different indeed where goods cannot be accumulated, where game or yams or berries must be consumed as they become available or go to waste.

The Patidar caste is, then, divided up into groups of villages that tend to marry more with each other than with other villages. These are not groupings of neighbouring villages because differences in wealth are not immediately related to the fertility of the soil, which is almost uniformly fertile. Differences arise rather from past and present investment in land, the degree of involvement in commerce, and historical relations with other villages; for example, in some cases wealthy Patidar in one village have bought up substantial areas of land from poorer Patidar in another village and permanently limited the capacity of subsequent generations there to improve their conditions, at least by the traditional practice of agriculture.

We find, then, that these intermarrying groups are scattered in the area, and three adjacent villages are, for example, very likely to have their strongest affinal relationships with three different sets of villages several miles away from them and from each other. It is quite possible in these circumstances that the Patidar of these three villages, unless they have interlinking commercial interests or casual friendships, may know very little of each other and have at best nodding acquaintances.

The situation as I have described it so far is from one point of view not so very different from the state of affairs in our own urban society. It is a notorious fact that we for the most part have a nodding acquaintance with the people in our neighbourhood—the inhabitants at our end of the street, the people who use the same shops—but we may not know their names and we neither know nor care with whom they have affinal relations. For our part, our affinal relations may be scattered across the country or over the world and are mostly with people of much the same economic conditions as ourselves, or of our parents where the two differ as they can sharply in our society.

The difference between ourselves and the Patidar on this score arises from the fact that they have different ideas about what constitutes a good, i.e. respectable, marriage. For them the notion that the bride is a gift from one family to another is not limited to a symbolic expression; it is enacted in a most practical way. A man who would contract a good marriage will give not only his daughter but also a substantial dowry. After the marriage, throughout his lifetime and in the lifetime of his sons, he and they will remain in a giving position. What this amounts to is that on ceremonial occasions of all sorts they will continue to give gifts to their girls' husbands and their families. Among the wealthier it is by no means unheard of that the bride's family will undertake, even at the time of marriage, to pay for the university education of her children.

Given the general tendency for intermarriage to take place between families of relatively equal economic condition, you may imagine that there is one very simple way in which the ideal sketched out in the preceding paragraph could be achieved with minimal hardship, and that would be by exchanging a son and a daughter for a daughter and a son. This was a possibility that I raised very early in my dealings with the Patidar. I raised it because the business of getting a daughter married often imposes heavy burdens, both emotional and financial, on a father. I have known men to travel around for weeks, make inquiries over months and even bankrupt themselves in order to get a good son-in-law.

My 'solution' was put to an old man in the village where I was living, and I can still recall after twenty years the look of embarrassed distaste that crossed his face as I spoke. His answer, delivered in the rather low voice of one who is obliged to speak of unpleasant matters, was: 'In such a situation the girl's brother (*sala*) and the sister's husband (*banevi*) would be the same, and that is not good.' This calls for a good deal of explanation, but for the present let us be sure that we understand the pattern of relationships. In the diagram opposite and elsewhere I use the conventional symbols, a triangle, a circle and an equals sign to signify male, female and marriage respectively, and unbroken horizontal lines to denote common descent from unbroken vertical lines. In a situation of direct exchange, A is the brother of B, the brother-in-law of C and the husband of D; equally C is the brother-in-law of A, the brother of D and the husband of B. It is a perfectly balanced reciprocal relationship, and in economic

$$
\begin{array}{ccc}
\triangle & = & \bigcirc \\
A & & D \\
& & \\
\bigcirc & = & \triangle \\
B & & C
\end{array}
$$

terms neither side is the loser when it comes to marriage expenses. Why, then, did this Patidar gentleman find it so distasteful a proposition?

The answer is partly given on p. 76. This would not be a good marriage precisely because it would be a symmetrical one; or, in other words, it is a bad marriage because neither side stands clearly marked as the giver of a bride. How can a family be said to have given their daughter when they have received in return a daughter from their in-laws? The Gujarati word for such a marriage is *avej*, and this also means trade or barter. I touch here on the whole matter of gift-giving and reciprocity which must be understood by anyone who studies or practises social anthropology. The seminal work on the subject was written by Marcel Mauss in 1925, when he was stimulated by Malinowski's reports on the Trobriand Islanders to publish his Essay on the *Gift* (English translation 1966). In 1949 Claude Lévi-Strauss underlined the significance of Mauss's ideas in a

major work, *The Elementary Structures of Kinship* (English translation 1969). Lévi-Strauss describes exchange as a 'total
phenomenon . . . comprising food, manufactured objects, and
that most precious category of goods, women' (pp. 60–1).

I do not propose here to do more than draw attention to this
important matter and, rather than attempt a paraphrase of the
lengthy accounts which should be read, I will give an example
from our own society.

Two men meet for a drink in a pub. One or the other says,
'What will you have?' It is almost obligatory for the first person
who gets to the bar to say this and the response of his partner
will vary according to the relationship, temporary or permanent,
between the two. If the other man has invited the first to meet
him for a drink, he may respond 'Let me get this', and very
likely the first man will let him make the first purchase. I say the
first purchase because, as every male British reader will know,
it must be followed by a second round, which in this case must
be paid for by whoever did not pay for the first one. The
obligation is not only upon number two to buy but also on
number one to accept. This is customary procedure and any
departure from it must be justified by a special explanation.
Number one must be known to be in a real hurry if he can leave
without having at least 'a half' or 'a short'. If he is only relatively
in a hurry he may say 'Just a quick one', and perhaps give due
warning of imminent departure by saying 'This must be my last'.
Again, number one can buy a second round having bought the
first if he is willing to accept and be accepted as the wealthier of
the two, and his relationship with his partner is such that this
'makes no difference'. This is the principle of reciprocity at
work, each person insists on being alternatively host and guest,
and both work to produce a balance. In understanding the principle of reciprocity social anthropologists argue that, in the
situation where our number one buys both drinks, number two
*reciprocates* by giving him, in that context, a superior status.

When more men are involved or longer periods of time—a
whole evening or even a lifetime of drinking together—the
reciprocity can be delayed. Two friends who drink together

regularly may agree that they have had enough even though one had bought X rounds and the other only X minus one. I have been very struck in such circumstances to note how the memory of the 'debt' lies, as it were, dormant in the mind of the 'debtor' so that the next time they meet he makes sure of buying the first round himself. In larger groups or 'schools' of drinkers the obligation to complete the cycle of reciprocity will vary in weight according to the intimacy of the group. Not only will a relative stranger, for example, feel the obligation to buy his round; the other members of the 'school' will feel obliged to accept his offer, however late the evening. Thus one can observe a group of men downing a pint of beer against the landlord's clock simply to ensure a complete cycle in which each one has been a host and all have been guests.

Let me observe further in connection with drinking 'schools' the way in which their membership works towards a relative homogeneity in the material standing of their members. It follows from what has been said that each member in a group of, let us say, six must be able to buy at least six drinks, of which some may be more expensive than his own. He must be prepared to cope with the odd stranger who may attach himself briefly, or a friend of another member. He must also be in a position to meet the expansion of the group from six to, shall we say, eight. Often enough it happens that a man is obliged to change his pub or his drinking hours when his usual 'school' has grown too big. I know landlords who strongly dislike the over-generous man who, by forcing others into reciprocal relations, creates buying obligations that can frighten regulars away.

Let me conclude this particular discussion with the remark that, despite persistent inquiries, I have not been able to discover a similar ritualised reciprocity among women in Britain. The difficulty women have in reciprocating a drink with a man suggests that reciprocal drinking between men is an expression of friendly rivalry of a kind which is inappropriate, conventionally, between the sexes. I will stick out my head and affirm that in most sections of our society a boy and a girl whose relationship is one of courtship will at best allow only token reciprocity from the girl. She may, for example, pay for one round of drinks and may even be allowed to go so far as to order the drinks herself at the bar.

Reciprocity is a basic feature of all human society. It rests on the principle that one gives and expects to receive in return, but this is not to be a commercial transaction. In a commercial transaction I dispose of things that I don't want as much as the things for which I exchange them. In giving a gift I give away something that I value to create a relationship. And note that the immediate return of an identical object, or of something blatantly worth the same price, defeats the purpose of my gift. The person who reciprocates a gift must assess the right period of delay, not too long and certainly not too short, judge the right moment and give something which is neither clearly more valuable than the original gift nor grossly of equal value.

We can appreciate this when we consider the most banal gift exchanges that take place in our own society—Christmas cards. Consider what your feelings are, however slightly they may be registered, when you receive a card identical to the one that you have sent. Or, to put it another way, if you had already chosen a card to send to someone but before posting it received an identical card from them, what prevents you from just going ahead with your original intention? And if you are sufficiently strong-minded and not deterred, why do you feel necessary to refer to the coincidence in an added message?

The paired injunctions marry outside one category and marry inside another give coherence and shape to a society. Amongst ourselves the strength of social class is to be measured by the number of marriages which take place within each class. Equally, social change in this area is indicated by the number of marriages which cross the bounds of social class, and the degree to which they do so. In our class society mobility is possible in theory, if less so in practice. In a caste society intercaste marriage is theoretically impossible, but in certain circumstances, as we shall see, this does occur. The contrast of caste and class on this score provides a simple illustration of the proposition with which I opened this paragraph. Our belief in human equality, however we practise it, and the value we set on ambition, success and the like make us think that the rigid rule of caste endogamy is some-how harsh, superstitious and even perhaps 'primitive'; certainly many people in modern India so regard it. To this extent we keep our social classes 'open' so that intermarriage is possible and does also occur, as do interracial and international marriages. In traditional India the status of castes rests upon religious criteria which apply over an area far wider than the social organisation. They are fundamental to the traditional cosmology; these values are reaffirmed by the insistence on caste endogamy and would be eroded by a significant increase of intercaste marriages.

Some readers of this book can construct from their own memories changes that have taken place in our own attitudes to marriage and class over the last fifty years, others can discover these facts from parents and grandparents. They can also range more widely by reading nineteenth- and twentieth-century novels and dramas with an eye to the relation between material achievement on one hand and marriage on the other. To what extent does self-improvement in the economic sense win social approval? To what extent is economic self-improvement ap-proved only when it is accompanied by cultural self-improvement in education, dress, manners, etc.? In what circumstances and periods are such a cultural development regarded as pretentious and the character concerned mocked for having ideas 'above' his or her station? How are such changes in economic and cultural condition related to marriage? At what point in our social history can a man who has come up in the world buy his son into a higher social class by sending him to the 'right' school, and how do such young men stand in the marriage market? In what circles and at what times was it considered worse for a woman to marry 'beneath' her than for a man? In this particular connection much of contemporary television drama deals in light or heavy vein with the theme of interclass marriage. It is significant that John Osborne's *Look Back in Anger* should have appeared with success in 1956 at a time when the upheavals and social changes set in motion by the war were beginning to achieve a general consciousness.

When we use literature in this way we must, of course, bear in mind the social position of both the author and his audience. We must not make the mistake of assuming that our authors are attempting to write social documentaries. Again, some authors, Dickens for example, do not have what I would call a developed sociological sensibility. Others have it to a high degree: novelists like Jane Austen and George Eliot could not write, it seems, without conveying a mass of social detail and relative social judgments. Jane Austen's novels are an excellent starting point for this inquiry. Note how specific she is about the financial details, income, inheritance and the like in relation to marriage in that section of English society, the provincial upper class, about which, for the most part, she wrote.

We may seem to have wandered a long way from central Gujarat and the Patidar, but not so. *Within* the Patidar caste we have already seen that there is a tendency for the caste to be divided into groupings based on relative economic equality and there is even a sense in which we can distinguish, again within the caste, certain gradations of culture broader than the economic differentiation. That is to say that several groups of intermarrying villages can share or emphasise certain cultural features that other Patidar would regard as superior or inferior. The kind of food that people habitually eat is a good example: those who cannot afford to grow or buy wheat will habitually eat millet. Fresh vegetables are also relatively costly and appear only occasionally in the diet of poorer families. This is not the simple economic fact that it seems to be; it is a social judgment because the inferior custom is so regarded by the very people who practise it. There may well be families in our own society who habitually use margarine (which is still served in what is called a 'butter dish') but buy butter for guests. This sort of behaviour is different from buying *special* food, i.e. food that is normally only consumed on special occasions.

Coming closer to the question of marriage, families at the

lower ranges of the Patidar cannot afford to confine their women within the house and to household tasks; their women work with them in the fields and have neither the time nor the resources to elaborate the varied cuisine that a woman in a superior village would have learnt from her mother. There are all sorts of dishes which are traditional in relatively well-to-do Patidar families which require vegetables that a girl from a poor family might never even have heard of.

With this value placed on a woman's labour goes the practice of widow remarriage, which is strongly disapproved of in higher families. Even for the poor, marriage is still a relatively expensive affair, and if a woman's husband dies the family cannot afford to waste her and she is usually remarried to one of her husband's younger brothers with little formality or ritual. In wealthy families the widow becomes a kind of recluse and lives out her days rather wretchedly, helping in the household chores. Her position is peculiarly sad and miserable if she has not given birth to a son. This disapproval of widow remarriage relates to the basic beliefs about the good marriage (see p. 76). A good marriage requires the gift not merely of a girl but of a virgin— the technical term is *kanya dhan*, literally 'virgin gift'. It is this gift which creates the alliance between the donor and the recipient, and it is a gift that cannot be given twice. What we have called widow remarriage is, strictly speaking, no marriage; it is simply the enjoyment of a sexual and economic utility. Here, as so often in the study of social hierarchy, we find that the system itself forces people at the lowest levels to engage in behaviour which is then cited as proof of the lowness of the people concerned and hence used to justify the system which represses them.

More generally and obviously, cultural differences corresponding to class differences within the caste are to be seen in housing, dress and dialect. This last feature is, I suspect, a relatively modern development resulting from the increased standardisation of the Gujarati language in the cities and the universities.

The broad economic and cultural distinctions do not remain

entirely static, and even if they were relatively static a century ago they are certainly not so now. Today it is possible, admittedly with some sacrifice, for a boy to prolong his education and move into a relatively safe job and receive regular wages. The diversification of employment and the creation of new sources of cash prevent the total ossification of divisions and, therefore, the ossification of the groups of intermarrying villages. A man who can count on a monthly wage of only £40 in our money is regarded as a highly desirable son-in-law by a man whose land only just keeps him above subsistence level. The man who moves into commerce or industry is in a position to pay a higher dowry when his daughter is married than a man whose present and future income is always dependent upon the vagaries of the grain market and the uncertainty of the monsoon.

I have explained what the Patidar father regards as a good marriage; in addition, this means marrying his daughter into a respectable family, people with whom the father and his kinsmen may hope to have good relationships. If therefore a man becomes relatively affluent he can choose to look further afield than his kinsmen for his sons-in-law. By offering an attractive dowry he can hope to marry one or all of his daughters into a superior family in a village outside the traditional group of his own. Once he has opened the door in this way, less wealthy kinsmen may hope to marry their daughters to the less wealthy kinsmen of the new affines; slowly a new pattern of intermarrying villages comes into being. Equally, those who come down in the world may not be able to maintain their affinal relationships with their traditional partners. They may have to give their daughters into slightly inferior families in other villages. To give a daughter to an inferior in rank is not considered good, and if a man is obliged to persist in making such inferior alliances, then those with whom his family had affinity in the past will break off the connection.

Some Patidar have tried to reduce their marriage expenses and at the same time avoid the direct exchange referred to above (p. 77) by practising a form of indirect exchange. Family I gives a daughter to family II, who in turn give a daughter to family III.

Family III then gives a daughter to family I. In the following diagram it can be seen that the arrangement does indeed prevent a situation in which a man's *banevi* and *sala* are one and the same person. A is the *banevi* of C and the *sala* of B; B is the *sala* of C and A's *banevi*; C is the *sala* of A and the *banevi* of B. Nevertheless those who believe strongly in the value and virtue of

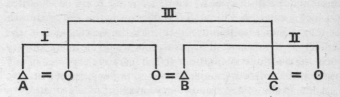

hypergamy still find this custom objectionable. They point out that this form of marriage poses a contradiction: the honoured affine of A, his *banevi*, is B; but B is the inferior affine of C, his *sala*; C, however, is also the inferior affine of A. Briefly, A honours B, B honours C and C honours A. How is it possible, say these Patidar, that I can respect someone as my *banevi* when he in turn respects as *banevi* someone who is my inferior affine, my *sala*?

The reader may by this point have began to think that there are contradictions in this sketch of Patidar marriage, and indeed this is true. If families of relatively equal economic condition tend to intermarry, how can they continue to regard givers of brides as inferior to wife receivers? If one village or lineage only received brides from another and never gave, the belief in relative superiority and inferiority would not be threatened. But they intermarry and, indeed, a lineage or village which refused to reciprocate brides would soon find that it was not being offered any.

The situation is saved by other changes that are taking place in the system of descent. I can best illustrate this from those villages in which all the Patidar are descended from one man and where this descent is genealogically demonstrable. It looks as though in the past these lineages preserved their solidarity for considerable periods so long as the members of the lineage were all of much the same economic condition. With increased wealth and numbers, splits developed as one section of a village lineage became wealthier than others and decided to dissociate itself from them. The men of this section would look to that point in the common genealogy at which their branch could be separated and then begin to call themselves collectively the descendants of the ancestor at that point, rather than the descendants of the founder of the village. This cessation would be marked by a discontinuance of contributions to the marriage expenses of any member of the larger group. Divisions, as I say, appear to have been few in the past. In one village, in effect now a small town with a total population of about 9000, I counted that after the founding of the village in the twelfth century six generations elapsed before three divisions emerged, and these new sections remained undivided well into the nineteenth century.

During the nineteenth century and increasingly in the twentieth the process of division has continued and the descent groups within the village who think of themselves as separate for the purposes of negotiating marriages have shrunk in size. This is even more apparent in smaller villages of heterogeneous settlement (see p. 73), where very often there is no recorded genealogy and no great pride in long descent. Here a group composed of the descendants of the great-grandfather can consider themselves as the marriage unit.

When the marriage units shrink in this way, exchange marriages can be concealed. If the marriage unit is large, say all the descendants of a man six or seven generations back, all the male kinsmen of a girl will regard themselves as givers in relation to her husband's family because they have all made some contribution to her marriage expenses. All the men who called the bride sister would be *sala* to her husband. Whereas it might be tolerable to accept a bride from that family in the next generation, it would not look well were they to receive one from the same generation. When, however, the marriage unit shrinks and perhaps approximates to the family in our society, then even the children of two brothers could be givers and takers in relation to one and the same family in another.

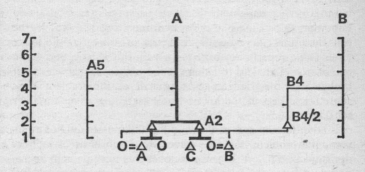

In the diagram above we have two lines of descent from A and B, both seven generations deep. At the fifth generation of A and at the fourth generation of B, there was a division in the descent lines such that A5 and B4 regard themselves as autonomous marrying units no longer associated with the marriages contracted by their kinsmen in A and B. As this process of division continues we come to a situation at A2 where two brothers marry a son and a daughter respectively to a son and daughter of B4/2. In the past this would have been regarded a direct exchange— the two brothers would have constituted a unit, and A would have been regarded as a *sala* of B and at the same time his *banevi*. When, however, the two brothers act independently and do not contribute to each other's expenses, then A does not feel himself bound by his relation to C and does not think of himself as the inferior affine of B. It should be stressed that the diagram represents an extreme development of what might occur in the future. Given the tendencies that I observed in modern Patidar society, such a development seemed a possibility and I discussed it with Patidar friends. They shrugged their shoulders and confirmed that in changing circumstances values also change and the terminology of kinship can be manipulated.

There is yet another contradiction between Patidar beliefs about marriage and their practice. If by and large the movement is towards giving daughters to equals or superiors, then surely somewhere along the line the system must break down. In the past there must have been a deficiency of women at the lower levels and a superfluity at the top. Again this is true, and it is a real source of anxiety to fathers at the highest levels who want husbands for their daughters. As we shall see, the problem is less acute for fathers at the lowest levels searching wives for their sons.

If other factors such as the class-like differences did not intervene, the problem might be solved by the formula of indirect exchange (see p. 85). In some societies this formula is in operation, but in such societies there is precisely neither such marked economic differentiation nor so strong a belief in hierarchy as we find among the Patidar. It is useful here, as always, to apply the formulae of other societies to the one that we are trying to understand: by finding out why it does not work, our attention is focused on the differentiating factors. The juxtaposition of class and caste was a simple application of this principle.

A system of indirect exchange which offers a comparison with the Patidar is a system that requires matrilateral cross-cousin marriage. According to such a system, a man's ideal mate is his mother's brother's daughter. The two are cross-cousins because their parents are siblings of different sexes. The system is called matrilateral because it is the children of a woman and her brother who are in question. (The children of two brothers or of two sisters are called parallel cousins and the patrilateral cross-cousins would be the children of a father and his sister.) This is an ideal and a formula, and I must stress this because some writers sometimes give the impression that a man must marry his mother's daughter or go celibate. The reader's understanding is not helped by the common diagramatic representation, shown below, which suggests the rather absurd likelihood that the mother in question has only one brother, or relative in that category, and that he for his part has only one son. The

```
A                      B                      C
△ = ○                  △ = ○                  ○ = △
 └─┬─┘                  └─┬─┘                  └─┬─┘
 △   ○                  △   ○                  △   ○
```

The children of A and B are parallel cousins to each other. They are the cross-cousins of C.

diagram represents a formula, the simplest expression of the ideal. The reader may indeed choose to think simply of a matrilateral marriage system and regard the cross-cousin element as a symbol, signifying in the formula that the women of the mother's side in a man's own generation are good marriage partners for him. Hand in hand with this injunction, the father's sister's daughter, a man's patrilateral cross-cousin, is the symbol that the women related to him through his father are barred. The reader may pause here to reflect why the father's sister's daughter is the suitable symbol and not the father's brother's daughter.

What are the minimal conditions we need if the formula is to be operated? Obviously we need more than one exogamous group, but how many more? Apply the formula to a society that is divided into two exogamous descent groups, A and B. The founding ancestor of A took his wife from B. Their son cannot marry into A and he must marry into B and therefore with his mother's brother's daughter. Where did his mother's brother get his bride? Two groups are clearly not enough; we need a third, C, which can provide wives for B, who can produce girls of A. However, the men of C must also marry, and marry according to the rule. What is the solution? Obviously the men of C must find brides in A.

I asked earlier why the father's sister's daughter is a better symbol of prohibition than the father's brother's daughter. The first answer is that the father's brother's daughter is a member of the exogamous descent group and there can therefore be no question of marrying her. The second answer you should now be in a position to see is that the father's sister's daughters of the men of C will be in the descent group B. If the men of C could marry them as well as the women of A, what would these latter do?

This subject could take us very far afield and the reader can pursue it in various specialised monographs. Let us return to the Patidar. They do not allow marriage with cousins of any sort; nevertheless they present a problem similar to that hypothesised on p. 88, namely the problem created by a flow of women in one direction only. Can we apply the same solution?

At first sight it would not be impossible, even allowing for the class–like differences that I have mentioned. In the large wealthy villages where the founding lineage has grown and split into several sections, there will be found families quite as poor as those in inferior villages. If the related but separate marriage units are not concerned, because they do not feel themselves contaminated by association with the marriages made by their poor kinsmen, why should this circularity not occur as in the following diagram?

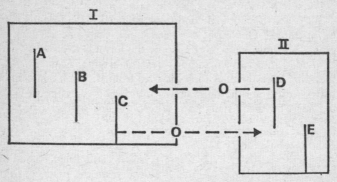

Villages I and II are of unequal status. In village I there are three descent groups with varying status such that A is superior to B and B is superior to C. In village II there are two descent groups of differing status. It is suggested that descent line B receives brides from D but would not reciprocate them; however, a hidden exchange could occur were descent groups E to receive brides from C.

In fact, this is how discrepancies within groups of inter-marrying villages are actually handled, and one of the Gujarati words for such groups is *gol*, which also means circle. Such an arrangement between the poorest lineages in villages at the top and bottom of the hierarchy of villages would, however, not be acceptable to the Patidar. First of all, even the meanest family in a wealthy village is governed by the standards of the majority. Secondly, even if it were not, or were, sufficiently desperate to ignore them, it remains dependent upon wealthier kinsmen for all sorts of patronage—jobs, loans, etc.

I should say that just once in Gujarat I came across a Patidar family from a very wealthy and highly regarded village which was eking out its existence in a village largely populated by a lower caste. It was by chance that I came across it and, for all I know, there may be others and, indeed, many such. The family had adopted the solution examined above and married its daughters to men of lower villages.

The extreme plight of this family illustrates the difference between the pragmatic solution of a human problem with its social cost and the social solution of a social problem. In the matrilateral system that we have looked at briefly, there is a positive injunction making for the circulation of women; in the case of the Patidar the principle of hierarchy works strongly against circulation beyond a limited range, and those individuals who seek to solve their problems in this way must pay heavily for it.

What, then, actually happens to the unmarried men at the bottom and the unmarried girls at the top? For the men, the solution is not so hard: they marry girls of lower castes. According to caste theory this is a very shocking thing, and many popular accounts give the Western world a simplified version by presenting the theory of caste divorced from the practice, from what people really do. These intercaste marriages are feasible and tolerated for various reasons. First of all, many other Patidar in a poor village are sympathetic. If they have not been in this predicament themselves, they know that they might have been or might yet be. Then again, descent is patrilineal and the children of such marriages *will* be Patidar, even though they are not of pure descent. Further, their closest kin and affines are likely to be people who have grandmothers or mothers of similar origins and they will not therefore reject or despise them. Finally, they do not constitute a sub-group of 'half-breeds', such as tends to emerge in racialist societies. A poor man with several sons and daughters will find recognised Patidar for the girls and try to ensure that the eldest son at least marries within the caste. Then, if he cannot find Patidar brides for the remaining boys, he will have recourse to women of a lower caste. By obeying the minimal requirements of the caste the family remains unambiguously within it. I have said that it is through marriage that society perpetually recreates itself, and this extreme case clearly illustrates the point.

The situation of fathers of girls at the highest levels is altogether different: it is unthinkable that they should marry into inferior families and maintain their position in the traditional society. There is no doubt that when a man has many daughters he is likely to suffer considerable anxiety until they are all married. In the past it was not unknown for men and sometimes the girls themselves to be driven by despair to suicide. There is some suggestion in the historical evidence also that in the more distant past the Patidar practised a kind of eugenics by neglecting female infants.

A sort of aristocratic pride mitigates the situation somewhat. In many of the wealthy families the practice of accepting girls with high dowries from lower families is disapproved of and there are some who say that such marriages never turn out well. In such families people prefer to marry among equals, and will only make an inferior marriage when they are obliged to do so. We have here a situation not unlike that of the poor father mentioned above. Now the father endeavours to marry his sons and daughters with the families traditionally allied to him; he may, however, marry one son or more 'down' if the dowries that their wives will bring in are necessary to enable him to meet the marriage expenses of his daughters. Among such 'aristocratic' families there have also existed for many years formal agreements to keep marriage expenses within reasonable limits. I should add that such agreements are today imitated at lower levels of the caste.

Finally, we must remember that the wealthier Patidar especially live in a modern society where ideas critical of the past, of the inferior status of women and even of religious orthodoxy are prevalent. Boys and girls go to universities not only in various parts of India but also abroad, and their fathers are often university graduates. Increasingly at this level of Patidar and Indian society it is generally being recognised that compatibility of temperament and freedom of choice are more important than caste regulations. Young people of similar educational background, especially in the cities, marry as individuals do in our own society. These marriages, based on the recognition that the nascent socio-economic classes are creating new cultures, making for ties stronger than the older culture of caste, reflect the changes taking place in Patidar and Indian society today.

## Summary

In Chapter 1, talking about marriage among the Nuer, we saw that this institution played an important political role. In this chapter we stressed the social importance of marriage in our own society and went so far as to say that *human* society, as opposed to any other kind, is founded upon marriage. Human society begins when the group bans marriage within itself (the so-called incest taboo) and forms marriage alliances with other groups. For this reason all societies have rules of *exogamy*, that is to say rules which forbid marriage within certain limits. But all societies also have rules of *endogamy* which require or encourage marriage within certain limits. The strength and the relation of the rules of exogamy and endogamy will vary from society to society according to the internal organisation of that society; even in our own society we were obliged to admit that informal, tacit rules of endogamy helped to perpetuate distinctions of class, race and nation.

We examined these general propositions in the light of one particular example, the Patidar of Gujarat in western India. There we saw a large endogamous caste in which all members, outside the limits imposed by exogamy, could theoretically intermarry. We saw, however, that there were considerable differences of income in this caste and that these were reflected in a tendency for the caste to be split up into groups of villages of relatively equal economic standing which, in fact, intermarried. At the same time we saw that the Patidar have definite notions about what constitutes a good marriage and that this encouraged hypergamy as men tried to 'buy' their daughters into superior families by giving large dowries. The examination of the problems which this belief makes for the Patidar led us into the all-important matter of gift-giving and reciprocity, which also serves to introduce matters discussed in Chapter 4. In the present context reciprocity is important because not only in India is marriage an important form of gift-giving; much important social anthropological work in recent years has developed the idea that the giving and the exchanging of women is one of the most central activities in society. Among the Patidar we understand why their ideas of what constitutes a 'good marriage' prevent direct exchanges and at the same time that in their attempts to achieve this ideal they are caught up in certain contradictions; they are saved from these by simultaneous social changes which are making for a reduction in the size of the marrying unit.

In conclusion we examined, in abstract terms, a common form of marriage. This introduced the terms 'cross-cousin', the children of siblings of different sex; parallel cousins, the children of siblings of the same sex; matrilateral, on the mother's side; patrilateral, on the father's side. Using these terms we referred to a marriage between a boy and his mother's brother's daughter as matrilateral cross-cousin marriage.

# Reading notes

Evans-Pritchard, E. E., *Kinship and Marriage among the Nuer*, Oxford, 1951. See especially Chapters II and III.

Fox, R., *Kinship and Marriage*, Pelican, 1967. A general introduction to the subject with a useful bibliography.

Freud, S., *Totem and Tabu*, English translation, London, 1919. This classic of psychoanalytical literature should be read in conjunction with Fox or preferably Lévi-Strauss (see below).

Hocart, A., *The Life-giving Myth*, London, 1952, Chapter XXII. A brief, sensible introduction to the problems of translating kinship terms.

Homans, G., and Schneider, D., *Marriage, Authority and Final Causes*, Glencoe, Illinois, 1955. A critique of Lévi-Strauss (see Needham, below). I draw attention to this controversy largely because it may help the reader in understanding Lévi-Strauss. It also illustrates the divergence between the American and the Anglo-French traditions in the 1950s. The debate is touched on by Fox (above).

Lévi-Strauss, C., 'The Family' in Shapiro (ed.), *Man, Culture and Society*, New York and Oxford, 1960. This is a clear and convincing account of the problems involved in the use of the word 'family'. The author discusses the Nayar amongst others and the article should also be read in conjunction with Chapter 2.

Lévi-Strauss, C., *The Elementary Structures of Kinship*, English translation 1969. The original French edition appeared in 1949 and has become the formative work for this generation of social anthropologists. At the time of writing some scholars are blaming Lévi-Strauss for their own early uncritical enthusiasm: this is a common phenomenon in intellectual history—the book will remain a classic.

Mair, L., *New Nations*, London, 1963, Chapter 3. An introduction to the study of marriage and social change.

Needham, R., *Structure and Sentiment—a test case in social anthropology*, Chicago and London, 1962. The importance of this book at this stage is summarised in its opening sentence: 'This book is about the possibility of explaining social institutions by reference to individual sentiments.' It is a trenchant critique of Homans and Schneider (above).

Pocock, D., *Kanib and Patidar*, Oxford, 1972.

# 4

# Economic Anthropology

Before reading this chapter, write an essay outlining what you understand by the term 'economics'. To what extent is it a specialised activity engaged in by economists. When you yourself say that this or that course of action, purchase or use would 'not be economical', what do you really mean and by what criteria do you assess the economy of your behaviour? Or, if you think of yourself as an economical person or not economical, what precisely have you in mind? How does your usage of the term square with your understanding of it in some such phrase as 'the National Economy' or the newspaper headline 'Government Economists Urge Spending Cuts'? Think also about your behaviour; if you carry out any household activity on the grounds that it's cheaper to do it yourself, how do you assess relative costs? Does it actually cost less money to make your own bread, grow your own vegetables or make your own clothes once you have taken into account *all* the expenditure involved? What about your time; has it any economic value in the hours that you are not gainfully employed? Finally, what is the largest sum of money that you would borrow from or lend to a friend or relative. Would you think of paying or charging interest? Think about the difference between those situations in which you would expect interest to be paid and those in which you would not.

\*       \*       \*

On 16 October 1841 Sir Robert Peel, then Prime Minister, wrote to Queen Victoria advising her about the succession to the Mastership of Trinity College, Cambridge. The retiring Master was Dr Wordsworth, and in his letter Sir Robert names among three suitable candidates Wordsworth's son Christopher, who was at that time Headmaster of Harrow School. Sir Robert said of him, 'he is a highly distinguished scholar, but his success as Headmaster of Harrow has not been such as to overcome the objection which applies on general grounds to the succession of a father by a son in an office of this description'.

Before proceeding any further, think about the word 'objection' in this quotation and your own reaction to it. I think I would be correct in assuming that Sir Robert Peel's logic in arguing against the appointment of Christopher Wordsworth seems sound and sensible; but why should we think so? Could it not equally be argued that if Christopher Wordsworth was as good a candidate as any, it would be unfair to discriminate against him solely on the grounds given? Nevertheless, in considering this case, or imagining a similar one in our own time, we tend to think along the same lines as Sir Robert Peel and suspect that there must be, or appear to be, an element of corruption in the appointment of a son to his father's office. A candidate who is in all respects well qualified may well be passed over on this ground alone. We know, nevertheless, from our own past and from the workings of other societies that the principle of heredity has often been used to settle the appointment of people to very high office, and we have no reason for supposing that leaders and officials chosen in this way were any worse, by and large, or less effective than others selected by other criteria.

What, in fact, we encounter here is an example of a more general belief prevalent in Western society that we *ought* to separate activities and institutions and the more we do so, the better. The proposition which we might find in a newspaper headline 'Keep Politics out of Sport' would appear to most of us to be expressing a desirable moral injunction. Equally, most of us find ourselves puzzled when religious denominations determine political affiliations. Again, most of us would feel that some generous donation to what we call a 'charity' was tainted if the donor expected to gain some social advantage thereby.

The findings of social anthropologists increasingly underline the fact that this tendency and desire to separate is a distinctive feature of Western belief. The difficulty we experience in appreciating that this is a *peculiar* feature of our *belief* is a major stumbling block for the student of social anthropology.

To the extent that we think we ought to separate areas of life into distinct compartments we tend also to think that it is so separable. By this I mean that if we think that we can separate politics from religion or from economics in our own society, then we go on to conclude that we can separate these activities in other societies. From this it is an easy stage to the assumption that there really are separate areas, radically different kinds of activity, a set of labelled boxes, so to speak, into which we can sort the different 'facts' of other societies.

If we proceed in this way we run into two kinds of difficulty. On the one hand, we may find that another society does not seem to have the facts that would fit into a particular box and therefore we say that they do not have, for example, a religion, a political system or law. Perhaps more distorting is the danger that we chop up the institutions and activities of other societies to force them into our boxes. A very simple example of this would be abstracting a belief and activities associated with that belief in an invisible masculine, moral, if not indeed benevolent, power, and giving this belief and activities the label 'religion' while distributing a whole lot of associated beliefs in other invisible powers, outside man or within man, into other boxes such as 'magic', 'politics', etc.

What has all this to do with economics? I suggest that the 'economic' is one of the two largest and strongest boxes that the Western mind has created. The other one is 'religion', and it may be significant that we have designed the first to contain material things of this world and that the other we tend to reserve

exclusively for immaterial things of some imaginary or supernatural world.

The growth of the idea of the 'economic' as a separate area of
activity governed by its own laws and quite distinct from politics,
religion, family ties, morality and, indeed, everything else that
goes on in society is a long and intricate story. Here I can only
work on the assumption that the reader will, on reflection, agree
that the word 'economy' in the phrase 'national economy'
connotes a separate world of activities, of natural forces and even
of reason which has nothing to do with religious affiliation,
family affairs or morality.

Essentially, I suppose, we think of the economic domain as
being the world of markets and prices, profits and rates of
interest; a mysterious domain which the vast majority of us can
neither understand nor control. We do not think of ourselves as
occupying an economic domain except in a passive capacity. This
is an understandable mistake because the economic domain in
which we actually live is probably less special and separated.
Our attitudes towards our own money are much more related to
the rest of our social being than the economic sphere that we
think exists; and yet we would agree that money is pre-
eminently, we think, a feature of precisely that economic sphere.

Let us consider some examples. If we borrow some money
from a relative or a close friend, we do not think to offer them
interest and we should be hurt or shocked were they to ask for it.
Nevertheless, thinking in 'economic terms', we must admit that
the money loaned could as well have been invested for profit.
Equally, if we lend someone else money, we experience loss only
if they fail to repay it or do not pay it when they said they would.
It is quite possible that someone who has an overdraft at the
bank or a mortgage on a house can lend someone else money on
which, in strictly 'economic terms', he himself is already paying
interest. It still would not occur to him, necessarily, to bring the
two facts together and to tell his friend or relative to go and get
their own overdraft.

When we entertain guests to a meal, whether at home or in a
restaurant, we expend more than we would were we eating alone

or in the family. Certainly, if we are prudent, we spend no more than we can afford and to this extent contain the operation within our own economy; for all that, we recognise that our action is not an 'economic' one. Not many of us may have felt the pressure to incur exceptional costs imposed by the social status of our guest(s), but very few of us have not, at some time or another, given in to the urge to translate great affection or love into a costly or even extravagant present of some sort.

From the point of view of 'economics' much of our behaviour in expenditure and consumption is irrational, but we remain, for all that, economic beings and conduct our economic affairs with relative success or failure no greater than those of nations; unlike nations, we do not split off our economic from our social selves.

Karl Polanyi, an economist and a major influence in the development of economic anthropology, was making a similar point when he wrote of Ancient Greece:

> 'Only the concept of the economy, not the economy itself, is in abeyance, of course. Nature and society are bound in locational and appropriational movements that form the body of man's livelihood. The seasons bring around harvest time with its strain and its relaxation; long-distance trade has its rhythm of preparation and forgathering with the concluding solemnity of the return venturers; and all kinds of artefacts, whether canoes or fine ornaments, are produced and eventually used by the various groups of persons; every day of the week food is prepared at the family hearth. Each single event contains necessarily a bundle of economic items. Yet for all that, the unity and coherence of those facts is not reflected in men's consciousness. For the series of interactions between men and their natural surroundings will, as a rule, carry various significances, of which economic dependence is only one. Other dependences, more vivid, more dramatic, or more emotionalised, may be at work, which prevent the economic movements from forming a meaningful hold.'

In short, man engaged and has always engaged in economic

activities, for all that he has not always had the idea of an economic sphere.

In the same essay Polanyi distinguishes between what he calls embedded and disembedded economies, and this distinction is essential for our understanding of both our own society and traditional non-Western societies. I have suggested that most people in Western society live in two economies. The one they think of when 'economics' is mentioned is the official, remote and even mysterious economy which affects them from the outside; the other, which they actually operate, is apparently less rational and is affected by morality, affection, bonds of kinship and friendship, and the like. This realisation can provide a starting point for understanding the difference between the disembedded and the embedded economy.

The disembedded economy is the historical creation of Western capitalist society, which in its turn rests upon certain assumptions about the nature of man and his material transactions; these are derived from the idea of the market, in which everything is a commodity having a price related to demand and to supply. Man, when he operates in the market, is supposed to have only two motives—hunger (demand) and the desire for gain (supply). Polanyi argues that this exclusive emphasis on the market and on the motives and nature of market operations was what gave birth to the idea of a distinct 'economic sphere' in which the loyalties and values of day-to-day life were not allowed to enter. He reinforces this by questioning the fundamental position given to hunger and to gain as *the* motive forces:

'This new world of "economic motives" was based on a fallacy. Intrinsically, hunger and gain are no more "economic" than love or hate, pride or prejudice. No human motive is *per se* economic . . . hunger and gain are here linked with production through the need of "earning an income". For under such a system, man, if he is to keep alive, is compelled to buy goods on the market with the help of an income derived from selling other goods on the market . . . thus all incomes derive from sales, and all sales—directly or indirectly—contribute to production. The latter is, in effect, *incidental to the earning of an income*. So long as an individual is "earning an income", he is, automatically, contributing to production. Obviously the system works only so long as individuals have a reason to indulge in the activity of "earning an income". The motives of hunger and gain—separately and conjointly—provide them with such a reason. These two motives are thus geared to production and, accordingly, are termed "economic".'

But the market is not the one sole and universal institution which man uses and has used to get his sustenance, nor are hunger and gain universally the predominant motives which order the way in which he does so. In the societies studied by social anthropologists we find economic activities so embedded in a variety of other institutions that it is impossible without distortion to separate out an 'economic system'.

The classic study of an economy embedded in society is Bronislaw Malinowski's *Argonauts of the Western Pacific*. Although this was first published in 1922 it remains a central work for any student of social anthropology. The book deals with a wide-ranging form of trade which in Malinowski's time prevailed across a considerable area—roughly eastern New Guinea northwards to the Trobriand Islands and eastwards to Rossell Islands. This system of trade was known as the *kula*: 'It looms paramount in the tribal life of those natives who live within its circuit, and its importance is fully realised by the tribesmen themselves, whose ideas, ambitions, desires and vanities are very much bound up with the kula.'

Malinowski's name is permanently associated with the Trobriand Islands, where he carried out his most significant research. Although his account of the *kula* is presented from the Trobriand point of view, it is remarkable that the rules and customs of the *kula* are identical over the wide area in which this trade prevails, despite the social and cultural differences of the various tribes that participate in it.

First a word on the salient features of Trobriand social

organisation. They are a matrilineal people, the women moving at marriage to live with their husbands. At marriage the family of the bride incur a permanent obligation to provide the bulk of food consumed in her household and to perform services of various kinds for the husband. Although initially this may seem to conflict with the relatively high status of women in Trobriand society, it can be appreciated that the husband is by this custom made heavily dependent upon his wife and her family. Malinowski tells us that if she is not well treated the wife can simply leave her husband, in which circumstances he would be destitute. The basic residential unit among the Trobrianders is the village, the important kinship affiliation the clan. The Trobrianders are distinctive in the area for their beliefs about rank and status, which are closely associated with clan organisation.

The Trobriand Islanders believe themselves to be descended from four mythical ancestresses who originally emerged from the ground. These clans are divided into sub-clans, which in turn are ranked in prestige. When a man of a high-ranking sub-clan combines this rank with the position of village headman, he is a person of considerable power. Malinowski tells us that such men are treated with marked deference and have their own insignia of rank and authority. In their presence other people, 'commoners', do not presume to stand higher; they crouch when the chief is standing and sit when he sits. In the days of warfare such a chief could command the allegiance of the population of several surrounding villages. In days of peace he can rely upon these villages for labour. By comparison the ordinary headman of a village who does not belong to a sub-clan of high rank occupies more of a foreman's role, co-ordinating activities, and depends upon the counsel of his peers.

These chiefs are linked with their tributary villages by marriage. The chief marries a wife from each village in the area of his influence, usually from the family of the headman of that village. He thus enjoys to a greater measure than the average husband the benefits of Trobriand custom. Malinowski tells us of a chief in the past who had forty wives and received with them something between 30% to 50% of the produce of the district.

The popular notion of primitive chiefs living in luxury on tribute and treating their people almost as slaves does not bear much examination. The Trobriander chief is expected to pay for the various services that he receives from his villages, even though these services cannot be refused. Malinowski stresses another chiefly expenditure which arises from the chief's authority. The strongest sanction of this authority and power is his open exercise of sorcery. Whereas commoners would not dare to be known to practise sorcery, the chief has at his disposal the best sorcerers of the area, and for these specialists he also has to pay.

This brief account of the Trobriander chief brings to the fore the intimate association between rank and power on the one hand and wealth on the other; although the association is seen in its extreme form in the chief, it is fundamental to Trobriand society. Malinowski draws our attention to the industry with which the Trobrianders work their gardens. He shows that they produce more than they can eat or even dispose of in a year, and add to their labours by an insistence upon the aesthetic appearance of their gardens.

'Another notion which must be exploded, once and for ever, is that of the Primitive Economic Man of some current economic textbooks. This fanciful, dummy creature, who has been very tenacious of existence in popular and semi-popular economic literature and whose shadow haunts even the minds of competent anthropologists, blighting their outlook with a preconceived idea, is an imaginary, primitive man or savage, prompted in all his actions by a rationalistic conception of self-interest, and achieving his aims directly and with the minimum of effort . . . the primitive Trobriander furnishes us with . . . an instance contradicting this fallacious theory. He works prompted by motives of a highly complex, social and traditional nature, and towards aims which are certainly not directed towards the satisfaction of present wants, or to the direct achievement of utilitarian purposes. Thus in the first

place, as we have seen, work is not carried out on the principle
of the least effort . . . again, work and effort, instead of being
merely a means to an end, are, in a way, an end in themselves.
A good garden worker in the Trobriand derives a direct
prestige from the amount of labour he can do, and the size of
the garden he can till.'

This prestige reward for labour is important when we understand how little the average Trobriander farmer enjoys of the
fruits of his labour. Approximately three quarters of what he
produces goes in tribute to his chief, as part of the collective duty
of his village, and in supporting his sister's husband and her
family. The reward comes with the harvest, when farmers compete with each other in displaying their crops and enjoy public
appraisal. Malinowski underlines the fact that basic ideas about
manhood are related to horticultural skill. There should be
nothing puzzling about this to members of our society who
associate virility with the capacity to kick a ball up and down a
field.

We must, however, remind ourselves that if the Trobriander
must give so much to his wife's family and to his chief, he also
receives in his turn. This return is of two kinds: first, there is the
produce that his own wife's family must send in substantial
quantities; second, there are the gifts which from time to time
his sister's husband makes to him. These are neither regular nor
of the same magnitude as the produce that was received. They
are important, nevertheless, because they draw our attention to
this fundamental aspect of Trobriand society—the gift. Although
a man is obliged to supply his sister's family, this is treated not
as a simple payment of any sort but rather as a gift. The produce
that goes to the chief and the labour performed for him are also
obligatory cesses; nevertheless the chief will give gifts in return
for them. These gifts are not, to our way of thinking, equivalent
in value to the goods or services received.

This idea of the need to give and to reciprocate gifts is at the
heart of the Trobriand economy and the *kula*. The *kula* is in its
detail an extremely complex affair, and what follows here is

inevitably simplified. Across a wide area, comprising several quite distinct cultures, two classes of artefacts are exchanged— white arm-shells and red shell necklaces. Wherever these are exchanged, they are exchanged such that the necklaces circulate to the north and the arm-shells to the south; the effect of this, were one to look down on the map of these scattered islands, is that the red necklaces would be seen to move clockwise and the white arm-shells anti-clockwise.

What is the meaning of this activity? The full answer lies, of course, in Malinowski's account. Briefly, these exchanges create relationships of obligation to give and to receive. Each man engaged in the *kula* has a limited number of people with whom he maintains these relationships; a commoner may have only a few, a big chief may have hundreds. *Kula* partners may be local; the average man may include his affines and perhaps even a chief or two. In either case special bonds of service and assistance come into being as a result of the *kula* relationship. But *kula* relationships overseas are even more important; they offer hospitality and protection for the traveller.

'Men living at hundreds of miles sailing distance from one another are bound together by direct or intermediate partner-ship, exchange with each other, know of each other, and on certain occasions meet in a large intertribal gathering. Objects given one, in time reach some very distant indirect partner or other, and not only kula objects, but various articles of domes-tic use and minor gifts. It is easy to see that in the long run, not only objects of material culture, but also customs, songs, art motifs and general cultural influences travel along the kula route. It is a vast, intertribal net of relationships, a big institution, consisting of thousands of men, all bound together by one common passion, for kula exchange, and secondarily, by many minor ties and interests.'

I shall return to the strict *kula* exchanges of necklaces and arm-shells shortly. Before doing so, it is necessary to point out that trade, still conducted in the manner of gift-giving, accompanies the *kula*. When the canoes set off on their often hazardous journeys, they are loaded with goods which it is known are desired by the *kula* partners. Even so, Malinowski stresses that this trade is secondary because the *kula* is the main aim for the Trobrianders. They distinguish *kula* exchanges from ordinary barter, *gimwali*, in which people can and do haggle for advantage. It is nevertheless striking that men who are *kula* partners to each other do not engage in this *gimwali*, although each may barter with members of the other party who are not his partners.

In describing the *kula* objects, the arm-shells and the necklaces, Malinowski compares them with the Crown Jewels in Edinburgh Castle which he saw after the completion of his fieldwork. He describes the Curator's account of them, how this had been worn by this king or that queen on such and such an occasion. The *kula* objects no less have such personal histories, and with age and circulation they increase their prestige and value. We do not even have to think of royal regalia but of some quite trivial object which, because it was once in the possession of some famous personage, is auctioned for a sum many times in excess of its utility value.

*Kula* exchanges are not immediate; the partners may not exchange from hand to hand like two mistrustful children who will only effect a swop if it is instantaneous. A few minutes or a few months elapse before the exchange is made and neither partner adverts to the value of the object given. A man may have given his partner a rather remarkable arm-shell and the partner may not at the time have a necklace of sufficient value to give him in return. Even so, he will affect not to notice the object, let alone betray his embarrassment. Even a year later the partner may still not have acquired a suitable necklace; he will then give an admittedly inferior necklace as a token of good faith, for which he receives a small arm-shell in return; the original obligation to give remains and at the same time gives birth to what may become a series of lesser exchanges.

A man has several, perhaps many, *kula* partners and can decide what he will give to whom. This freedom has for its effect the possibility of varying the strengths of his relationships. If it becomes known that a man is in possession of a first-class arm-shell which has its own name and a distinguished history, his partners will flock to present him with gifts that are explicitly solicitory. Only if the current possessor of the arm-shell proposes to give it to a particular partner will he accept his gift, and, perhaps after one or two more such, part with the arm-shell. The recipient then gives him more food, which must be returned on some suitable occasion.

This prime institution of the *kula* expresses the central values of Trobriand society and the economy which is embedded in it. Possession, use and enjoyment take the place of absolute ownership. It is significant that, whereas our own highest valuables tend to be static and locked up, the Trobriand valuables *must* circulate. While they are in the possession of a man he enjoys the prestige which they confer and at the same time he accepts the obligation to give them.

'A man who owns a thing is naturally expected to share it, to distribute it, to be its trustee and dispenser. And the higher the rank the greater the obligation. A chief will naturally be expected to give food to any stranger, visitor, even loiterer from another end of the village. He will be expected to share any of the betel-nut or tobacco he has about him. So that a man of rank will have to hide away any surplus of these articles which he wants to preserve for his further use.'

It is possible that this emphasis upon the duty of giving and the prestige which attaches to giving more than one has received may be interpreted in a romantic fashion, and the Trobriander may appear to represent some ideal realisation of St Francis of Assisi's injunction 'It is in giving that we receive.' Malinowski's account makes it clear, however, that the Trobrianders have their due share of human meanness, avarice and hostility. To suppose otherwise would be as silly as to assume from a reading of an economics textbook that the average Western man or woman is quite incapable of generosity.

In his account of the *kula* Malinowski frequently refers to the days before Western administration affected life in the Trobriand

Islands, but apart from occasional references we know little about this. It is interesting therefore to examine briefly another economy in the Pacific about which we have more historical information, though less ethnographic detail.

Roviana is a coastal strip in New Georgia, one of the Solomon Islands. In the mid-eighteenth century it had established itself as a major centre of head-hunting and slavery, which were, as we shall see, interdependent and related to certain fundamental beliefs of the Roviana people. Certainly by the nineteenth century Roviana had established itself as an indigenous colonising power. Its war canoes travelled in large flotillas carrying warriors across considerable distances, and they were widely feared. It has been suggested that the people of Santa Ysabel Island, a voyage of well over 100 miles to the east, developed their tree houses as a defence against Roviana warfare, and Guadalcanal Island, over 200 miles to the south-west, was within the regular slaving route.

The central sacred act in Roviana, as almost everywhere else in the world, was sacrifice and, what is much less common, there the best sacrifice was a human one. These blood sacrifices were performed for the satisfaction of ancestral spirits, and slaves were required as victims. Equally important were the spiritual associations of skulls. The skulls of their own ancestors and, more especially, the skulls of dead chiefs and warriors were the repositories of *mana*, spiritual power, but the heads of slaves, particularly captured warriors, had powerful *mana* also. Just as a Trobriander chief would display his pile of yams, so the Roviana chief would point to his pile of skulls as evidence of his power. Skulls were also needed for the sacred decoration of houses and of war canoes.

The warriors of Roviana did not plunder indiscriminately and certain areas and islands which produced artefacts, particularly weapons, were visited for the sake of trade. The Rovianians supplied canoes and shell money, which was a universal currency, in exchange for these artefacts. As slaves were involved in the manufacture of shell money and canoes, this was an added reason for acquiring them.

Slaves were needed not only as labour to build war canoes but more generally to release the manpower of the warriors. No less important was the need to perform human sacrifice when a canoe was launched, and it was quite possible that the very slaves who had built a canoe would then be killed as it was launched over their living bodies.

Competition between chiefs and lineages for the prestige which came with increased *mana* was the impetus to build bigger and bigger canoes and to embark upon more widely ranging expeditions. More warriors and canoes were required and, both for the voyages themselves and for exchanges, more shell money was also needed. More canoes launched required more sacrifices and, therefore, a large reserve of slaves for this purpose, in addition to the increased numbers required for manufacture. The more successful the expedition, the greater the display of skulls at its conclusion and the greater the stimulus to general emulation.

This expanding system was held in check by the need to maintain peaceful relations with those on whom Roviana depended for trade goods. With the coming of the European trader this check was destroyed. In the early and mid-decades of the nineteenth century, traders brought arms and ammunition which they traded for *bêche de mer*, sandalwood, copra, ginger and, later, slaves. This had a dual effect. The warriors of Roviana were no longer dependent on their traditional trade allies for weapons and increasingly turned on them both for slaves and for skulls. Some of the areas nearby which had traditionally been protected by trade interests were now completely depopulated. The guns also made it possible to kill many more people, more quickly. One account tells us that on one expedition so many potential slaves were caught that the Roviana head-hunters preferred the value of skulls to the value of slaves and decapitated their victims *in situ* for the sake of a full cargo of skulls.

Events which occurred between 1890 and 1900 give a summary of the extreme effects of European contact. A British commander, intent upon destroying the head-hunting cult, sacked and burned Roviana, destroying the thousands of skulls which had been accumulated through the years. For the next ten years the then chief dedicated himself to the restoration of what was for him and his people a spiritual treasury and power-house. Having exhausted his traditional fields he made a major attack on Santa Ysabel Island, using for the purpose two British-built boats to carry an invading force of 500 men armed with some 400 rifles and 9000 rounds of ammunition.

After British annexation in 1893 head-hunting was made illegal and progressively brought to a halt. In many areas the effect of this was shattering and it was accompanied by a rapid depopulation for no evident reason, such as an epidemic. The anthropologist Rivers, pointing to the severe destruction not only of an economy but also a whole way of life, attributed the decrease in marriage, decrease in children per marriage, and increase in childless marriage and the general death rate to the fact that the people had lost all interest in living.

Economic anthropology is a relatively recent branch of the discipline and the lines of its orientation are still the subject of debate. There are those who so emphasise the differences between modern Western and traditional or 'primitive' societies that it becomes impossible to effect any general comparison, and there are others who maintain that the concepts of Western economists will serve to analyse the economic behaviour of all societies past and present.

The reader is already in a position to translate some of the facts given in this chapter into Western economic terms. One contributor to the current debate has listed some tentative basic concepts and definitions which, in his opinion, would enable a general theory of economic process to emerge. Economics, he writes, is the study of economising, and economising is the allocation of scarce resources among alternative ends. 'Resources' here are understood to be scarce by definition; if they were abundant they would not need allocation. The 'ends' to which resources are allocated are defined as the satisfaction of the various wants human beings may have. One end is said to be alternative to another when the resources that satisfy one such end could equally satisfy another. 'Goods' are defined as anything tangible or intangible which may satisfy a human want, and 'production' is any activity that uses resources to create goods and make them available. Some 'goods' do not directly satisfy a human want but assist production and these are defined as 'capital goods'. Finally, 'consumption' is defined as the use of a 'good' in satisfying a 'want'.

We could apply some of these terms to the facts at our disposal. We heard of the Trobriander farmer allocating a resource (his labour) to the production of goods (yams) for three kinds of consumption—eating, meeting affinal obligations and display, all of which satisfy Trobriand 'wants'. We could say that the Trobriander chief accumulates capital goods, which he allocates as resources for the creation of further capital goods—canoes used for *kula* exchanges. The highest goods of Trobriand society —famous arm-shells and necklaces—are, we must suppose, 'consumed' temporarily by the man who has them in his possession, since this possession satisfies his human want. Or is it the case that the satisfaction he derives from exchanging them for more desirable objects makes this the act of 'consumption'?

Equally, turning to Roviana, we can point to the highest social want, sacrifice and human skulls and the 'production' of slaves, which can be in their turn both 'goods' and 'capital' goods. We could go further if we wished and compare the increase in head-hunting after the introduction of firearms with a boom in our society associated with a drop in the exchange value of slaves, but it may be thought that in all these translations we are really only using the language of economics figuratively and for the sake of description.

If we were to attempt an analysis using these terms the situation becomes more complicated because, to take the example of the slave, he or she may be at once a production unit—making a canoe—a unit of exchange like a canoe, and a consumable good. Or should we say that the living slave is rather a capital good which is used to produce a good—his skull? Certainly the massacre mentioned above demonstrates the use of resources— other people—by a productive activity—decapitation—to produce goods—skulls—and the allocation of a scarce resource—space on the war canoe—to satisfy the end—a cargo of skulls—rather than the alternative end—a cargo of slaves.

I do not intend here to enter into controversy but rather to draw the controversy to the reader's attention. It may well be that the use of the terminology I have listed depends upon our own wants and ends. If we are interested in the specificity of particular cultures, how they cohere as meaningful systems, we shall insist upon what we have called the embeddedness of the economic activities. From such a point of view we shall perhaps be less concerned with breaking up these activities according to the concepts of a Western economy. If, however, we are concerned with comparison for the sake, ultimately, of some universal truths about Man's economic activity, we may have recourse to some mutation of the terminology of economics. But for this to occur, I suspect that the division between economics as an intellectual discipline and our experience of our own economies will have to be overcome (see p. 100).

The problem with which we started was that Western society appears to sustain two kinds of economy—the public and official economy of the academics, and the domestic or private economy of the individual. At the extreme it appeared that the individual's private economy was not strictly 'economic' at all, because the individual is swayed by 'irrational' interests such as affections, personal relationships and the like.

This is not just an intellectual problem. Karl Polanyi points to it as one of our fundamental moral problems. Basically he is attacking the Western tendency to 'separate out', and his argument is that whereas man in general values possessions to the extent that they ensure social goodwill, social status and social assets, the 'economic' society subordinates these social values to the values of production: '*Man's economy is, as a rule, submerged in his social relations.* The change from this to a society which was, on the contrary, submerged in the economic system was an entirely novel development.'

In the 'economic' society, 'economic' motives are considered

to be the *real* ones and others—love, hate, pride, honour, etc.—
because they are not conducive to production or interfere with it,
are somehow regarded as less than *real*:

> 'Honour and pride, civic obligation and moral duty, even self-
> respect and common decency, were now deemed irrelevant to
> production, and were significantly summed up in the word
> "ideal". Hence man was believed to consist of two components,
> one more akin to hunger and gain, the other to honour and
> power. The one was "material" the other "ideal"; the one
> "economic", the other "non-economic"; the one "rational",
> the other "non-rational".'

One does not, I think, need to demonstrate that people in our
society will nevertheless continue to have affections, loyalties,
ambitions, aesthetic preferences and the like. And this being so,
it is easy to see that if all our social values are put into the category of the non-rational, or idealistic, we are perpetuating a split
in our consciousness which can make us slightly ashamed or even
downright guilty. Our social being tells us that we produce in
order to live. The imposed ideology of the market tells us rather
that we should live to produce.

Several anthropologists following Karl Polanyi have tried in
their different ways to correct the language of economics by
comparing our own way of looking at things with the 'embedded'
quality of economic activity in traditional societies. Of these
Marshall Sahlins is the most relevant to our present purpose.
The value of his argument is that he does not oppose a mechanical and impersonal Western type of economic activity to a communal face-to-face system of primitive exchange. He shows that
both kinds of activity occur in so-called primitive societies, and
he offers a spectrum of reciprocities which ranges from the
gratuitous gift on the one hand to exploitative relations on the
other. He defines this spectrum by discussing these extremes and
the mid-point between them: reciprocity which could be described as concealed, reciprocity which is explicit or balanced, and
negative reciprocity.

Concealed reciprocity is perfectly exemplified by our own idea of the gift, and by the daily sharing of food in the household, by hospitality as well as by a variety of other actions in which the obligation to return is diffuse and unspecified both as to the time within which the return is made and as to the amount that is returned. Consider, for example, the gifts given within a family on birthdays and at Christmas in relation to their actual cost. As a child comes to consciousness it is taught to expect presents on these special occasions, and these toys, and later perhaps parties, represent a real financial sacrifice on the part of the parents. The parents have no expectation of a material return from the child; nevertheless the child does learn to reciprocate and by the time it is seven or eight it will be beginning to give in some way or other, by making something or by acting in some way. Even the apparently comical situation in which the child asks for extra pocket money in order to buy a gift for one of the parents is instructive because it highlights the difference within a family between giving as an expression of relationship and the expenditure of mere cash. In later life when the children are married and perhaps have children of their own, we find that the situation is reversed. In most families the greater financial cost of gifts now falls upon the younger adults and the grandparents are most likely to revert to token gifts. Whatever the situation may be in any particular family, it remains the fact that within the family we do not give in order to receive, nor is there any expectation that the cash value of the gifts exchanged should be equivalent. Certainly, by and large, the failure to give on any particular occasion does not sever the relationship and, in fact, failure to remember an anniversary is considered more hurtful. Sahlins writes:

'The material side of the transaction is repressed by the social: reckoning of debts outstanding cannot be overt and is typically left out of account. This is not to say that the handing over of things in such form, even to "loved ones", generates no counter obligation. But the counter is not stipulated by time, quantity or quality: the expectation of reciprocity is indefinite.

It usually works out that the time and worth of reciprocation are not alone conditioned on what was given by the donor, but also upon what he will need and when, and likewise what the recipient can afford and when. Receiving goods lays on a diffuse obligation to reciprocate when necessary, to the donor and/or possible for the recipient.'

Balanced or explicit reciprocity approaches more closely to our own academic notion of the 'economic'. In such situations the continuance of the relationship is contingent upon the recipient recognising his obligation to make a return gift which is regarded as the equivalent of what was originally received. In many cases like is exchanged for like: the best example of this is the exchange of women between intermarrying groups. On the material level balanced reciprocity is exemplified by much of the material discussed on pp. 103-9, with the exception of *gimwali*.

The difference between this type of reciprocity and the preceding one is that the continuance of social relations depends upon the exchanges in a way that within the family, or equivalent group, they do not. Nevertheless, balanced reciprocity is not a simple 'commercial' exchange. Certainly people can find new partners if their traditional partners consistently let them down by failing to reciprocate brides, or material objects in the *kula*; but such a break in relationships is considered to be a bad thing and is accompanied by ill feeling. The contrast with the commercial transaction is clear. If you shopped regularly in some supermarket and then discovered that another offered the same goods at lower prices you would have no hesitation in changing your shop, and you would certainly not feel under any moral obligation not to do so, or experience any embarrassment. On the other hand, your relationship with your local grocer or newsagent may be instructively different. In my experience it is quite common for people to feel an obligation to buy certain kinds of goods from the people with whom they regularly deal. This does not mean that they, any more than partners in the *kula*, are irredeemingly bound to their local greengrocer, but it does mean that they may experience some slight embarrassment if they shop elsewhere. If you are in the habit of buying your vegetables from one particular shop, could you, without giving the matter a moment's thought, buy your potatoes elsewhere for a change and, without concealing them, march into your usual shop to make the rest of your purchases? In the local shop and in the supermarket you are engaged in a commercial transaction, but your relationship with the former is tinged with moral considerations not unlike those which are more formally and strongly expressed in a situation of balanced reciprocity.

Often enough this relationship is expressed by the small trader himself in a variety of ways, such as granting short-term credit, by giving the odd ounce over weight, by levelling down the odd halfpenny, advising on quality and imminent price rises, etc. To the extent that this sort of behaviour creates 'goodwill' it is commercial behaviour. Nevertheless, when we contrast it with the impersonality of the supermarket, we can see that it is a different *type* of commercial activity. One final example of balanced reciprocity in our own society is the relationship of drinking partners in a pub; such a relationship can tolerate all sorts of temporary imbalances, but it is inconceivable that such a relationship could exist between someone who consistently drank large gins and someone who regularly drank beer.

Marshall Sahlins defines his 'negative reciprocity' as follows:

'Negative reciprocity is the most impersonal sort of exchange. In guises such as "barter" it is from our point of view the "most economic". The participants confront each other as opposed interests, each looking to maximise utility at the other's expense. Approaching the transaction with an eye singular to the main chance, the aim of the opening party, or of both parties, is the unearned increment. One of the most sociable forms, leaning towards balance, is haggling conducted in the spirit of "what the traffic will bear". From this, negative reciprocity ranges through various degrees of cunning, guile, stealth, and violence to the finesse of a well-conducted horse raid.'

At first sight it may be difficult to understand how profit achieved by violence or theft can be called reciprocal at all. We have to remember that we are here dealing with a *spectrum* and appreciate that these extreme forms are at the limit. By this I mean that even the most exploitative relationship can be said to be negatively reciprocal to the extent that the exploiter has an interest in maintaining the existence of the 'partner' that he exploits; it is a question of not killing the goose that lays golden eggs. Nevertheless it must be obvious that people, especially when they imagine themselves to be in positions of unlimited power, do not always calculate their own interests so nicely. When two societies are at war they can be said to be engaging in negative reciprocity to the extent that each has an interest in preserving something in the other which it hopes to possess. As the war intensifies, national survival takes increasing precedence and both sides aim more towards total destruction of each other. On another and altogether more trivial level, the commercialist who consistently indulges in sharp practice will soon find that he has destroyed the field of his own operations.

Sahlins is fully conscious that his spectrum may be, as he puts it, 'too widely set'. And he reminds us that actual exchanges occur at all points in the spectrum 'not directly on the extreme and middle points'. Equally, all types of transaction may be found in one particular set of relationships. The husband who does not pass on a wage increase to his wife but who is generous in other ways has simultaneously a relationship of concealed reciprocity and negative reciprocity with her. Hospitality of the 'invitation to dinner' type can be an act of gratuitous generosity; it can be an example of balanced reciprocity when convention dictates that the guest will take his turn as host within a reasonable period; and finally, to the extent that the host expects to exploit the relationship for financial gain, hospitality can play its part in negative reciprocity. The lavish gifts and expensive entertainments which feature so prominently in corruption cases are interesting examples precisely because of the complexity of the relationship of negative reciprocity involved. A straight bribe is altogether simpler because it is, in fact, an example of balanced reciprocity.

T–E

Sahlins tests the value of his typology by exploring the possibility that different kinds of social circumstance encourage one or other kind of reciprocity. Of the various possibilities that he examines, one is particularly relevant for us. He offers the following proposition: 'The span of social distance between those who exchange conditions the mode of the exchange.' Social distance is quite different from physical distance, and this must be understood before we can proceed. Social distance is measured by social values and interests and by the degree and complexity of social interactions. A full definition and discussion of this concept can be found in Evans-Pritchard's *The Nuer*. The reader can, however, come to understand it by a simple experiment: select half a dozen points in your own locality which, on the map, are equidistant from the place where a friend lives, making sure that some are located between that place and the town centre or shopping centre and others further away from it. Ask your friend to list, without thinking too much about it, the chosen points in order of their proximity. You will usually find that those points which lie between the friend's residence and the centre are thought of as being nearer than those which do not. Equally, you can check with a watch your own notions of the distance between places. You will invariably find that the familiar road seems the shorter. Moving away from physical space we can say that the social distance between you and your next-door neighbour may be greater than the social distance between you and your friends, who may live 5 miles away, or your colleagues at work etc.

Sahlins examines his spectrum of reciprocity in relation to a particular kind of social distance—kinship distance—and he sets out to demonstrate that concealed or diffuse reciprocity is associated with kinship proximity and that negative reciprocity becomes increasingly likely as kinship distance increases to a point where there is an encounter with non-kin.

'The reasoning is nearly syllogistic. The several reciprocities from freely bestowed gift to chicanery amounts to a spectrum of sociability, from sacrifice in favour of another to self-interested gain at the expense of another. Take as the minor premise Tylor's dictum that kindred goes with kindness, "two words whose common derivation expresses in the happiest way one of the main principles of social life". It follows that close kin tend to share, to enter into generalised exchanges, and distant and non-kin to deal in equivalents or in guile. Equivalence becomes compulsory in proportion to kinship distance lest relations break off entirely, for with distance there can be little tolerance of gain and loss even as there is little inclination to extend oneself. To non-kin—"other people", perhaps not even "people"—no quarter must needs be given: the manifest inclination may well be "devil take the hindmost".'

In our own society kinship distance is a simple affair easily calculated. Our siblings are closer to us than our first cousins, and our first cousins are closer to us than our second cousins. In societies in which kinship is like an arterial system the community determines the degrees of proximity and distance. In one society we may find that the social distance between a man and his mother's kin is less than the distance between him and his father's kin, and this may well be reversed in another society. In some parts of India, for example, a man will refuse to accept hospitality in the house where his daughter or sister is married; if he does accept hospitality he will on his departure insist on making a gift, often of cash, far in excess of the value of the hospitality that he has received. When, on the other hand, he visits the family of his wife he will be entertained to the hilt of that family's capacity. Among the Nuer, as we have seen, a married man will, out of respect, avoid the company of his wife's parents. Complexities of this nature must be borne in mind when following Sahlins' demonstration.

Sahlins represents the 'typical' tribal situation as a set of concentric circles. At the centre is the house, or homestead; next comes the lineage sector, and as we move outwards we pass through the village, tribal and intertribal sectors. The movement from the household to the intertribal sector corresponds to a movement through the spectrum from concealed reciprocity via balanced reciprocity to negative reciprocity.

At first sight it might seem easy to dismiss Sahlins' demonstration as one of those cumbrous expositions of plain common sense to which social scientists are often prone. The more our relationships approximate to the familial type, the more our exchanges become diffuse; the further away they move from it, the more 'economic' they appear. But consider it in the light of the caveats advanced above (pp. 120–1). It is society that determines the sense of social distance and the morality appropriate to relationships. Western industrial society makes us more mobile and much less bound by the ties of kinships or neighbourhood than mankind in general has ever been.

This situation imposes a choice upon the individual. He or she can, as many indeed do, perpetuate the split between the self and 'others-like-me' on the one hand and any other wider community on the other. As a result of such a choice, transactions with the world of self or 'others-like-me' will tend to vary between the two poles of concealed or balanced reciprocity. Transactions with the wider community will inevitably therefore be conceptualised as relations of negative reciprocity. A person living in such a moral universe may be scrupulous about paying in some way a share of the petrol cost when a friend has given a lift but think nothing of avoiding payment on public transport. Equally, debts to friends and local shopkeepers may be scrupulously settled, while debts to large concerns, whether these are public or private, tend to be regarded as lying at some point between the poles of balanced and negative reciprocity.

Alternatively, the individual can survey the whole range of his or her material transactions and the rationale, at once moral and economic, which supports them. A very simple but useful exercise would be to examine your own concept of the 'gift' in practice over the last twelve months. Did you expend equally on all gifts? What were the reasons for the differences in expenditure? Did you expect a return gift, and if so of what sort and when? From these considerations you could turn to those transactions which seem to come more strictly under the heading 'économic'. What thoughts and circumstances lead you to settle or defer, or perhaps even avoid, which transactions?

Because many of us are brought up to accept unthinkingly the kind of division in our moral universe that Polanyi criticises (see p. 115) the exercise suggested may not be an easy or comfortable one. It may even be thought that I am presenting one view of human transactions as morally superior to the other. It is not part of social anthropology's business to preach a morality. What it can try to do is to heighten consciousness and leave the individual more free to choose how to live in the light of that.

## Summary

The main theme of this chapter was the current debate in social anthropology about our approach to non-European and traditional economies. On the one hand, there are those who think that the concepts of Western economics can be applied directly or with minor modification; on the other, there are those who think we must find a new approach because in many societies 'economic' activities are so embedded in a complex of non-'economic' values that it is impossible to separate them. We observed at the outset that the term 'economics' tends to denote for us an area of life which, like the 'religious', is split off from our day-to-day understanding and our day-to-day affairs. We had, then, to recognise that each one of us has his or her own economy which might appear irrational in the eyes of a professional economist; but it would only be thought irrational to the extent that our personal economic behaviour is related to all our other values and relationships: unlike nations, we do not split off our economic from our social selves. We then looked at Karl Polanyi's distinction between the 'embedded' and the 'disembedded' economy and at his argument that the disembedded economy, which is the product of Western capitalist society, rests upon the idea of the *market*, in which everything is a *commodity* having a *price* related to *supply* and *demand*. Polanyi pointed out that this was neither the only nor the inevitable way of conducting human transactions.

We turned then to look at a classic study of an embedded economy—Malinowski's *Argonauts of the Western Pacific*. Malinowski wrote about the Trobriand Islanders and their participation in a relatively vast system of trade called the *kula*. Malinowski was himself a critic of the notion that rational self-interest governed man's production and he showed how the Trobrianders produced surplus to maintain their matrilineal kin, to present to their chiefs and to display for their own prestige. This brought to the fore the idea of the gift and of reciprocity both in Trobriand society and in the *kula*. In the *kula* reciprocity is expressed in the obligation to circulate red shell necklaces to the north and white arm-shells to the south; seen as though we were looking down on a map, this would mean that the necklaces moved in a clockwise and the arm-shells in an anti-clockwise direction. The exchanges of these objects, which vary in their prestige according to their history, size and beauty, created bonds of moral obligation between widely separated groups. Within the context of these exchanges ordinary trade, as we should call it—*gimwali* to the Trobrianders—was carried on, but those who were *kula* partners could not *gimwali* with each other; they would *gimwali* with those who accompanied the partner.

We then looked briefly at Roviana in the Solomon Islands because this gave us the opportunity to see what happens to an economy when external factors intervene and produce change. We saw that European traders introduced new values and guns which destroyed the relative balance of the head-hunting complex. The new ability to accumulate more slaves and heads made for an inflationary situation and hitherto protected areas were devastated. Even a major attempt to suppress the trade by destroying the spiritual treasury of accumulated skulls only made for an unprecedented expansion of the raids.

In conclusion we returned to the current debate among social anthropologists about the future development of economic anthropology. We examined the possibility of applying some of the concepts of Western economics to the Trobriand and to the Roviana material and found ourselves involved in a complex game of translation which, it was suggested, was not very profitable. This leads us back to Polanyi and an appreciation that the moral problem posed by the split in our own thinking between the disembedded 'official' economy and our personal embedded economies was more important than the intellectual problem. Briefly, the disembedded economy generates notions about human reality which perpetuate a split between, say, affection on the one hand and self-interest on the other; between rational and non-rational behaviour; and between 'economic' and 'non-economic' behaviour.

We then examined one attempt to correct the language of economics in the light of the preceding material and reflections. Marshall Sahlins' attempts to overcome the split by showing that there are degrees of embeddedness and disembeddedness in all societies and that these degrees can be represented by a spectrum of reciprocities ranging from the gratuitous gift, via a mid-point of balanced reciprocity, to negative reciprocity. Sahlins tested out his spectrum in a variety of ways, and we looked at the way in which different notions of reciprocity came into play according to the degrees of social distance in our own society. This in its turn led us to appreciate that our attitudes to our 'economic' transactions and the way in which we do or do not carry them out tell us something about the moral universe which we choose to construct for ourselves.

## Reading notes

Firth, R., *Themes in Economic Anthropology*, Association of Social Anthropologists (ASA) Monographs, No. 6, London, 1967.

Forde, D., and Douglas, M., 'Primitive Economics' in Shapiro (ed.) *Man, Culture, and Society*, Oxford, 1960.

Hocart, A., *The Life-Giving Myth*, London, 1952, Chapter X.

LeClair, E. E., and Schneider, H. K., *Economic Anthropology*, New York and London, 1968. The controversy over this subject is well aired in Part Two, section IV, and V. E. E. LeClair's proposals will be found in the latter section.

Lévi-Strauss, C., *The Elementary Structures of Kinship*, English translation London, 1969. Chapter V, 'The Principle of Reciprocity', sets 'economic' exchanges in the context of kinship and marriage.

Mair, L., *New Nations*, London, 1963, Chapters 2 and 5.

Malinowski, B., *Argonauts of the Western Pacific*, London, 1922. It is in this work that Malinowski gave his account of the *kula*. It is a substantial volume well worth reading in its entirety; if time is short, read Chapters I–III.

Malinowski, B., *Crime and Custom in Savage Society*, London, 1926. This book and the one next listed are mentioned for those who might be interested in acquiring a deeper knowledge of Trobriand society.

Malinowski, B., *Coral Gardens and their Magic*, London, 1935.

Mauss, M., *The Gift*, English translation London, 1954. The original French version was published in 1925 and established the wider human significance of Malinowski's *Argonauts*, published three years earlier. Mauss' *The Gift* is widely accepted as a classic of social anthropological literature and is very well worth reading.

Melitz, J., *Primitive and Modern Money—an interdisciplinary approach*, Massachusetts and London, 1974.

Polanyi, K., *The Great Transformation*, New York, 1944. 'Marketless Trading in Hammurabi's Time', 'Aristotle discovers the Economy', 'The Economy as Instituted Process' in *Trade and Market in the Early Empires*, K. Polanyi, C. M. Arensberg and H. W. Pearson (eds.), Glencoe: The Free Press, 1957.

Polanyi, K., *Primitive, Archaic and Modern Economies*, ed. G. Dalton, New York, 1968. This is a very useful collection of Polanyi's essays taken both from the two works previously cited and from less accessible publications.

Rivers, W. H. R., *The History of Melanesian Society*, 2 volumes, Cambridge, 1914.

Rivers, W. H. R. (ed.), *Essays on the Depopulation of Melanesia*, Cambridge, 1922. Rivers' own contribution 'The Psychological Factor' is Chapter VIII. It is worth mentioning here that Rivers was a distinguished and influential figure in the British social anthropology in the first two decades of the twentieth century. He had a breadth of imagination and sensitivity greater than that of his most well-known student, Radcliffe-Brown.

Sahlins, M., 'On the Sociology of Primitive Exchange', see M. Banton (ed.) in reading notes for Chapter 1. The essay is reprinted as Chapter 5 of the work next listed.

Sahlins, M., *Stone Age Economics*, London, 1974. A highly congenial collection of essays, more significant than the title suggests.

Singh Uberoi, J. P., *Politics of the Kula Ring*, Manchester, 1962. This is a reassessment of Malinowski's work in the light of later developments in social anthropological thought. It is a very good example of what can be done without setting foot outside the study or library. More particularly, Professor Uberoi brings the Trobriands into comparison with the so-called 'stateless societies' discussed in *African Political Systems* (see reading notes for Chapter 1).

Tippett, A. R., *Solomon Islands Christianity*, London, 1967. I have used this secondary source for the Roviana material as much for the interest of the book as for the intrinsic value of the material. Tippett is a missionary who makes good use of social anthropology. Whether the reader sympathises with his aims or not, the book is an excellent example of what is called 'applied anthropology'.

# 5

# Political Organisation and the Birth of a Nation

Before reading this chapter, write an essay answering the question 'What is Politics?' Is it a special sort of activity that some people go in for? Do you think of it as a disruptive or a unifying activity? What about international politics: do you think of this as being different in some way from domestic politics? You yourself engage in economic activity, but do you also engage in political activity? Does the proposition that man is a political animal make any sense to you? Finally, what does the word 'nation' mean to you? Does membership of a nation impose duties or confer rights and, if it does, how do these rights or duties relate to the rights or duties which emerge in other areas of your existence?

\* \* \*

An official, if somewhat outdated, definition of political organisation provides us with a good starting point. It will be found in *Notes and Queries on Anthropology* produced by the Royal Anthropological Institute:

'In its widest sense the political organisation of a people embraces, on the one hand, the whole complex of institutions by which law and order are maintained in the society, and, on the other, all the institutions by which the integrity of the group is maintained in relation to neighbouring communities of a similar kind and protected against attack from without. Thus political organisation includes the legal institutions by which the juridical rights of every member of the society are safeguarded and his juridical obligations enforced ... The organisation of local, i.e. village, town, tribal subdivision, government, and the system of tribal or national or state government. It embraces also the military or other organisation by means of which offensive or defensive action is taken against enemies who threaten the unity, security, or independence of the society, either from outside or from within.'

This definition reflects the thinking and writing of British social anthropologists in the pre- and immediately post-war era. The modern classics of social anthropology which are the products of that generation laid their emphasis upon the maintenance of solidarity and order. This is particularly reflected in the final sentence of the definition, where internal forces making for change in the established political organisation are equated with external enemies. It is not, however, the case that in these older monographs the question of conflict is not faced. Nevertheless the tendency is to ritualise such conflicts and to present them as being ultimately functional to the continuing solidarity of the traditional organisation. Rivalries between chiefs or the sons of a chief, for example, are often represented as being of the same order as the 'conflict' between Labour and Conservative parties in our own political system. According to our own theory this 'conflict' is certainly functional to the continuance of our democracy: after an election the defeated party takes on the role of opposition in Parliament and, by its participation in Parliament, is recognised as contributing to the government of the country in the widest sense.

The contribution that internal conflict makes to the continuance of a traditional system is not to be ignored, but the analysis of political life cannot be limited to that alone. In the post-war period interest began to turn towards the mechanics of the political process, the ways in which people in different societies actually achieve influence and power as opposed to the way in which they are said to achieve them. I can best illustrate this shift in attention by referring once more to the Nuer, the most distinguished example of the earlier approach. In his dis-

cussion of the political system of these people Evans-Pritchard
refers to certain men in Nuer society who are known as *tut*,
bulls. Such people were highly respected members of their
communities and took a prominent part in settling affairs and
arriving at decisions, they were able to attract kinsmen to live in
their byres and to rally support for raids upon the neighbouring
Dinka. Evans-Pritchard takes great pains to insist that these
'bulls' had no defined status, powers, or sphere of leadership . . .
no political status' This insistence results from Evans-Pritchard's
determination to limit the word 'political' to the regular and to
the institutionalised; for him the emergence of 'bulls' is not a
political phenomenon because particular 'bulls' are vaguely
defined and ephemeral. A modern social anthropologist would
certainly include the 'bulls' in his analysis of the political system;
he would be concerned to examine the circumstances favouring
their emergence, the effects of their undoubted power and influence on the more regular and blatant decision-making procedures, and the effect of their presence on traditional affiliations
and loyalties. He would be concerned to examine the reasons for
their ephemerality and perhaps even go so far as to speculate on
the circumstances which might make their power more permanent, even inheritable.

The study of the political life of a particular society is, then,
not to be limited to political institutions and more or less
consciously held theories of how those institutions work. It
must include also the hidden or implicit ways in which power
and influence are achieved and used. To take an example from
our own society, it would be a simple matter to describe the way
in which the average committee works, the role of the chairman
and secretary, the procedures of approving minutes and working
through agendas, the rules governing the proposal of motions
and amendments and voting. A social anthropologist studying the
concept 'committee' in our society would obviously have to
acquaint himself with the general theory about the way in which
committees work, which I have sketched out. He would also
no doubt recognise that, by and large, practice corresponds to
this theory. He would, however, go on to study the unwritten

rules upon which the functioning of any committee depends
fully as much as it does upon the theory. He would try to understand what makes for a 'good' chairman, and the effects of prior
discussions on the formal debate in the committee room. He
would study the ways in which chairmen arrange the agenda
and, without blatantly appearing to do so, prolong or curtail
discussion on particular items. He would observe the ways in
which external affiliations such as age, class, sex, race or religion
were consciously or unconsciously reflected both in the committee's discussions and in its decisions. I myself am also interested in the kind of language people use in the committees and
the way in which this is related both to the size of the committee
and the seating arrangements. Let me give an example: the
closer that people are sitting to each other, the less likely is it
that they will either use the special 'language' of committees or
be offensive to each other. Let us suppose that a particular member knows in advance that he will wish to oppose the line adopted
by the Chair and that in so doing he will have recourse to the
whole battery of committee language—points of order, questions
of clarification, amendments, and amendments to amendments.
Such a person, if he is to be effective, must locate himself as far
as possible, even in a small room, from the Chairman and preferably sit near or next to people who sympathise with his
views. Someone who is opposing the 'official line' would be
imprudent were he either to use the casual language of day-to-
day affairs or to sit close to the Chairman; in such circumstances
the Chairman can thwart him either by insisting upon formality
of procedure or, perhaps more subtly, by appealing to him as a
commonsense human being, as Jack or John, not the 'previous
speaker' or 'the poser of the motion'. Formal language and
physical distance are in a way depersonalising, and the conscious
use or unconscious operation of this principle in any committee
must be observed in any analysis of the proceedings.

In sum, then, the social anthropology of politics is concerned
with the formal theory expressed by the people concerned and
the regular institutions which are said to embody and implement
this theory and also with the implicit or unwritten rules govern-

ing the way in which power and therefore the capacity to make effective decisions is gained or lost by individuals or groups.

I fear that many people may imagine that once we move out of the sophisticated world of state politics into that of the 'pre-literate' or 'primitive' we shall have to do simply with powerful hereditary chiefs exercising an almost despotic power. It is questionable whether such figures existed before Western traders, bringing guns and political support, created them. In fact, were we to attempt a general picture of the traditional 'chief' from our own history and from the observations of anthropologists we would have to emphasise his dependence upon the people whom he is said to govern, who include his own kinsmen. We should find that the government of the chief operates very much through consultation and consensus and that an important characteristic of any effective chief was his capacity to be generous in material things. Where there are no precise political boundaries or a political force capable of coercing loyalty, people can vote with their feet. By their generosity, as much as by their military valour, chiefs can seduce the populations of their rivals. Coming down to the particular, we can even find an example of something which is not dissimilar from our own constitutional monarchy. In a study of the kingship of the Shilluk of the Nilotic Sudan, Evans-Pritchard demonstrates that the king of the Shilluk was more of a sacred figure symbolic of the unity and values of Shilluk society than a ruler. He embodied the life of the nation and Shilluk society, which is believed to be one of those in which the king was killed before he could decline into the weakness of old age. Whether or not he was actually killed is still a matter for discussion; nevertheless anyone who reads the historical plays of Shakespeare can find in them vestiges of the view that the fortunes and health of the king affected in some mysterious way the health and fortunes of his people. In other societies we find that the secular power of the chief is heavily qualified by the spiritual power of other officials, such as priests, or individuals believed to have divine-like powers. Again, the Old Testament provides excellent illustrations of the balance and the conflict of power between the king and the prophets.

In this chapter I propose to give the history of the development from a traditional system of chiefly government based on kinship to something which resembles the modern nation as we know it. The reader should note in this development how the three prerequisites of central power are achieved. For a secure central government to emerge the tribal affiliations of kinship and locality have to be broken down and replaced by a higher loyalty, and a military or police support which is dependent solely upon that central power and nobody else must be built up. This has been the formula of dictatorship whether we observe this in our times or read about it in the history of the Roman emperors. Even Western parliamentary democracy, to the extent that it requires strong centralised institutions, must at the last resort have the power to command a loyalty which transcends that of family or neighbourhood. The essential difference between this and a dictatorship is, of course, that a democratic society has built into it a series of checks which prevent any particular government from assuming absolute power, and the requirement that the government must offer itself for re-election or dismissal at regular periods.

It is safe to assume that most people have heard of the Zulu of South Africa and that a number of them will have heard of Shaka, or Chaka, the Zulu chief, sometimes popularly referred to as the 'Black Napoleon'. In this chapter I am going to discuss Shaka and his people because their history both brings to the surface some of the matters which social anthropologists study in the field of politics and corrects some popular notions about African societies and African history.

The Zulu are one of a family of societies and they emerged relatively late to play an important part in the history of South Africa. They belong to the Nguni-speaking peoples who once inhabited the coastal area of South Africa from Port Elizabeth to Lorenço Marques, between the Drakensberg Mountains and the sea. As late as 1965 it was estimated that there were some seven million Nguni speakers in all Southern Africa, of whom some were in Swaziland and some in Rhodesia but the vast majority in what is now the republic of South Africa.

To say 'Nguni-speaking' is not to suggest that the language is entirely uniform; in fact, the differences in dialect are as marked as they were in this country, especially in the rural regions until very recently. There are still today old people in Sussex and Northumberland who would initially have difficulty in communicating and would be equally unintelligible to an inhabitant of Birmingham or Exeter. In the histories of the Nguni we hear of people who were able to converse with relative ease 'after two or three days'.

The whole notion of uniform language, correct grammar, standard speech and the like is a modern one in Europe, as it is in Africa. The factors that determine the selection of one dialect out of a whole family vary from place to place; communications, trade, military centres, even fashion and, of course, fortune can all have a hand in the choice. Thus an obscure dialect of northern Italy became an universal language of scholarship, and thus also the fact that in the nineteenth century missionaries wrote down and studied two Nguni dialects have given these—Xhosa and Zulu—a greater stability and permanence in South Africa.

As with dialect, so with the people that speak them. Shaka was fifth in descent from a man called Zulu, the younger son of Malandela who moved with his family into the coastal territory some 400 years ago. Zulu settled in the Mfule valley some 60 miles from the coast, about 100 miles north of Durban. Zulu's older brother, Qwabe, settled nearer the coast and founded the Qwabe people, who have by no means achieved the same place in history as their cousins.

To understand the emergence and the importance of the Zulu we have to understand something of the social and political organisation of the Nguni-speaking peoples.

Nguni society was divided into clans, and clans were composed of all those who claimed descent from a common ancestor and between whom marriage was strictly forbidden. The effects of this exogamy were controlled by the custom that when two lineages were sufficiently remote from their common ancestor a chief in one lineage could marry a girl in another and thus create a new clan. In this way several clans could claim a common ancestor and a remote kinship no longer ruled by exogamy.

The clan was not a local group. As among the Nuer, the clans were represented across the tribal territory, but the clan which had the greatest number in a territory provided the chief of that territory and enjoyed the greatest prestige.

The territories of a tribe were ruled by chiefs and were inhabited by lineages of the clans. These were agnatic descent groups of varying time depth, from three to as many as nine generations, which occupied a common homestead or cluster of homesteads. The homesteads were constructed on ridges and the disposition of the huts were governed by the practice of exogamy and the principal of seniority.

The huts of the homestead were arranged in an arc facing east; the mother of the head of the homestead or, if she were dead, his senior wife occupied the 'Great Hut' at the centre of the arc facing the cattle byre. The huts of the junior wives and of the wives of other members of the homestead were arranged in order of rank on either side. It is important to note here a difference between commoners and chiefs. Whereas the first wife of a commoner was also his senior wife, among the chiefs the first wife to be married was the 'right-hand wife' and her son, 'the right-hand son'. The wife whom a chief married later with the subscribed cattle of his leading supporters was the 'Great Wife' and the 'mother of the country', and her son would normally succeed to the chieftainship. The inevitable rivalry between the eldest son and his half-brother, who might be several years his junior, was a perpetual source of fission in the politics of the Nguni.

The homestead of related lineages might well cluster together along a ridge, but they would also be associated with the homesteads of friends and affines. One custom making for this diversity was that of circumcision. Traditionally all the boys or young

T–F

men who were circumcised together would constitute a sort of brotherhood and, as it was the custom for them to be circumcised together with a prince of the chief's house, they and their families would often constitute his retinue and settle where he settled.

It is worth noting finally that the Nguni were remarkable for their receptivity towards strangers; to take an extreme example, even Europeans were integrated. The Cape route claimed many shipwrecks and even as early as 1554 survivors of a wreck came across survivors of earlier wrecks who were so content that they refused to return to Europe. Two men who survived a wreck in the early eighteenth century became the founders of the Lungu (Abelungu) clan, i.e. the whites, and a woman in their company married a local chief.

At this distance of time it is impossible to know what the relationship was between the different chiefdoms. We know that they varied in size, between 1000 and 350 000 people, and could muster from 150 to 6000 fighting men. Some of the larger chiefdoms were subdivided into sub-chiefdoms; in other cases related chiefdoms recognised some sort of precedence based on seniority of descent. In some chiefdoms it would appear that there were both sub-chiefs, who owed a feudal duty to their superior and administered justice subject to his appeal court, and other *junior* chiefs, who merely recognised the seniority of the head chief.

For the anthropologist as for the historian of South Africa the most important feature of the traditional political system was the availability of land. It is clear that the Nguni, like so many other people, were able for a considerable period of their history to assume an unlimited universe, and the nature of their political organisation reveals this. Either because men had quarrels or simply because a particular population had increased beyond the resources of a particular locality, whole groups would secede from the parent body and find land enough not only for their settlements, their cattle pasture and agriculture but even for the hunting which the Nguni particularly relished.

Nguni records show how, time after time, new settlements and chiefdoms came into being when the 'right-hand son' seceded from the 'great place' of his father.

In 1651 a decision was taken in Holland and in 1652 an action was taken in Africa which contributed to the emergence of Shaka and the constitution of modern South Africa. The decision of the Dutch Netherlands East India Company was to establish a refreshment station, and the action which followed a year later was the landing of Jan van Riebeeck at Table Bay, where the foundation of modern Cape Town was laid.

The new refreshment station was to service Dutch ships returning from Java, but this function inevitably bred others. African cattle acquired by trade could not meet an increasing demand for fresh meat; the lack of skilled horticultural labour made it difficult to meet the prime need for fresh vegetables. Despite the original intentions of the Company not to establish a colony, local demand brought in Dutch *burgers* and *boers* from Holland, slaves from the Dutch East Indies, Germans, and French Huguenots after the revocation of the Edict of Nantes in 1685. By 1700 the original colony had absorbed all the population it could take and new settlers were obliged to farm inland. By this time the future had been shaped; notably the distinction between 'Afrikaners' and Europeans had emerged, that is between the settlers and the Company servants who were only temporary residents. Three of the fundamental ingredients of the South African Republic emerged at this time: the vision of South Africa as the haven of persecuted Protestantism; the birth of the Cape 'coloured' population, born of sexual liaison between the white settlers, the Malays and the indigenous population; and the origin of the category 'poor white', which has been an important consideration in the shaping of modern South African domestic policy.

From being a refreshment station the Cape settlement became a colony, and as it became a colony it engendered its own needs and aspirations independent of the original function. Not only were new immigrants encouraged to settle inland but also the less advantaged whites of the colony moved eastward, where they could at once enjoy greater opportunities for material gain and be less under the eye of authority. Inevitably raiding for cattle and for ivory developed and, as the farms around the colony increased and expanded, they pushed the lawless element ahead of them.

Successive governments, Dutch and then, after 1795, British, tried to prevent or at least control this expansion eastwards, but with no success. By 1835 the colonist population had moved 400 miles from the Cape and was laying claim to land just east of the Kei river, about 100 miles into the territory of the Nguni-speaking Xhosa.

The invasion of 'native' territory by white colonists is often rendered as a kind of rape, or at best a seduction of 'innocent savages' by means of beads, baubles and alcohol. Such an understanding of the situation is often over-simple and certainly misrepresents the case of the colonists and the Nguni. So far from resisting or even being reluctant, the Nguni moved as eagerly towards contact as did the whites. They were particularly interested in acquiring horses and guns, but they were also quick in response to European missionaries and to Western education.

The tragedy of the situation resulted from the failure to recognise the close relation between their political organisation, their economy and their conception of infinite space. They needed land for agriculture and grazing; they knew that the over-use of land for such purposes weakened it and, to that extent, were more sophisticated than many *boers*, who tended to overgraze their pastures; therefore they needed more land than was actually in use at any one time. In addition, they were devoted to hunting and tended to be prodigal, sometimes killing more than they could eat.

These needs combined with Nguni political notions implied infinite expansion. Conflicts between fathers and sons and between brothers was traditionally minimised by the fact that a secession by one party to open up new land was regarded as a normal procedure. Like many people who exist and have existed in the world, the Nguni had no notion of land as property which could be owned in perpetuity by individuals or groups. Their society was a society of kinsman, not, essentially, a society of the inhabitants of a territory. A Sudanese friend pointed the difference for me years ago when he said 'For us the land is like the air we breathe, we use it and pass it back.'

These social factors, combined with the Nguni readiness to take advantage of new relationships, were sufficient to ensure contact with the colonialists. The fact that the latter were as hungry for land themselves, and moreover had a very different view of land-ownership, was enough to ensure conflict. To this has to be added an increase in population which could only accelerate the expansion process. One of the possible factors making for population increase is instructive as an example of an apparently fortuitous good which contributed to an ultimate misfortune: this was the introduction of maize.

Maize had been brought to Africa from America by the Portuguese and its cultivation had spread among the Nguni in the eighteenth century. Maize matures more rapidly than the traditional staple crop, sorghum (a rather inferior kind of millet), yields heavier crops and is a good deal more nutritious. But maize takes more from the soil than sorghum and requires more rapid rotation. It may therefore not only have increased the population but also have heightened the demand for land.

The effects of these internal and external pressures on some of the Nguni were similar to those which we observe elsewhere; in short, it is the emergence out of a polity based on kinship of a state based on territorial possession. This was apparent among the northern Nguni, among whom the Zulu are the most famous. But the emergence of Shaka and of the Zulu state was dependent upon earlier developments.

It would appear that, deprived of space for expansion and given a rising population, tensions in the Nguni political order could no longer be reduced by secession. The dissident were obliged to fight out their quarrels and the vanquished, having nowhere to go, were obliged to submit to the stronger. The details of this development are now lost. What is certain is that towards the end of the eighteenth century a man called Dingiswayo of the Mthethwa tribe ousted his brother from the chieftainship and initiated important changes.

Traditionally, Nguni armies were territorially based, so that on most occasions the men of one locality fought side by side. Dingiswayo now recruited his regiments from age groups *throughout* the chiefdom and created age-regiments with distinctive insignia and colours. The importance of this change cannot be too strongly stressed. In the movement from politics based on kinship to state organisation, the crucial step is the creation by a leader of support that is independent of other ties, whether this is an army or a bureaucracy.

To what extent Dingiswayo was a revolutionary we cannot say at this distance of time. We should not, however, fall into the error of supposing that non-European societies are incapable of innovation without some external model. At the same time the most vigorous leader cannot effect changes without favouring circumstances. It is evident, in fact, that these northern Nguni tribes had been undergoing a process of social change before Dingiswayo; this fact is witnessed by the abolition of the rite of circumcision. What the reasons for this were, again we do not know, but we can assert with confidence that the lapse of so important a ritual, central to the definition of manhood, indicates simultaneous changes across a wide range of beliefs and relationships. In a sense what Dingiswayo did was both re-storative and revolutionary. In creating the new regiments composed of age-mates he reintroduced, now at a tribal level, the notion of solidarity between coevals which before had been effected, at the local level, by the group circumcision of young men.

Certainly the new military organisation was successful. Practising the limited warfare which was characteristic of the Nguni, Dingiswayo's campaigns were aimed to ensure the submission rather than the annihilation of the enemy. Apart from the recognition of Dingiswayo's supremacy the conquered tribes were required to supply men for his army, and these were recruited on his new principle. Thus a regimental army was created

which now transcended even tribal ties; a further step towards
a state had been made.

By the time of his death *circa* 1818, Dingiswayo had created a
confederacy modelled on the larger Nguni chiefdoms, which extended across some 800 square miles. One of the smaller units of
this confederacy was the Zulu, a small tribe of about 2000
people.

Shaka of the Zulu was born in about 1787. Zulu tradition
records that his birth was irregular in that his mother, a girl of
the Langeni tribe, became pregnant by a Zulu chief, Senzangakona, before marriage. According to Zulu tradition Shaka's
mother did not find a happy or permanent place among the
Zulu even after she had been accepted as a bride. Shaka's childhood was spent among his mother's people, the Langeni, and
among his mother's mother's people, the Qwabe, descendants of
Zulu's elder brother. Some records suggest that subsequently,
first with his mother and later alone, Shaka resided with various
other tribes. Certainly his later adolescence was spent among the
Mthethwa army at about the age of twenty, *circa* 1807.

Shaka was clearly a highly successful warrior under Dingiswayo and he is credited with various military innovations, including the invention of the stabbing spear to replace the
assegai or javelin which could only be thrown once and could in
its turn be thrown back by the enemy. In order to increase their
speed he made his soldiers go bare foot; he also imposed
celibacy on the young men and devised the encircling tactics, or
pincer movement, by which one regiment would engage the
enemy from the front in the traditional manner while two others
would spread out on either side 'like the horns of a bull' to surround them. His major departure from Nguni custom was the
practice of total warfare, in the sense that he aimed to break
permanently the capacity of the enemy to fight, and when he
thought fit he would by massacre destroy the tribal identity by
eliminating men, women and children of the ruling house.
Those who were taken prisoner were divided from their fellows
by incorporation into various age-regiments.

The preceding account anticipates somewhat on Shaka's development. In about 1816, when he was some twenty-nine years old, Dingiswayo appointed him chief of the Zulu. Senzangakona had died and had been succeeded by his son Sigujana. The new chief was murdered shortly after his succession by Shaka's half-brother, the son of his mother by another marriage. Obviously Shaka's autonomy and power to innovate, evident before he assumed the Zulu chieftainship, were now enhanced.

During Dingiswayo's lifetime Shaka limited his military excursions to his own area. But Dingiswayo was killed while on campaign in 1818 and without him his confederacy rapidly crumbled. Some of the dependent tribes submitted to Shaka, who was now the strongest power in the area; others he reconquered for his growing empire. Dingiswayo's heir was killed and replaced by a chief who recognised Shaka's supremacy.

Shaka died, assassinated by his own kinsmen, in 1828. By that time he had created a state which extended over nearly 20 000 square miles and stopped short of Natal. It has been estimated that at the peak of his career he controlled an army of 40 000 men. In the state Shaka was commander-in-chief, law giver and supreme judge at his headquarters or capital, Bulaweyo. He retained some traditional hereditary chiefs under him and in some areas appointed his own men. All chiefs were, however, constantly checked for their loyalty and required to attend at Shaka's court, where he would play one off against another. Bulaweyo became the symbolic centre of the kingdom where the entire army congregated annually for the first-fruits ceremony. On this occasion a traditional ceremony which formally had only local associations was made a national feast. In accordance with this movement Zulu customs and language became national ones, and Shaka's subjects, whatever their original tribe, became Zulu.

As his power increased Shaka developed his regimental system and he added to it regiments of women. The new regimental system was used to weaken still further the old ties of tribe and locality. Some fifteen regimental barracks were located at different points in the kingdom, all built to one plan. The male and female regiments lived in segregated quarters and the sexes were allowed occasional intercourse, which stopped short of procreation. Men were allowed to marry only in their forties and even then were obliged to take their wives from designated female regiments.

The traditional homesteads were thus depleted of many of their young men and women, but they survived and adults returned to their natal homestead when they married and were demobilised or put on reserve. The homesteads also continued to produce the bulk of the nation's grain.

Shaka's achievement in state-building, accomplished in something over ten years, is amazing; its side effects are equally significant in the history of South Africa. Because of his practice of total warfare many populations fled rather than confront him in battle. These refugee freebooters disrupted the societies into which they moved and in some cases conquered; elsewhere they established themselves as separate chiefdoms beyond the range of Shaka's army. Among the latter was Sobhuza, who retreated northwards and laid the foundation of modern Swaziland. Where the local population fled, had been massacred or absorbed, ruin was left behind. By 1824 Shaka's armies had devastated south of the kingdom an area which stretched 125 miles down to the Mzimkhulu river and extended between the Drakensberg Mountains and the sea. The cattle had been taken, the grain looted or burnt and the surviving population fled further to the south. We may note that this scorched-earth policy tended to become a general military tactic under the Nguni after Shaka.

I will conclude with a brief account of Shaka's character as far as such details can be known. Early travellers give us a picture of the Nguni which may well have been influenced by ideas about the 'noble savage'; even allowing for this, the authors are explicit in contrasting the Nguni with other peoples for their generosity to strangers, their lack of slavery and their practice of limited warfare. Shaka does not emerge as a typical Nguni, but we must remember that considerable changes had taken place among the northern Nguni by the time of his birth. He was clearly a ruthless man who did not hesitate to kill, sometimes by torture, either to enforce discipline or to spread terror. Some accounts suggest that towards the end of his life he even began to take pleasure in killing for its own sake. Some questions arise about his sexual life. He did not recognise any legitimate heirs and it is not known whether he had illegitimate issue. His own reason, given to traders, was that he wished to avoid rearing up rivals to his own throne. We may wonder, nevertheless, whether his insistence upon sexual abstinence in his army was not so severe as to suggest that there was more to it than discipline or some theory of the sublimation of sexual energy. Some have suggested that he was impotent, or even that he was a latent homosexual, or that he suffered some trauma as a result of a delayed pubescence. His reaction to the death of his mother lends support to a pathological diagnosis of his character. Like everyone else, he believed that all deaths were the result of sorcery and that the sorcerers had to be found out and punished. We are told that, even allowing for exaggeration, the number of people executed on this charge after the death of his mother are to be numbered in thousands. In this connection we should note that one at least of the relatives behind his assassination in the following year, his paternal aunt, believed that Shaka had murdered his mother himself. A final indication of Shaka's psychopathology is the report of an increasing hypochondria in his later years expressed in a morbid fear of declining vitality. With all this he was a man of original and inventive mind, a highly efficient organiser capable of sustained energetic effort over long periods.

In conclusion I would like to look at just one aspect of Nguni history and compare it with situations in other societies—the relation to the terrain. This is not a simple matter of geographic determinism; different peoples interact with the same environment in different ways. Nor is it a matter of technological efficiency alone; social values also play their part. People and land interact: on the one hand, people may know the skills of fishing and agriculture but not exploit the possibilities of these skills if their heart is in cattle. Equally, a cattle-owning people deprived for whatever reason of pasture land will be driven, if they are to survive, to exploit their new circumstances in new ways. Climate and the times of harvest will affect many social activities such as marriage, warfare, trade, etc. Facility of communications and availability of game among hunting peoples will determine the intensity of interaction between groups; these and many other factors of the environment must be taken into account in any full understanding.

We say that the history of the Nguni-speaking peoples takes place between the Drakensberg Mountains and the south-east coast of South Africa, and the effects of population movement can only be to the north and south; we note also the lack of any major natural barriers to this movement. Given the expanding nature of their traditional polity they were bound to intermingle a great deal with each other and with other people. Their terrain was rich enough to maintain their mixed economy of herding, agriculture and hunting, and they were enabled to tolerate population increase to an extent which a more hard-pressed society could not have done.

In the study of political organisations there are perhaps two interconnected features of the environment which are particularly important, and these are the relative ease of travel and communication on the one hand, and the natural limits imposed upon the size of local settlements on the other. The Nuer (see Chapter 2) represent an extreme and interesting case. Their land has been described as 'throughout the year hard on man and beast, being for the most part of the year either parched or a swamp'. In the dry period between November and April their clay soil retains enough moisture to support the grass on which their cattle feed; in the wet period between May and October the flat land is flooded and they and their cattle take refuge on the ridges and knolls where their homesteads are built.

The alternation of these two main seasons is severe and sudden. When the rains stop the sun rapidly dries up the flood water and by the middle of November the grass is dry enough to be fired. This is a critical time, for the soil may not always retain enough moisture to sustain the new crop of grass. As the dry season proceeds to its climax in March and April the Nuer are obliged to travel further and further afield for water supplies and in this process congregate together by the most enduring of these. As the drought progresses the camps become larger and larger and may finally contain several hundred people. When the rains return these camps break up and the people return to their homesteads, where they may effectively be isolated at the height of the rainy period. In the dry season therefore, and increasingly, whole tribal sections of the Nuer meet to renew relationships. Thus every year the Nuer man or woman is reminded of tribal affiliation and renews participation in tribal culture. At this time also the unmarried young have the opportunity to meet and the bases of subsequent marriages are often established.

This example from the Nuer has been much simplified and it should be remembered that, sharp as are the transitions from one season to the other, each season has its own climax, before and after which its effects are less severe. This is particularly true of the wet season, which at the outset and towards the end allows for more social interaction between settlements than the above suggests.

Finally, we can note that the Nuer grow millet and, indeed, depend on it for porridge and for beer; but they lack any knowledge of crop rotation and are obliged to shift their settlements when the soil is impoverished. Again, they could supplement their diet with the wild game in which their territory abounds, but they show no great skill or interest in hunting and, indeed, regard game as shameful food to be eaten in secret by those who have not enough cattle. Equally, although they eat fish and each tribe guards its own fishing areas, they despise people who depend on fish and they have not developed any technique for fishing other than with the spear.

A situation which is sometimes compared with that of the Nuer is that of the Eskimo, about whom Marcel Mauss wrote a classical study based on literary sources. He was probably the first to note how the rhythm of social life is affected, in the case of the Eskimo markedly, by seasonal variations. In the summer Eskimo families are scattered in individual tents, while in the winter they join together in larger conglomerations with perhaps as many as six families in one long-house, with which is associated a central hall for the male members of the group. The quality of social life varies also. In the summer the only religious rites are those of birth and death, which in the nature of events cannot be delayed. In the winter their religious life is intense. In the summer each family governs its own economy, while in the winter there is a communal economy. In the summer government of the family is patriarchal, in the winter the father's authority gives way to the communal authority of the clan elders. Mauss expressed his understanding in a way which most modern social anthropologists would accept. It was not the case that the season were the immediate determinants, they operated, rather, by their effects on the social densities involved, and the given densities were related to technological circumstances, in this case the lack of snow-shoes which prevented the Eskimo from pursuing their game as it moved towards its winter quarters.

I will give one final example of the environmental relation which will also serve as an interesting comparison with the Nguni. This is the case of the Plains Indians whose descendants still live, albeit in restrained circumstances, in their traditional territory, very roughly between the Rocky Mountains and the Mississippi River, including adjacent parts of Canada.

As far as the early evidence can guide us, we see the original Plains Indians living in relative isolation, each tribe enjoying the illusion of infinite space. It is certain that traditionally they used dogs for transporting goods on a kind of sledge and that they hunted buffalo with spears and on foot. When exactly horses were introduced to the Plains we do not know. The evidence suggests that the Spaniards brought them from Europe and that they spread from the Spanish settlements in New Mexico northwards and were well established among the Plains Indians by the end of the eighteenth century. It is even more difficult to pinpoint the time at which firearms were introduced, although some must have come from the Spaniards. The major influx of firearms is associated with the expansion of the European fur trade and the development of the Hudson Bay Company, which received its royal charter in 1680. Guns were among the prized trade goods that were exchanged. People who came to be known as the Plains Cree, for example, originated in the east near Hudson Bay and in response to the European need for furs turned trappers. In the eighteenth century they moved with European guns westwards into the Plains, dislodging the indigenous population. By the end of the eighteenth century firearms were common among the Plains Indians.

It is not possible in a little space to detail the short- and the long-term effects of these two innovations, the horse and the gun. Among the short-term effects was a change in the pattern of marriage. Polygyny was permitted amongst most tribes but was practised on a modest scale. With the introduction of guns and the fur trade, polygyny increased. This was for the reason that the preparation of hides was women's work and a man who had several wives could keep his processing in step with the increased slaughtering made possible by his horse and gun. It is estimated that the maximum number of wives for one man among the Blackfoot rose from six in the 1780s to twenty or more in the 1840s. This development stimulated the need for horses, because these had become the prime object for bride wealth, and this in its turn heightened the motives for intertribal horse raids and war. The new mobility given by the horse, the lethal power of the gun and the demand for fur combined to ensure that the buffalo were overhunted. By 1880 the beast was almost extinct. With the buffalo went the inflated polygyny and, of course, much else besides.

The fur trade brought other tribes, in addition to the Cree, into the Plains and generally accelerated the development of a problem. Even without it, however, the Plains cultures were caught up in change. Now that they could hunt buffalo in greater numbers and cover wider areas, their contacts with each other increased; young warriors might be away from home for two years or more on their excursions. With the growth of potential conflict with distant strangers implicit in this expansion went the need to establish far-flung alliances with people who could provide support and shelter to hunting and warring parties. With the decline of the buffalo, and after 1880, the warrior's occupation had gone and we have a situation similar in some ways to that of the Nguni. In this case a relatively recently developed form of organisation was folded back on itself; the young generation of men who expected to show their manhood in external military activities now found themselves living in decreased territory. Inevitably conflict arose between them and the older chiefs, and this only added to the general distress of a people who, within a few generations, had been reduced from complete independence to the status of barely tolerated pensioners of a white government.

## Summary

In this chapter we recognised at the outset that the study of political systems must, if it is to take account of realities, appreciate the existence of conflict. We see that conflict does not necessarily make for change but, in favouring circumstances, can do so. Nor should we limit our analysis to the surface institutions; we have also to take into account the implicit rules upon which the functioning of any political institution depends. In approaching non-European polities we have to be on our guard against simple notions of omnipotent chiefs of the sort that occur only in fiction or films.

After these caveats we turned to the study of the emergence of the Zulu kingdom and the power of Shaka. First, we looked at the traditional set-up among the Nguni-speaking peoples of the west coastal area of modern South Africa. The most notable feature of their traditional political organisation was the way in which chiefdoms could divide, and we saw how dependent this system was upon the availability of land for expansion. The same held true for traditional Nguni notions about hunting and their form of agriculture. We then looked at the events which made for the founding and development of the Cape colony, and we observed the expansion of the white population westwards

towards the Nguni and briefly noted the effects upon the Nguni
of being penned into a confined area. This was followed by an
account of Dingiswayo of the Mthethwa, who in the eighteenth
century was able to make important changes in Nguni military
organisation and who, as a result, established a large confederacy
which included a small tribe called the Zulu, the tribe of Shaka.
We looked at Shaka's career and at the implication of further
changes that he introduced. We saw that if he was to become a
paramount chief he had to create ties of dependence upon himself which cut across those of the old chiefdoms or of traditional
neighbourhoods and kinship, and we noted the effectiveness of
his regimental system in doing just this.

In conclusion we considered the relevance of terrain in the
study of political systems and looked briefly at the Nuer, the
Eskimo and the Plains Indians of North America. In the case of
the latter we were able to go a little further and to examine the
effects upon them of the introduction of horses and guns, and
later of white expansion in the form of the fur trade; we saw
how their polities were, like those of the Nguni, dependent upon
the idea of unlimited space and that they could not cope with
their internal conflicts when this idea was no longer practicable.

## Reading notes

Bailey, F., *Stratagems and Spoils*, Oxford, 1969. Compared with those
studies which deal with the principles which organise political institutions, Professor Bailey's work is an attempt to discover the rules governing the success or failure of political behaviour. It is a stimulating
book written with an eye on the non-specialist.

Brown, D., *Bury My Heart at Wounded Knee*, London, 1970. A his-
tory of the white expansion into the American west and its effect on the
Indians, culminating in the notorious massacre of the Sioux at
Wounded Knee.

Driver, H., *Indians of North America*, Chicago and London, 1961.
This is a comprehensive comparative description of native American
cultures from the Arctic to Panama. It is essentially a reference work:

the chapters are devoted to topics—Subsistence, Marriage and the Family, Crafts, Clothing, Language, etc.—rather than to the various distinct cultures. The reader has to rely heavily on the index to collect information about any one particular people.

Evans-Pritchard, E. E., *The Nuer*, Oxford, 1940. Compare the author's summary account of his analysis (pp. 261–6) with the analysis itself.

Evans-Pritchard, E. E., 'The Divine Kingship of the Shilluk of the Nilotic Sudan' in his *Essays in Social Anthropology*, London, 1962.

Frankenberg, R., *Village on the Border*, London, 1957. This is referred to by Bailey (see above) and could be usefully read in conjunction with Bailey's book.

Gluckman, M., *Custom and Conflict*, Oxford, 1955. A simple example of the 'conflict makes for harmony' school of thought.

Gluckman, M., 'The Kingdom of the Zulu of South Africa' in *African Political Systems* (see reading notes for Chapter 1).

Gluckman, M., 'Kinship and Marriage among the Lozi of Northern Rhodesia and the Zulu of Natal', in *African Systems of Kinship and Marriage* (see reading notes for Chapter 1).

Lowie, R., *Indians of the Plains*, New York, 1954. A brief, readable account of these peoples by a distinguished American anthropologist of the older generation.

Mair, L., *New Nations*, London, 1963. Chapters 1 and 4. A discussion of African political systems under colonial rule, and the effects of decolonisation.

Mauss, M., '*Essai sur les variations saisonnières des sociétés éskimo*' in *Sociologie et anthropologie*, selected essays of Mauss with an introduction by Lévi-Strauss, 2nd edition Paris, 1966.

Mutwa, C., *My People*, London, 1969. The author is a modern Zulu and the book presents the views of the black historian. His account of the Xhosa should be compared with Wilson (see below).

Pedersen, J., *Israel—its life and culture*, 2 volumes, Oxford, 1940. Anybody interested in gaining anthropological insight into the Old Testament should read this remarkable and exciting work. For the discussion of Kings and of Prophets, see Part III in Vol. 2.

Ritter, E. A., *Shaka Zulu*, London, 1955. This is a novel based on the life of Shaka. The author has used documentary evidence and the main lines of his account are reliable. Nevertheless this enjoyable novel inevitably contains much imaginative reconstruction.

Weber, M., *The Theory of Economic and Social Organisation*, London, 1947. The reader should now be in a position to use the material given in this and the preceding chapters in relation to Weber's types of authority (see reading notes for Chapter 1).

Wilson, M., and L. Thompson (eds.), *The Oxford History of South Africa*, 2 volumes, Oxford, 1969, 1971. The accounts of the Nguni in general, the Xhosa and Zulu in particular, and of the growth of the Cape Colony will be found in Volume I, South Africa to 1870.

# 6

# Belief and Action

Before reading this chapter, write an essay on your understanding of the words 'religion' and 'ritual'. If you regard yourself as a religious person, what would an irreligious person be like? Conversely, if you do not think of yourself as religious, what does that mean? Either way, is ritual necessary to religion or can there be secular rituals? Think seriously what is meant when we say of someone that they take a walk, clean their teeth, go to Bingo or attend to bills 'religiously' every morning, every Friday or whenever. More generally, can 'belief' be 'rational' and what does it mean to talk of 'having faith in science'? Do you believe in luck? Do you believe in chance? Is there a difference? Consider your own rituals of dressing and eating: when do you wear which clothes and when do you eat which foods, and to what extent are your responses determined by the presence or absence of other people? To what extent is your eating or dressing flexible or rigid, and in what social circumstances? When is it permissible to serve vegetables in the saucepan instead of a vegetable dish? Who do you allow to see you in your dressing gown or equivalent and who not? What foods typically 'go' with the following meals—lunch, dinner, tea, high tea, supper? In what circumstances do you use some or all of these terms? Finally, try to think of other areas of your behaviour which vary according to social circumstances—sitting, walking, greeting, laughing, etc.

\*　　　\*　　　\*

Two contrasting events that occurred while this work was being drafted will serve very well to open up the theme of this chapter. The first occurred in Trafalgar Street, Brighton, which runs under Brighton Station forecourt. Two youths were walking down the street, one drinking a carton of milk which he had just finished as I saw him. He looked around for somewhere to get rid of it and reached up to put it tidily on one of the ledges in the supporting arches of this subway. This was during the high summer in Brighton, a time and place for littered streets. I was initially amused by this fastidious action but then reflected on the significance of it as representing a fundamental feature of human nature—the need for order.

The second event was a snippet of an interview heard on the radio. An artist had decorated an old church with brightly coloured pictures of biblical stories, using local parishioners as models and setting the scenes among the day-to-day objects of the contemporary world—television sets, cars, washing machines and the like. Would not, the interviewer asked, the colours and the modernity upset the congregation as conflicting with what he called the 'essentially religious character' of the building. This was as good an example as any of a distinctive feature of modern European and perhaps especially Anglo-Saxon Protestant society. The religious is regarded as special and clearly identified by certain characteristics which set it apart from 'normal life'.

Because many people associate anthropology with the study of strange beliefs, superstitions and the like, and because many social anthropologists encourage this by projecting the notion that the religious is a separate sphere of human existence, a sphere in which otherwise rational people can appear to believe the daftest things, I am tempted to the extreme position that the young man with his milk carton was acting religiously and that the BBC interviewer should have spoken of superstition rather than religion. A more sober and useful approach, however, would be to argue that the concept 'religion' is not merely useless in our attempt to understand humanity, it can positively impede us.

The history of a word does not necessarily reveal its true

meaning, but it can often help us to understand its modern usage better. In the case of the word 'religion' we find its earliest meaning in the Roman sense of that which is incumbent or required—a sense which survives oddly in the modern 'she goes to Bingo religiously every Friday', or ludicrously 'he goes to church religiously'. In the early Christian period the word 'religion' got linked with a particular kind of organisation, an *ecclesia*, or exclusive church, such that by the fourth century AD people could write of true and false religions. This was combined with the growth of a division, too long and complicated to pursue here, between reason and faith, between the natural and the supernatural which through the centuries brought us to our current opposition of the religious and the secular, the sacred and the profane.

The history of the word 'religion' is paralleled in India by the history of the word *dharma*. In the earliest texts and for centuries, this word in its widest sense denoted the order of the universe and, more narrowly, the nature and duties of men. It was possible for the universe and for men to behave according to *adharma*, not *dharma*, but if everyone and everything obeyed the inner law of its nature then the world was governed by *dharma*. It is only in recent centuries, and more rapidly in the nineteenth and twentieth centuries, that we find the word *dharma* connoting a private adherence of an individual to a world view based essentially on supernatural premises.

This development of the ideas of the supernatural is of fundamental importance. It probably originated in the works of St Thomas Aquinas (1225–74) and the earliest uses of the word in English are in the early sixteenth century. The significance of its emergence is underlined by Durkheim in one of his most important works published originally in 1912 and translated in English as *The Elementary Forms of the Religious Life*, where he makes the evident point that people cannot develop the notion 'supernatural' unless they have first created a prior notion of the 'natural'. This itself is a quite peculiar development in Western society which would repay study. All that we can affirm here is that by the thirteenth century, in the immensely in-

fluential writings of Aquinas, we find a clear distinction between
the objects of science and the objects of faith; a critical distinction for the subsequent development of European thought
both about the 'religious' and about the 'scientific'.

And yet the century before Aquinas saw great developments in
what we would call science within a framework which we might
call religious but which most of us would call superstitious—
the system of thought that today survives in impoverished form
as astrology. The scientists of the twelfth century were remarkable for the ingenuity with which they wove together Christian
theology, Greek and Arab world views and theories, and the
findings of their own inquiries, into a magnificent harmonious
scheme in which God presided over planets, whose movements
governed not merely human temperaments but also different
parts of the human body, the seasons, the properties of minerals,
animals and plants. A last great attempt to create a synthesised
world view before a crack in the universe was to widen into a
gulf.

Among modern social anthropologists there is none who has
provided stronger ethnographic evidence for this Durkheimian
point of view than Evans-Pritchard, at least in his earliest period.
In 1936 he published an article 'Zande Theology' based on his
first major fieldwork among the Azande of Central Africa. In
the article the author considers a Zande word *mbori* which
earliest travellers, missionaries and others had rendered 'God'
or 'Supreme Being' and had described as 'a personal God, a
kindly creator and father, moral ruler and judge of the universe,
to who men pray in humility and faith'. Evans-Pritchard cautions
against such translations and, in the light of his own experience
of the Azande, writes:

'In treating of religion . . . we have only to translate primitive
religious terms into our own language, and our interpretation
of them is already made by the very process of translation.
Once we have translated Zande words into such English
expressions as "Supreme Being" and "soul", the notions and

feelings these words evoke in us already intrude to colour our apprehension of the meaning they possess for the Azande. Merely by translating "Mbori" as "Supreme Being" we ascribe to him supremacy which implies for us personality, omnipotence, benevolence and others.'

How does the anthropologist set about the business of arriving at a true translation, it being recognised that it is only faithful translation that we can aim at? Evans-Pritchard's article ex-emplified the method. The social anthropologist makes it his business to collect every context and instance in which a word is used, on the assumption that usage is not fortuitous or arbi-trary, that one and the same word used in a variety of apparently diverse contexts means the same thing and that the full meaning of the word is the sum of its contexts. This is a primary methodo-logical procedure. Only secondarily will the social anthropologist have recourse to the notion of analogy, extension, figurative expression and the like. To take an example at random, I suggest that in the two sentences 'O god, my father' and 'O God, my Father', the one suggesting surprise, perhaps alarm, and the other being a prayer, the word 'god' in the first contributes to our understanding of the word 'God' in the second, quite regardless of the theological beliefs or disbeliefs of either speaker. A closer look at the Zande material will clarify this.

Evans-Pritchard found that the Azande had very vague no-tions about *mbori*: it figures in their myth of creation and is associated with unusual or surprising features of the landscape and with situations of unusual danger, such as epidemics. I say 'it' because the Azande do not ascribe human gender to *mbori* but a neutral gender: whereas men and women have the pronouns *ko* and *li* respectively, *mbori*, certain heavenly bodies, vegetables and tools have the pronoun *u*. Evans-Pritchard found that the Azande were generally rather bored with *mbori* as a topic of conversation as compared with their intense interest in the discussion of witchcraft.

Earlier missionaries and travellers had credited the Azande

with deep 'religious' feelings and pointed for evidence to their frequent prayers to *mbori* and the number of times that it figures in the names given to children, such as Who-is-as-*mbori*, *Mbori*-sees-you, Thing-of-*Mbori*, *Mbori*-is-very-good. But Evans-Pritchard discovered that this was rather as though everyone in Britain who gave their son the name Christopher thought of the child as Christ Bearer. He questioned one man who had called his son Mborizingbare, or *Mbori*-has-closed-my-lips. What had happened was that when, according to custom, he was asked to give a name to his new-born child he went completely blank and said the Zande equivalent of 'I can't think', '*Mbori* has sealed my lips'. We may imagine some such custom among ourselves and conjecture that the name 'God-knows' would be as common as 'John' and no more pious in intent.

Evans-Pritchard also noted that *mbori* was referred to when the Azande were pressed for the reasons and origins of things and institutions: 'Why do you do this'? 'Because my father instructed me.' 'Why did he instruct you thus?', 'Because the ancestors did it.' 'Why did they do it?', 'Because it was always done so.' 'Why was it always done so?' '*Mbori*.' The reader can sympathise with any informant being pestered by a social anthropologist in this way and can imagine himself finally exploding with 'God knows' or a less polite equivalent term. Would they not be surprised to have profound piety attributed to them on this account, let alone, in the event of an alternative phrase, being attributed with a belief that the act of coition was the ultimate cause of things?

Or put yourself to examine the causal chain which reveals the destiny of some happening in your own life—a car accident, a marriage, a financial windfall or whatever. Let us take the car accident and let us imagine that we have examined the possibility of mechanical failure, the state of the weather and the road, and even the state of mind of the driver, and pressed on to ask why the driver was at that particular point on the road when he collided with the other car. The answer might be that both drivers regularly commute between Brighton and Worthing, both leave their houses at set times and invariably reach that point in the road at that particular moment. But why on this particular day should the combination of circumstances amount to a collision? Sheer chance, we say, or bad luck. In short, we can look at any event and bombard it with explanatory procedures, geographical, climatic, psychological, statistical, until, in the face of the persistent question 'Why?', we exhaust our capacity to explain and say 'sheer chance'; or some might say 'God knows'.

The difference between the devout believer and the unreflecting atheist at this point is not great. When the believer has recourse to God as the ultimate explanation of some human disaster he or she is not referring to God the loving, just and merciful, but to God the impenetrable, ultimate cause, the impersonal premise of all being. The unbeliever no less is paying tribute to some blind force that ultimately determines existence. I say 'at this point' there is no great difference. I am not saying that there is no difference between belief and unbelief in a whole range of other matters. Nor is Evans-Pritchard saying that the Azande believe that a blind fate governs their universe. What he is drawing our attention to is a pattern of human thought which it is initially difficult for anyone raised in a monotheistic tradition to comprehend. In the following section I shall expand upon the implications of monotheism.

To start with, the reader must appreciate that monotheism is a peculiar and I think unique development in the whole history of mankind. It is the creation of the ancient Hebrews, and from them it shaped the Christian and Islamic worlds. And by monotheism we do not mean a belief in a sort of king or emperor God who rules over lesser gods in some sort of divine feudal system in which these lesser gods have spheres of relative autonomy; nor do we mean a belief in some ultimate principle sustaining the universe but independent of it and unconcerned. Monotheism is perfectly expressed in the Muslim formula 'There is no god by God'—*La ilāha Il-la'Lahu*—and in the tradition which derives the word Allah from *ilah*, a deity, plus the definite article *al*, thus *Al-ilah*, Allah—*the* God. Allah has ninety-nine names which list the glorious attributes—Ar Rahman, the Merciful; Ar Rahim, the Compassionate, etc— and the dread attributes—Al Mumit, the Killer, Al Khasiz, the Abaser, etc. A muslim may pray to Allah under the name of the attribute to which he appeals, but he does not pray to some separate manifestation or section of divinity. Allah is Al Wahid—the One.

We can study the growth of monotheism in the Old Testament, as the Christians call it, or simply the Jewish Bible. The story is of the evolution of a lineage deity, Jahweh, the God of Abraham and his son Isaac, and his son Jacob, to become a national God. This change goes together with the changing of Jacob's name to Israel, so that Jahweh becomes the god of the children, descendants or nation of Israel. Initially Jahweh is at war with and proves himself more powerful than other gods. Later he claims absolute obedience against other gods and finally comes to be regarded as the one only God. It is interesting to note that even in the famous declaration which we call the Ten Commandments we do not find the pure monotheistic statement that we find in Islam and which was yet to develop in Judaism. In both versions, *Exodus* Chapter 20 and *Deuteronomy* Chapter 5, we do not find the affirmation 'I am *the* God'; rather it is a demand for loyalty, 'Thou shalt have no other', which is a different thing.

Parallel with this development we observe how the gods of other peoples are first weaker than Jahweh and finish up as false gods; in other words, the ideas about Jahweh develop still further, such that he becomes not merely the national deity of the children of Israel, but *the* God of all peoples.

This development of monotheism in Judaism gives another essential peculiar characteristic of monotheism: God is the God of all people and therefore should be accepted by them. The world knows what impetus this belief has given nations in the Islamic and Christian traditions to spread and to convert or impose upon other nations not merely a theology but also institutions and culture. That there was no similar Judaic expansion is to be attributed to the Roman conquest and the Diaspora.

To deal with the implications of the development of monotheism in any detail would require more than one substantial volume. It has affected not merely our ethical systems but also ways of thinking that appear to have nothing to do with theology —politics and science. All that I am concerned to achieve here is the realisation that the vast majority of those who read this book have been brought up in a cultural tradition which is a sport on the tree of human experience. Certainly the geographical, political and even numerical spread of monotheistic culture is enormous, but this must not blind us to the fact that in qualitative terms it is a unique departure in human thought. From it we derive the split between the natural and the supernatural and such misleading terms as polytheism, animism and the like.

To return to the Azande: they are not monotheists who believe that *mbori* is like God the Father, or Allah. *Mbori* is not a governor of the universe, nor is he an almighty blind will. Evans-Pritchard sums up his own account:

Finally it emerges, that the notion of *Mbori* furnishes a remote cause for anything and everything in the world. *Mbori* is the horizon of Zande thought, an ambient haze into which every chain of causality ultimately fades ... If you take a Zande back step by step to the limits of his knowledge you will reach *Mbori*, whose name takes the place of understanding. He is the horizon that rounds off knowledge and tradition. He made the sun and the moon and the stars, the rivers and plains and mountains, men and beasts and birds and trees. When Azande do not understand something, it is vaguely explained by citing *Mbori*. Man and woman beget children but Azande perceive that they alone will not account for conception because some people do not beget children, or wait many years before conception takes place. Conception also depends on *Mbori* and if it were not for his participation children would not be born. What is the cause of monstrosity?

Azande do not know but say, "it is the affair of Mbori". Who made the curious phenomena of nature, smooth holes in rock outcrops, an expanding and contracting tree-root in a rock face, long luxuriant hair of men? "*Mbori* made it", say the Azande.'

*Mbori* is, then, the ground of Zande experience, the base and limit of their explanatory power. Consider the matter of childbirth. The Azande believe that conception takes place when the male semen and the female mucus combine. They believe that both these substances contain soul, and the relative strength of soul in either determines the sex of the child—a man whose soul is stronger than his wife's will beget a male child. If one or other partner lacks soul the woman will not conceive. They argue that women must have this power in their mucus because they notice that some children resemble one parent more than another. The semen and the mucus 'thoroughly mix with each other' and thus, even though the strong soul of the man has produced a son, the child may have facial features like the mother.

The Azande fully recognise that conception cannot occur before sexual maturity, and they attribute a boy's first ejaculation to the fact that the semen accumulates at the root of the penis and forces its way out. Both the semen of men and the mucus in women originate in the prostate and womb respectively, and the Azande attach no significance to the testicles. In the early stages of pregnancy the foetus is not fully attached to its soul and it is strengthened by the mother's blood, and after birth by her milk. Should a man's mother's brother have occasion to curse his nephew in later life, he pinches his own nipple and blows on it to show that the maternal clan has played a part in the boy's nurture. Similarly, a paternal kinsman slaps his thighs and blows on his penis when cursing a son or a paternal nephew. Zande knowledge includes an understanding of the relation between fertility and menstruation, and, from their study of animals, they have fairly precise notions about the development of the foetus at its different stages. Starting as a tiny thing 'like a lizard' huddled up, it becomes progressively a full human being, lacking only teeth when it is born. Their understanding of the excretory function of an unborn child is expressed when they say that its anus remains closed until the midwife opens it. This she does with her little finger shortly after birth.

In addition to this knowledge, and more, of cause and effect, and favouring circumstance, the Azande say that the fundamental cause of the whole process is *mbori*, from whom the soul in man and woman derives. They believe that other things such as hostility, witchcraft, magic and, of course, abortion can interfere in the process and that all these ultimately originate from or are explained by *mbori*.

I have given this detail about Zande theories of gestation in a fairly confident belief that they are not much more unprecise than the notions of many readers. If popular surveys are to be believed the Azande may indeed have more correct notions about the whole process of birth than many in our own society. Even the sophisticated reader may not instantly recognise the significance of the presence or absence of nuclear chromitin in the blood cells of the unborn child: it is what the Azande would call female soul.

We and the Azande know that certain causes will produce certain effects and we have more or less precise notions about the sequence of events. Both we and they know that this sequence can be upset by unforeseen accidents, the effect of which we can understand. A bad fall or illness at certain stages of the pregnancy can have serious consequences. But beyond our capacity to foresee or to understand, other things can interrupt pregnancy or disrupt the natural sequence, and in this knowledge we know that despite all expectation and precaution something that we call fate or chance can frustrate our hopes at any stage.

When we drive a car, switch on a light, put the potatoes on to boil, we know that we might by chance have an accident, blow a fuse or have a power cut. We do not, for all that, lead our lives in the constant expectation of these things. On the contrary, we act from day to day on a whole mass of assumptions to the effect that B will always follow A. But we do so partly because we have in some cases a partial or total understanding of the system which we are operating, and in the majority of cases we accept the authority of our society which is mediated to us through doctors, mechanics, electricians, etc. Some of our actions are a mixture of faith of this order and experience. We know that we have to flip the light switch to turn on the light and we may even recognise the idiosyncrasies of our own particular switches. Should this act fail we know that we have either to buy light bulbs or to mend a fuse. Mending a fuse is probably the limit of the average reader's knowledge of how the system works; the rest is taken on authority. In great things and small, it is when our expectations are not met that we have recourse to some alternative system of explanation and, when all else fails, to chance.

Like ourselves the Azande know that ultimately everything is contingent on fate or *mbori*; in this sense *mbori* underpins all their more specific knowledge. At the same time *mbori* is at the limit of their knowledge because they only have recourse to it when all other ways of accounting for events have failed.

The Azande use various systems with which they make sense of the world and some of these are, as we should say, operational and some gratuitous. I shall be dealing with the apparently gratuitous systems later in the section because they are the ones that may strike the Western reader as the most esoteric. For the present I will limit myself to the operational. By operational system I mean no more than the process whereby certain things are related to others systematically for a purpose. For example, the Azande, like all human beings, have some sort of pharmacopoeia and have presumably experimented and learnt suitable remedies for the majority of the minor ailments that afflict them. I have to say 'presumably' because that branch of anthropology which deals with non-Western medicine is very young and the problem is largely ignored in most anthropological literature.

The Azande believe that all sickness is attributable to witchcraft, but this does not mean that they run to a witchdoctor every time that they are ill. Like us, they doctor themselves for minor ailments according to their experience and the accumulated knowledge of the past. Evans-Pritchard writes:

> 'Their reference of sickness to supernatural causes (does not) lead them to neglect treatment of symptoms . . . they possess an enormous pharmacopoeia, . . . and in ordinary circumstances they trust to drugs to cure their ailments.'

It is only when drugs fail that they have recourse to oracles to find out who is bewitching them.

We also have general theories about the causation of illness and our traditional remedies. The difference between us and the Azande is that we tend to have several theories of causation instead of one—germs, viruses, diet, emotional conflict, climate: and we have various remedies—the well-tried cough-mixture, stomach tablets or a couple of aspirin, an early night, a cup of tea, sea air, sweating it out, feeding a cold, etc. If, say, we believe in germs, we can still speak of catching cold in the rain or in a draught and swear by any one of countless popular remedies. We would be hard put to it to explain the relation between our chosen remedy and our favoured theory of causation.

The Azande have recourse to oracles if they do not get better or if they get worse. I shall discuss later how they cope with witchcraft. If the oracles cannot help there is another set of beliefs about sorcerers against whom remedies are limited. Finally, a man may die and his death is, as we would say, caused by his illness but according to the Azande also by witchcraft or sorcery, and ultimately by *mbori*.

Operational knowledge, whether directed towards the curing of sickness, the building of a hut or the making or a weapon, rests on and is supported by a prior system of understanding which I have referred to as gratuitous. It is to be understood that I use this word in opposition to the Western notion that systems of thought always have practical ends in view. In fact, I shall show that they are not truly gratuitous at all.

One of the most important developments in social anthropology in the last twenty-five years has been the recognition that, if man is to be understood at all, he is to be understood as man the meaning-maker. This turn of phrase is clearly borrowed from earlier definitions which represented man as primarily a tool-maker, a weapon-maker or a hunter. What we have come to recognise is that it is his intellect which sets man apart from the animals, and that through the use of his intellect he makes meaning of his universe. This recognition is paralleled by a methodological shift: the earlier anthropologists and other social scientists were disposed to look upon the behaviour of other men as objectively as possible and to give an account of it in a variety of mechanical terms. With the new realisation came the appreciation that the starting point for any field worker was to find out what sense people themselves make not only of the universe but also of their own society. It was recognised, in short, that all peoples in the world have their own theories and views of society, their own indigenous anthropologies.

This development did not come as a sudden revelation and, indeed, its history can be traced back into the pre-World War II period. Nevertheless its formulation is associated with one particular scholar, Claude Lévi-Strauss, who most clearly expressed this point of view in his two books *Totemism* and *The Savage Mind*. In the first chapter of the latter work, appropriately entitled 'The Science of the Concrete', he drew attention to the vast variety, richness and apparent uselessness of systems of classification in non-European societies:

> 'Every civilisation tends to over-estimate the objective orientation of its thought and this tendency is never absent. When we make the mistake of thinking that the savage is governed solely by organic or economic needs, we forget that he levels the same reproach at us, and that to him his own desire for knowledge seems more balanced than ours.'

Lévi-Strauss goes on to quote from one of his authorities:

> 'These native Hawaians' utilisation of their available natural assets was well nigh complete—infinitely more so than that

of the present commercial era which ruthlessly exploits the few things that are financially profitable for the time being, neglecting and often obliterating the rest.'

And another:

'The acute faculties of this native folk noted with exactitude the generic characteristics of all species of terrestrial and marine life, and the subtlest variations of natural phenomena such as winds, light and colour, ruffling of water and variation in surf, and the currents of water and air.'

In discussing these complex systems of classification among 'primitive' peoples, Lévi-Strauss is concerned to emphasise the fact that discrimination and classification almost for their own sakes are prior to practical utilisations. It is necessary to emphasise this because the canons of Western scientific thought tend to make us believe that we analyse phenomena for practical purposes only. Lévi-Strauss is drawing our attention to man's fundamental propensity to put order into his universe in excess, so to speak, of any 'practical' need. It is in this sense that such classifications are 'gratuitous', although they are only 'gratuitous' from the point of view of Western scientific thought.

But we are not all Western scientists, nor, indeed, are all Western scientists scientific all the time. We have to recognise that all of us are every day operating classifications of the universe for which we have no rational or practical 'use'. We have already seen how an atheist or an agnostic can share a category with the Azande; other more commonplace examples are found in our day-to-day reactions to authority in various forms, which include our relations with subordinates, the way in which we behave in the street, or on the bus or tube, our behaviour towards those younger and those older, to those of the opposite sex, our basic assumptions about what constitutes food and what does not, and the very way in which we eat—these all rest upon *a priori* classification of the world about us.

Let me give an example of the kind of thing I have in mind, taken from a student's essay. He reported that in his early adolescence he had a running battle with his mother about the

G—T

kind of dish that their dog should eat from. She used to buy dog meat from the pet shop which was cooked in an old saucepan not otherwise used, and the dog was served on his own dish. The quarrel arose over the leftovers from human meals. If the mother had her own way she would scrape the plates onto the dog's dish, whereas the boy was more likely to put down one of the plates which the humans had used. His mother's argument about germs and the notorious indifference of dogs about where they poke their noses seemed to him quite irrational. He argued that if washing a plate meant washing a plate, then this risk of contamination could only be temporary; moreover, he pointed out that the dog's dish, the cat's saucer and the plates used by the humans were all washed together in the same water, and dried with the same tea towels.

The student recognised later that what he had been trying to do was to confuse two classes—the human and the animal— which were not merely fundamental to his mother's personal anthropology but universal. She could, had she been so inclined, have turned the argument back upon him by questioning the rationality of his current notions of suitable masculine attire, attitudes towards men's work as opposed to women's and so on. What is significant and symptomatic for us is that both mother and son felt that they could only argue their cases in the language of rationality, having recourse to 'scientific' notions. Most of us react in the same manner when the way in which we classify the universe is questioned and some cherished assumption or mode of behaviour is labelled as, what indeed it literally is, prejudice. If we were to recognise that the greater part of our existence is devoted to making *sense* of the world rather than telling the *truth* about it, then, perhaps, when universes clash either the argument would take place at the level of genuine human understanding or there would be more tolerance. This is by no means a plea that each man should do and believe as he pleases. I myself find the assumptions behind a racialist anthropology repulsive, but I would not waste time arguing with a racialist about the rational grounds of his belief. I would, of course, try to refute such evidence as he produced, but I would be more concerned to show him that ultimately his arguments rested upon a *wish* to believe, even in the teeth of the evidence, than that what he said was true. We should remember, however, that any such demonstration must go hand in hand with a complementary recognition on my part that I also have a *wish* not to be convinced by any evidence that he might adduce. Such wishes rest upon classificatory judgment about what constitutes the human: by and large, the anti-racialist will tend to stress the biological similarities between humans, whereas the racialist is more likely to attach importance to cultural and social differences. It is not unusual to hear a racialist refer to members of another race as being 'like animals' or 'not human'.

The purpose of the preceding section was to stimulate the reader to engage in some systematic introspection. Try to think, and, preferably, write down, what foods you consider are appropriate to what occasions and to what times of day; what kinds of dress are proper in what contexts; what objects, foods, clothes, ornaments and utensils of all sorts properly 'go together', and which do not; what objects can be intimately shared with others, and with whom, without passing through the ritual of washing— towels, tea cups, shirts, dresses, underwear, tobacco pipes, cigarettes, etc; what are the limits of physical intimacy appropriate to lovers, friends, siblings, children and parents, and what parts of another's body may be touched when it is clothed or when it is unclothed; is it the case that you would not hesitate to touch someone's clothed forearm to emphasise a point but not their hand, and yet think it rude to wear a glove when that same hand is to be shaken?

When we distinguish between what we think about life and the world around us and what we think we know about it, we tend to regard the latter as science and relegate the former to some such category as superstition or religion. It is no less the case with action: purposive action based on some theory of material causality is a *real* act, whereas acts which are based on theories of symbolic association or historical re-enactment are *rituals*. The chemist in his laboratory going through the normal procedures when setting up an experiment does not think of himself as engaged in a ritual any more than the priest, consecrating a wafer, thinks of himself as performing a scientific act. Here as elsewhere we must be on our guard against imposing upon other peoples the distinctions that we ourselves find convenient. It has to be admitted that many social anthropologists, past and present, have done us no service by marking off among the peoples that they have studied a discrete area of behaviour which they have called 'ritual'. Almost without exception they have implicitly or explicitly associated 'ritual' with a belief in supernatural power, and even those few who have realised that the concept 'supernatural' is unhelpful have not much improved the situation by substituting the word 'ceremony'.

The classical study of 'ritual' was by a Frenchman, Arnold van Gennep, who published his *Les Rites de Passage* in 1908, which appeared in English translation as *The Rites of Passage* in 1960. The title indicates the focus of van Gennep's interest and the nature of his theory. He saw primitive society as composed of a host of social conditions or stages such that at any given time groups or individuals are clearly defined as, for example, children and not adults, or as adults but not elders. In addition to this human aspect, society comprises space: there is not only the territory of the tribe but also the territory which is inhabited by the village as opposed to the bush, the inside of the domicile as opposed to the outside.

So far it might seem that van Gennep did no more than anticipate Lévi-Strauss in saying that primitive, traditional man insists upon a tidy universe in which there is a place for everything and everything is in its place; a universe that does not tolerate ambiguity or confusion. But van Gennep was concerned with human actions and the ways in which both these categories were maintained and the ways in which individuals or groups moved from one condition to another. Is there anything in common between the 'ritual' that moves a boy or girl into man-

hood or womanhood and the 'ritual' that moves them from
the condition of not being married to the condition of being
married?

Arnold van Gennep aimed to demonstrate that all rituals
involving changes in condition shared a common tripartite
structure or pattern. They could be divided into three subdivisions – separating rites, rites of the transition and incorporation rites. What he meant was that the movement from one stage
or condition to another is accompanied by a rite that cuts away
the previous condition, after which the individual or group has
no identity other than that of being in-between. This 'in-
between' condition is marked by rites of the transition, which
are followed by rites that incorporate the individual or
group into the new condition—status, role, membership or
whatever.

Let me illustrate van Gennep's theory from my own experience in India. When two parties are agreed upon a marriage, the
informal agreement is ratified by a series of actions which are
cumulatively binding on them both. These actions include visits
between defined categories of kin and the exchange of gifts of
specified kinds. This bundle of rites has the effect of shifting the
young couple from the condition of the unmarried towards that
of the married, but like our own custom of engagement the marriage can still be called off. Again, as amongst ourselves, the
later that the engagement is broken, the more serious the matter.
The rites of the transitional phase are more brief or seldom last
more than a few days: they comprise the segregation of the bride
to be, the eating of special foods and the bathing and anointing
of the young couple, and conclude as they are seated together
opposite the Brahman before the sacrificial fire. Incorporation is
a lengthy affair and calls for separate treatment.

Traditionally the couple are regarded as married at a particular
point in the ceremony performed by the Brahman, that is when
the groom leads the bride seven times round the sacrificial fire.
Were either boy or girl not to do this, folklore has it, they would
not be married. This is only a matter of folklore and occurs in
tragic tales of folk-heroes who, for some noble reason, leave the

ceremony before taking the seven steps. Following van Gennep I would regard this crucial stage as marking the end of the rites of transition and only the beginning of the rites of incorporation, not the act of incorporation itself.

There is one important qualification to this general statement. After the seven steps the girl has the status of a married woman in the important sense that, were her husband to die the next day, she would be regarded as a widow, a woman who could be married, if at all, only with inferior ceremony. Despite this the new wife has yet to be fully incorporated into the family of her husband.

In the past the bride would not go to her husband's house immediately and the ceremony was followed by a series of rites known as the 'bringings'—the girl, suitably accompanied by attendants bearing gifts, is brought three times to her husband's house. On the first two occasions she stays for a brief period and it is hoped that she will become pregnant during this time. The third 'bringing' should be that occasion when, having given birth in her father's house, she brings her baby to the home of her husband. As in so many societies the birth of the child, especially if it is a boy, sets the seal on the marriage and concludes the rites of incorporation both of the young couple into marriage and of the bride into her new family.

It would be as well to point out that in the modern India of towns and cities the rites of engagement are often truncated or dispensed with, as are the post-nuptial 'bringings': the modern bride will often join her husband immediately in a house or apartment of their own. The birth of a child is also, of course, no longer essential.

From the example that I have given, as from van Gennep's own exposition of his theory, it is clear that different societies and the same society at different times distribute the emphases differently on the three phases of passage. When boys are made into men, especially when this is accompanied by some operation such as circumcision or by instruction, the period of transition is longer than that of separation or incorporation. In the ceremonies surrounding death we find in many societies, as we might expect, firm emphasis upon the separation of the dead person from the land of the living accompanied by slight and vague notions about his or her subsequent condition.

The term *rites de passage* has become part of the jargon of social anthropologists, but interestingly it tends to be applied only to the rites surrounding initiation from the condition of childhood into adulthood. This is because van Gennep has not been fully understood and those who followed him tended to interpret his argument as being essentially about the movement of *individuals*. A careful reading of van Gennep shows that he was much more concerned with the dynamics of *society*, and even the way in which society could be said to protect itself from individual manifestations.

To understand this we have to go back to the view of primitive society that van Gennep shares with Lévi-Strauss, a society in which the concern is for classified order. The rites of passage are, above all else, the means by which a society reaffirms its classifications. Let us consider, for example, this very business of the initiation into adulthood. Later writers have tended to identify this initiation with puberty and to regard it as a 'crisis' in the life of the individual, a crisis for which the rite is supposed to provide some sort of psychological support. Van Gennep is careful to insist upon the difference between physiological puberty and what he calls 'social puberty', which are essentially different even if, in fact, they may converge in time. We can easily see why this must be so when we reflect (*a*) that most often it is groups not individuals that are initiated, (*b*) that in some societies several years may elapse between one initiation ceremony and another, and (*c*) that the age at which individuals achieve puberty is variable.

In a society that lays store and value by the distinction between children and adults, this distinction must be socially defined and even enforced; it cannot, to put it another way, be left to the vagaries of individual physiological development. The same is true of marriage: if this is left to individual taste and preference, as it largely is in our society, no clear categorical distinction emerges between the married and the unmarried, and, indeed, in our society this *is* a distinction which is fast losing significance. In most other human societies marriage is an essential stage in the human development, carrying with it important rights and obligations; it is also the means by which whole groups create or reaffirm their alliances; it cannot be a haphazard affair left to individuals. It is not surprising therefore that we normally find both that marriages are arranged, or at least confined within a range of choice, and that, with the rare exceptions of institutionalised celibacy, all are expected to have passed through the prescribed rites of marriage by a certain age.

It might be thought that if society can overrule human development and preferences, as in the initiation to adulthood and marriage, death is the one physiological fact that cannot be so regulated. First of all, let us reflect that the majority of deaths do indeed occur when they are expected—in old age—and, secondly, that the ceremonies surrounding death are the occasion for making important affirmations about the human condition. Another French scholar, Robert Herz, is a pioneer in the development of our understanding of the activities surrounding death. Herz's essay draws our attention to a widespread phenomenon—dual mortuary rites. In the simplest terms his argument can be reduced to two propositions: in most societies there is a rite that deals with the immediate physiological fact, and this is followed soon or much later by a rite that effects the social death of the individual. Between these two occasions the soul is sometimes thought of as lingering near or around the home, its kinsmen are regarded as being in a dangerous condition and then life is subject to particular regulations.

Traditionally in our own society a dying person would receive the 'consolations of religion', which after death would be followed by the laying out of the corpse, the 'waking' or 'watching' of the laid-out corpse and then the burial. The whole complex of mortuary rites was worked through only when the period of mourning was complete; then, we might say, the dead person was truly dead, the surviving spouse free to remarry, and close kin free to wear normal clothing and to enjoy themselves.

Several elements of this complex are referred to in Shakespeare's *Hamlet*. The ghost of the dead King complains that he died 'Unhouseled, disappointed, unaneled', that is without having received *housel*—the sacrament—unprepared by confession and without extreme unction. Because of this he is doomed 'To walk the night, And for the day confined to fast in fires' until the sins of his lifetime 'are burnt and purged away'. Earlier in the play we have a reference to 'the funeral baked meat' which was prepared for the mourners at the wake, and the indecent haste with which the widow has remarried. In this play we also find reference to the harm that unquiet ghosts can do to the living and the pre-Christian idea that the dead do not rest until their debts (in this case revenge) are paid.

In our own time much of all this has gone, but the complex survives on the death of a monarch or important statesman. This is significant because in almost all societies we find that the social status of the deceased is a measure of the scale and duration of the mortuary rites. Typically, an old man who died 'full of honour' would receive more attention and would be mourned by more people and for a longer period than a woman, and at the extreme end of the scale an infant might be buried without ceremony.

Through its rites or ceremonies a society draws or redraws the lines of its classifications and affirms what is important to it. What is not necessary to the maintenance of its distinctive profile may be left to a greater or lesser extent to the vagaries of human will or physiological growth. However distasteful some people may find the fact, the evidence for the decline in significance of marriage in our society is the decline in marriage rites, and the decline of the mortuary complex is a sure sign that, unlike our ancestors, death is becoming non-significant for us.

Rites affirm important values and demarcations, they 'say' things through actions. But they *are* composed of actions and are not merely verbal formulae, nor simple 'enactments' of beliefs or myths. Rites *do* whereas words can only *say*. In the Catholic mass the priest adds a drop of water which he has previously blessed to the wine in the chalice and says:

'O God who hast wonderfully created and dignified human nature, and hast still more wonderfully restored it; grant that by the mystery of this water and wine, we may be made partakers of His divinity who deigned to share our humanity . . .'

The Catholic believes that in the Mass the bread and wine are transubstantiated into the body and the blood of Christ, which means that the appearance of the elements, the bread and the wine, remains the same while the substance is changed. In this particular part of the Mass the mingling of the water and the wine blends humanity (water) with wine (divinity), and thus the incarnation is re-enacted and this sacred chemistry is a prerequisite for the transubstantiation of the wine which follows. The force of this act comes out when we learn that in Masses for the Dead the water is not blessed and the prayer is omitted. The contrast enables us to understand that the 'humanity' referred to in the prayer is the humanity of the assembled congregation, whose nature is constantly being 'restored' by the act of incarnation. In the Mass for the Dead, however, the deceased is regarded as being outside the world and he or she is no longer a participant in the Mass but only the object of it.

The same sort of reasoning applies in coronations and investitures of all sorts: things—royal regalia, uniforms, medals and the like—which have significance in themselves are *put on* people, who thereby participate in the significance and value of these things. In Great Britain, for example, the ancient formula 'The King is dead, long live the King' establishes that there is no discontinuity in the monarchy. But it is not sufficient for the new King or Queen to be proclaimed; he or she must be joined to the regalia—in particular the crown, which is the symbol of the highest authority in our constitutional monarchy. Today we generally attach little importance to the fact that the monarch is also 'the Lord's anointed'; in the medieval period, if not earlier, the anointing of a King with a mixture of oils conferred upon him a sacred personality such that offences against his person could be regarded as sacrilegious.

Rites then, are, actions that *do* things which words cannot. Let us consider in some detail one example with which we are all familiar, an example that has the added advantage that it has nothing to do with the 'religious'—the formal hand salute. Let us note first that the word shares with 'salubrious' and 'salutory' a common origin in the Latin *salus*, health. *Salus* was so common a greeting that the ancient Romans would abbreviate *salutem dicit*, so and so greets so and so, in the initials SD, just as some of us at the end of a letter abbreviate 'Yours faithfully' to 'Yours etc.'. The modern military-type salute preserves this essence of greeting and well-wishing, despite its formality and the serious-ness with which it is given.

A salute in our society is not, obviously, just an ordinary greeting. Someone who saluted another in day-to-day clothing would probably only do so facetiously. I say in 'our society': Nazi Germany provides a significant counter example of a society in which the militarisation and subordination of the civilian population to the dictator was expressed in the 'Heil Hitler' salute. Amongst us a salute is exchanged between people who are wearing uniform; this is quite clear when we observe that the monarch only returns the salute of uniformed people when she is herself wearing uniform. What does the wearing of uniform mean? As the word 'uniform'—uni-form—suggests, it identifies those who wear it one with another. In addition, the uniform identifies in another sense those who wear it as separate from everyone else.

Salutes are associated not only with uniforms but also with the differentiation of ranks. In military organisations the differ-ence between the official dress of a Field Marshal and that of a Private is so striking that at first sight it obscures our apprecia-tion that they are both wearing a common uniform. Nevertheless the wearing of that common uniform constitutes those who wear it into a sort of fraternity of equals which is contradicted by the necessary internal distinctions of rank. This situation is reflected in the exchange of salutes. It is the inferior rank which salutes first and the superior rank which then returns the salute. In short, they exchange a formal greeting *as between* equals; and let us note that the superior rank is obliged to reciprocate the salute. The *exchange* of the formal greeting affirms the principle contained in the uniformity, while at the same time the *distinction* between those who initiate and those who reciprocate the greeting affirms the principle of rank. This interpretation of the military-type salute is strengthened when we reflect that equals in such organisations do not in normal circumstances salute each other and that people who are identified, in both senses, by a uniform but who are not distinguished by rank, for example postmen and traffic wardens, do not exchange salutes.

If the formal salute is limited to certain kinds of organisation, greetings or salutations with the hand are not subject to such limitation. Let us leave aside hand-shaking, which is a particular form because it involves body contact, and consider rather the greeting that we call a 'wave'. This is not easily observed in a busy town or city and can best be studied where there is a relatively large community of people who know each other more or less well; here also self-observation and introspection can help. The 'wave' can vary from a slight raising of the arm from the side accompanied by an upward movement of the hand through various positions, including something very close to the 'salute', to a position in which the arm is held straight above the head with the palm of the hand extended. If the reader considers and, indeed, tries out these various positions he will appreciate how many varieties of emotion can be expressed and how many additional messages are conveyed; not only degrees of warmth of affection but also signals, such as 'Stop, I want to talk to you', or 'Thanks', or 'Help!'.

The wave is then a very flexible form of greeting and at the same time one that is not universally exchanged in our society. We would not usually wave to someone with whom we had not some sort of friendly relation. According to old conventions two unrelated people of different sex would not wave to each other, for the gesture implies familiarity and even intimacy.

Relationships develop from formal acquaintance to friendship, and once more I must rely upon the reader's own experience. We have seen that outside military organisations equals can salute each other with a wave. What is the situation as between people who regard each other as being of unequal rank in some respect more or less well defined, for example employer and employee and the like? If we imagine that the two are on waving terms, which of them is likely to have taken the first step and initiated this form of greeting? I am confident that in the majority of cases it will be found that it is the 'superior' and that some apparently innate sense tells us that for the 'inferior', junior or whatever to wave first would be regarded as presumptuous' familiar, checky or something of that order. Whether between equals or non-equals there is, let us note, no obligation to reciprocate; personal temperament and physical circumstances are allowed to determine the mode of reciprocation, if indeed there is any.

Let us pause here and try to get some order into the situation. The reader should reflect on the two situations which I have sketched out and see whether he or she can tabulate the differences between them under two such headings as 'military organisations' and 'civilians', in such a manner that the contrasts are clear—for example, uniform is present in the one case and absent in the other.

Something along the following lines should emerge:

| *Military organisations* | *Civilians* |
| --- | --- |
| Salute | Salutation |
| Formal | Informal |
| Unambiguous | Ambiguous |
| Not between equals | Between equals |
| Must be initiated from below | May be initiated from above |
| Must be reciprocated from above | May be reciprocated from below |
| Associated with uniform | Not associated with uniform |

This sort of tidying up of the facts is always useful, not least

180 Understanding Social Anthropology

because it enables us better to note elements that we may have missed, or anomalies. I do not think that I have missed anything, but some more items may well occur to the reader. Tabulations of this kind also enable us to push the analysis further because an initial emphasis upon the differences enables us to see better what the similarities are. To start with, there are two which have not been mentioned so far; both salutes and salutations are carried out with the right hand, and both involve an *upward* movement of the arm. Such apparently trivial details must be noted because they make us think of other associations which the right hand has and also of what kinds of message we send with *downward* movements. We can, however, go further and say that what the two situations also have in common is that they both have to do with the play of equality and inequality in our society, even if they deal with the relationship in contrasting ways. Quite simply: in the Western world greetings of this kind have an equating effect; they break down the distinction between superior and inferior, and for this reason must be initiated by the superior. He is, so to speak, the guardian of his rank and reserves the right, according to judgment, personality and circumstances, to relax the relationship. In military organisations, on the other hand, the salute marks the differentiations of rank between those who wear a common uniform and as such are otherwise equated. If the superior officer were to salute the inferior first, this would be, as in the civilian world, an invitation to equality whereas the situation requires the assertion of rank, and for this reason the inferior initiates a salute. Nevertheless the salute is and must be returned; in this reciprocation, once rank has been asserted, equality can be recognised. The exchange of military or quasi-military salutes can be seen to be a subtle action in which two contradictory principles are combined and their contradiction resolved.

There is a great deal more to be said about the use of hand gestures, formal and informal; such a study would be only a small part of the complex and fascinating field opened by the consideration of body imagery and body symbolism in society—a field still largely unexplored. In the preceding paragraphs I have been concerned only to show that between a so-called 'ritual' act and day-to-day behaviour there is no qualitative gap. The difference is a matter of degree, and as the 'job' which actions have to achieve becomes more complex and important to the actors, so it is likely to become more stereotyped and precise, precisely because it is important and must be got right. No less important is the illustration of the fact that actions do what words cannot say; by action, divinity is mingled with humanity, rank and equality are synthesised, and a mortal human being is assimilated into the undying institution of monarchy.

Let me conclude by returning to more exotic material. Among contemporary social anthropologists none has developed the tradition of van Gennep or made significant advances in the understanding of 'ritual' action more than Victor Turner, who worked among the Ndembu, a matrilineal people of Central Africa. Turner's detailed analyses of the materials used by the Ndembu in their rites reveal that every bit of wood or leaf, the directions in which people face, each colour, every movement, and the component element of each action can be regarded as a word that takes on its precise significance, just as real words do, by its particular relation to the other words with which it occurs.

But they are more than words because they can be acted upon and put into action. Consider a very simple example: there is no way in which you can blend masculinity and femininity in such a way that they are and they are not distinct. As the immediately preceding sentence shows, mere words only make the problem worse! The Ndembu use a certain tree, *Diplorrhyncus condy-locarpon*—*mudyi* in Ndembu—for making such statements. When cut this tree exudes a white milky latex and the Ndembu say *mudyi* means breast milk, the mother's breast and the bond between mother and child, and, it follows, the principle of matrilineality. *Mudyi* also means 'woman' or 'female' as opposed to 'men' and 'masculine' and here its synthesising action is most clear.

In a matrilineal society men trace their descent through women and are members of the matrilineage. We have already seen (p. 46) that this can be a source of tension and even conflict.

Among the Ndembu this tension is heightened by the fact that marriage is virilocal, the wife lives in her husband's home. The *mudyi* tree is used in a variety of ways both to express and to transcend the conflict.

I will conclude by briefly outlining an example. The Ndembu practise male circumcision. This is obviously a masculine affair and the circumcision rites, the act of circumcision itself, constitute a statement that men, the men's world, are now appropriating male children and making them into men even at seven years old. After circumcision the young boy's position and rights in society are changed. The matrilineage needs circumcision because it needs men; at the same time the association of children with their mothers, and women generally, must be denied if they are to become men.

Turner describes the function and meaning of three kinds of tree which figure at three stages of the ceremony. First there is the *mudyi* tree, under which the boys are circumcised. They are then carried over a freshly transplanted *muyombo* tree, *Kirkia acuminata*, and finally seated upon a log of *mukula*, *Tterocarpus angolensis*, until their wounds stop bleeding. Turner analyses the full range of meanings which each tree has and then shows how certain of these meanings interlock, so to speak, to achieve the purpose of the ceremony—the maturation of the boys. The white secretion of the *mudyi* tree in this context is associated with the ideal of the matrilineage and motherhood. The *muyombo* has a 'dazzlingly white wood when its outer bark is peeled off' and secretes a clear gum which the Ndembu associate with tears and mourning. The *muyombo* is also associated with the *segments* of the matrilineage, that is with the disunity within the unity. Finally, the *mukula* tree secretes a red gum and brings in all the associations of 'redness' in Ndembu thought. Redness can be both good and bad—it can be mixed with white to produce health and success, and it can be mixed with black to produce witchcraft and evil. In this particular ceremony the blood of the circumcised boys becomes mature matrilineal blood by association with the gum of the *mukula* tree, which, say the Ndembu, 'is the tree of menstrual blood, of parturition, of maternal blood'. The name *mukula* is also derived from the verb *ku-kula*, to mature or grow older.

I have very considerably simplified Turner's analysis and must do so even more in summarising the significance which results from the relation of these three trees. Circumcised and still bleeding, the boys are carried away from the undifferentiated world of whiteness, via death and disunity, to maturity—the world where good and evil can mix and can be differentiated. There is, let me repeat, a good deal more being affirmed in these rites, and this is only one important theme in a complex symphony of actions and things which asserts certain fundamental values of Ndembu society, highlights certain basic conflicts both of the culture and of human nature, and works upon all these to bring about certain desired effects.

## Summary

This chapter was intended to be more provocative than 'instructive'. The business of the social anthropologist is to move towards totalities—relating, for example, the apparently discrete areas of politics and art, or kinship and economics. The argument of this chapter has been that the ways in which we use the terms 'religion' and 'ritual' encourage us to think that the ways of thinking and acting to which these words relate are special and call for special acts of understanding on our part. In order to provoke some reconsideration there was first of all a brief consideration of the word 'religion' and its history, and we saw that the word *dharma* has suffered a similar reduction in modern India. We then followed Evans-Pritchard's analysis of the Azande word *mbori* and saw that it was closer in meaning to English words like 'luck' or 'fate' than to 'God', 'Supreme Being' and the like. This view was reinforced by a discussion of the uniqueness of monotheism in the whole span of human thought. Our discussion of the Azande led us to make a point about theory and method. The theory, best expressed by Lévi-Strauss, is that man is before all else a meaning-maker, a classifier, a concept-builder: we can only understand what he *does* with his classifications of the universe after we know what they are. The reader was then invited to examine in his or her life the proposition that the greater part of our life is devoted to making *sense* of the world rather than telling the truth about it.

We turned then to the word 'ritual' and here again we were concerned to insist that if in our society this word refers to some special way of acting, then it is we who are peculiar in the world. First we looked at van Gennep's theory of the tripartite structure of rites—separation, transition and incorporation. We related this theory to the view of man the meaning-maker and appreciated that man has to work at keeping his conceptual universe tidy—birth, marriage and death, for example, must as far as possible be controlled according to the categories of any particular society, and the change elements of individual whim, physical need and physical decay must be kept within bounds if these categories are to be preserved. We then looked at marriage in India and took the occasion to emphasise the point that different societies stress different parts of van Gennep's scheme according to need and interest. The argument which emerged was that the complexes of action which we call 'rites' or 'ceremonies' are ways of reaffirming the lines of social classification. But acts *are* acts and can *do* things that words cannot; by an *act* we can mix wine and water, whereas we obviously cannot mix the words 'wine' and 'water'. We explored this proposition by looking at greeting and saluting in our own society and suggested that the act of greeting with the right hand, despite the variety of forms that it takes, copes with the contradiction in our society between equality and inequality. We saw that there was no discontinuity between the casual wave of the hand and the 'ritualised' salute, but we appreciated that, as the 'job' which the act does becomes more significant to the actors, so it is likely to become more formal and precise; it is important and must be got right. In conclusion we looked briefly at a circumcision ceremony among the Ndembu, as described by Turner, and saw how social values can be brought together in objects, the secretions of trees, and thus literally manipulated to solve problems—in this case to separate boys from their mothers in order to make them into men and then to return them as mature members of the matrilineage.

## Reading notes

Banton, M. (ed.), *Anthropological Approaches to the Study of Religion*, Association of Social Anthropologists (ASA) Monographs, No. 3, London, 1966. Here the reader will find approaches which differ from the one adopted in the preceding chapter: various writers either attempt to define 'religion' or make analyses which presuppose the concept. The notable exception is Turner (see below).

Crombie, A. C., *Augustine to Galileo*, 2 volumes, Penguin Books, 1969. This is a scholarly and reliable history of western science in the Middle Ages. It is recommended here for two reasons. First, a historical understanding of the emergence of modern science will assist the reader to an anthropological understanding of it. Second, this account of the way in which ideas from Greece, Arabia and India were assimilated and adjusted in the Middle Ages in Europe is to begin to understanding the reversal of this process in what is called 'westernisation' today.

Douglas, M., *Purity and Danger*, London, 1966. This is an important study which examines human notions of dirt and impurity in the context of man's need for order.

Durkheim, E., *The Elementary Forms of the Religious Life*, English translation London, 1915. Few of Durkheim's works have been so influential. The serious student is obliged to read this if later works and commentaries are to be understood.

Durkheim, E., and Mauss, M., *Primitive Classification*, English translation London, 1963. This work appeared in French in 1903 and stimulated the modern emphasis upon man's fundamental need for categorical order.

Eliade, M., *The Myth of the Eternal Return*, English translation New York, 1954. An exciting book mentioned here because it relates Western man's conception of time to the emergence of monotheism; more generally it has been influential in the social anthropology of time-reckoning.

Epstein, I., *Judaism*, Penguin, 1959. A useful historical introduction to Judaism and its development.

Evans-Pritchard, E., 'Heredity and Gestation as the Azande see them' and 'Zande Theology' in *Essays in Social Anthropology*, London, 1962.

Evans-Pritchard, E., *Nuer Religion*, Oxford, 1965. The Preface and Chapters I and XIII should be read. It would be a very useful exercise to compare the author's handling of the word 'God' in this later work with his discussion of the Azande published over twenty years earlier.

Evans-Pritchard, E., *Theories of Primitive Religion*, Oxford, 1965.

Gibb, H. A. R., *Mohammedanism: an historical survey*, London, 1949.

Gluckman, M. (ed.), *Essays on the Ritual of Social Relations*, Manchester, 1962. See Gluckman's own contribution for an extended critique and evaluation of van Gennep.

Gluckman, M., 'Rituals of Rebellion in South-East Africa' in *Order and Rebellion in Tribal Africa*, London, 1963. This essay was originally published in 1953 and has perpetuated the idea that 'ritual' is a special sort of human activity for which special reasons must be found; Gluckman's essay is the source of notions about social 'tension', 'repression' and 'catharsis' which will be found in later works.

Hertz, R., *Death and the Right Hand*, English translation 1960. A misleading title for two quite separate essays which appeared in French in 1907 and 1909 respectively. The study of the rituals of death and the study of the human tendency to associate moral characteristics to the right and to the left both contribute to our understanding of the way in which man orders the universe.

Hocart, A., *The Life-Giving Myth*, London, 1952, Chapters I, II, V, VI, VII, XIX, XX.

Holt, P. M., Lambton, A. K., and Lewis, B. (eds.), *The Cambridge History of Islam*, 2 volumes, Cambridge, 1970.

Leach, E. (ed.), *The Structural Study of Myth and Totemism*, Association of Social Anthropologists (ASA) Monographs, 1967. This collection contains an influential example of Lévi-Strauss' method in the analysis of myth and discussions of his work by various British scholars.

Leslie, C. (ed.), *Anthropology of Folk Religion*, New York, 1960. Substantial selections from the work of nine authors of varying value.

Lessa, W. A., and Vogt, E. Z. (eds.), *Reader in Comparative Religion*, London and New York, 1st edition 1958, 2nd edition 1965, 3rd edition 1972. These are useful compilations with substantial bibliographies. The contents vary from edition to edition and Pettazzoni's 'The Formation of Monotheism' was dropped from the third edition.

Lévi-Strauss, C., *Totemism*, English translation, London, 1964.

Lévi-Strauss, C., *The Savage Mind*, English translation London, 1966. *Totemism* (above) is a brief work which was intended as an introduction to *The Savage Mind*, and it should therefore be read first. *The Savage Mind* is tough going in parts and the reader may be contented for the present with Chapter I, 'The Science of the Concrete'.

Lienhardt, R. G., 'Religion' in *Man, Culture and Society*, ed. Shapiro (see reading notes for Chapter 1). This brief article is a useful account of various approaches to the study of religion.

Needham, R. (ed.), *Right and Left—essays on dual symbolic classification*, Chicago and London, 1973. A major tribute to the inspiration of Herz (see above) and an important work for the serious student.

Pocock, D., *Kanbi and Patidar*, Oxford, 1972. See Chapter IV, iii 'The Ceremonies of Affines'.

Turner, V., 'Three Symbols of Passage in Ndembu Circumcision Ritual' in Gluckman, 1962 (see above).

Turner, V., 'Colour Classification in Ndembu Ritual' in Banton, 1966 (see above).

# 7

# Witchcraft and Sorcery

This final essay differs from the preceding ones because it calls both for a greater stretch of the imagination and for a good deal more introspection. To start with, most people do not believe in witches or sorcerers; nevertheless these words do summon up images and, even if these are derived from childhood stories or popular fiction, you should try to put them in words. See whether the associations of the words sorcerer and witch are identical, or in what ways they differ. Next, take some personal accident or misfortune and insistently ask the question 'Why?' and 'Why me?' In this exercise you should behave like an irritating child that refuses to be satisfied with the answer. Next, consider some more general social ill—unemployment, drunken driving, inflation—but choose one that really concerns you. Do you agree that if more people behaved like you the world would be a better place? Are there not other people who are less reasonable or more selfish than you are? What sort of people are they? Or perhaps you think that, human nature being what it is, no one is perfect and that therefore we are all responsible, although some are a little more so than others. As a reasonable person you will recognise that there are certain misdemeanours and even crimes that are understandable in the circumstances in which they occurred. Buy any evening paper and study the court cases; mark out those offences in which you can imagine yourself in the place of the defendant given the circumstances of poverty, sickness, pressure or whatever. In relation to which offences does your imagination fall short, and what kinds of antisocial or criminal behaviour fail to strike the slightest chord of sympathy, or even evoke your disgust? To what extent do you spontaneously tend to describe such behaviour as 'inhuman', 'bestial' or 'fiendish' etc. What social categories are most prone to behave in such ways or commit such crimes? In conclusion, make a list of crimes which are humanly understandable in the above sense and those which are not, and spell out the criteria you have used in making the distinction.

\*       \*       \*

However much social anthropologists differ amongst themselves in their intellectual approaches, they all tend to share the habit of apologising somewhat for the words they use, for example 'primitive'. Typically, inverted commas, real or implicit, cluster around common terms such as 'politics', 'religion', 'economics' and words of exotic origin such as 'taboo' and 'totemism'. What these inverted commas are signalling is that ideally our common use of the words enclosed by them should be replaced by a more precise term or phrase which would correctly define the phenomena under discussion. And yet the inverted commas continue.

This is not always a vice, nor evidence of intellectual pusillanimity: it represents rather what I would call the benign dilemma intrinsic to this particular intellectual pursuit. The social anthropologist is trying to grasp the innermost heart, the specificity of the phenomena which he is observing, and almost simultaneously to express the general significance of it. But this general significance can only be expressed in his native tongue, which also expresses social beliefs and categories, and is therefore itself the proper object of anthropological investigation. To put the matter as concretely as possible: as our use of the word 'politics' is modified by our understanding of the phenomena to which we apply it, so it becomes a different thing each time we use it. Inverted commas, conscientiously and not lazily applied, express this ever-changing, provisional and relative quality of our definitions.

The more that the things we are trying to understand appear

remote from our day-to-day experience, the more heavily we must apply our inverted commas, because this remoteness makes it likely that the words we are going to use are riddled with suppositions and unexamined elements. They have not been tested, so to speak, by daily renewal in living use.

'Witchcraft' is certainly one such word and 'sorcery' perhaps even more so. We can all summon up images of a 'witch', most of them constituted from literary experience—fairy tales, or quasi-literary experience—theatrical or cinematic performances. With some confidence I can affirm that the majority of readers who have carried out the suggested exercise presented an image of the 'witch' as an old, ugly, thin woman; perhaps not so many but still a lot, and perhaps especially the younger, will have added such details as conical black hats, black cats, toads and broom-sticks. A few will have reversed the female image and conceived of a young, dangerously attractive woman. I bet, very safely in the circumstances, that not one in a hundred thought of the 'witch' as a man of normal appearance in, say, his forties.

The image of 'sorcerer' is less easily guessed at. I venture to suggest that where sex has been specified it is masculine, that the 'sorcerer' may have been represented as old and perhaps sinister-looking but not necessarily ugly. Compared with the 'witch' the 'sorcerer' has a vaguely 'scientific' air about him: one thinks, doesn't one, of pentagrams, alembics and elaborate chemical apparatus which replace the mucky cauldron of the 'witch'?

It is interesting to find that the *Oxford English Dictionary* lends support to the sexual differentiation of these two figures. It notes that the notion of masculine 'witch' is now only found in dialects, and has to add the female suffix -ess to sorcerer. Keith Thomas, a historian who has used anthropological material and insights to produce a magnificent work on popular beliefs in sixteenth- and seventeenth-century England, gives us some evidence from the period for the 'scientific' associations of sorcery. He cites a text from 1653 which defined sorcery as 'a thing or mischief which is distinct from witchcraft, as thus, witchcraft being performed by the devil's insinuation of himself with witches, . . . sorcery being performed by mere sophistication and wicked abuse of nature in things of nature's own production'. For an earlier period W. C. Curry points to the use of astrology and image-making for quite legitimate medical ends; but the power to cure by spiritual means also suggests, as we shall see, the power to cause disease.

The popular images of the 'witch' and the 'sorcerer' that we have correspond by and large to a quite remarkable extent with the findings of social anthropologists. We quite commonly find some sort of distinction between an essentially non-material and an essentially material source of harm. It is certainly not the case, however, that the distinction between the sexes is always found.

Another distinction is hinted at by Curry's reference to the use of images—wax models, for example—for both good and bad purposes. The seventeenth-century authority quoted by Keith Thomas explains that what makes the sorcerer evil is not so much the fact that he uses nature as the fact that he uses it for a wicked purpose: 'it is the evil of the end which is sorcery' (*ibid*). No such ambiguity attaches to the witch, whose malpractice is inspired by the devil and is unquestionably evil. We shall find many examples of this ambiguity opposed to an absolute evil.

The ambivalence of the sorcerer's materials, which *can* heal or be employed to a good end, suggests another generalisable feature, a distinction between motives which is related to the relativity of moral judgment in society. This situation is not unlike that when two officially Christian countries both pray to God to support them in the destruction of their enemies, whose cause is allegedly ungodly. The matter is well expressed by Professor Lucy Mair who, after citing several examples of spiritual powers, such as the power to curse, for socially approved ends, continues:

'All these ideas belong to the field of legitimate action against misbehaviour. In some circumstances one might include in this field the use of magic-charms and spells and objects believed to have mystical power. In the language of anthropologists harmful magic is generally called sorcery, and most sorcery is thought to be illegitimate. But it is possible in Africa to buy from a sorcerer protective magic which will keep thieves off your property, and in parts of New Guinea different families are believed to own different kinds of harmful magic with which they protect their own food crops. It is also possible in Africa, after something has been stolen, to get a sorcerer to make magic which will injure the unknown thief if he does not make restitution; an interesting variant of this idea comes from the Nyoro of Western Uganda, who have medicine to smear on the ruins of a house that has been burnt down, so as to punish the person responsible. The chiefs of the Trobriand Islands in New Guinea were generally supposed to employ sorcerers against anyone who threatened their authority.

Witchcraft in contrast is unambiguously evil. It may well be motivated: it is often ascribed to the ill feeling generated in some quarrel which is remembered when one of the parties falls sick or meets with some other misfortune. But it is always held to be unjustified: the witch may have good cause for anger, but if he had not an evil disposition he would not have expressed his anger in this way. It follows, of course, that the anger of a witch is by definition not "righteous anger".'

The pioneer and classical work on these matters is Evans-Pritchard's *Witchcraft Oracles and Magic among the Azande*, and later in this chapter I shall give a brief resumé of the salient points of this work. But before I do so, I have to clarify a rather tiresome point of terminology. In the discussion of our associations, the images of the 'witch' and the 'sorcerer' respectively correspond to Professor Mair's terminology. The reader will, I am afraid, inevitably be confused by the fact that Evans-Pritchard inverts the two words so that the 'witch' emerges as the less malevolent figure and the 'sorcerer' is the embodiment of malice. Here the importance of the inverted commas comes in.

We have seen that even our own vague notions about spiritual malpractice have some sort of shape—the 'witch' by and large female, the 'sorcerer' by and large male; the 'witch' motivated by malice or the devil, the 'sorcerer' being more scientific or technical in his operations, working good as well as harm. In order to understand spiritual malpractice in other societies we have to keep in mind the way in which these elements are related, rather than the shapes themselves. We shall try to see whether in societies other than our own there is a fundamental distinction between kinds of spiritual malpractice, rather than worrying ourselves about whether we are to call one 'witchcraft' and the other 'sorcery'. Again, we shall look for a distinction between purely spiritual sources of harmful power on the one hand and spiritual *cum* material sources on the other. Another important question worth asking, which is not suggested by our own notions in these matters, is whether there is a distinction between the existence of a social category as opposed to the lack of one. I mean by this that if there is a distinction between kinds of spiritual malpractice one of these may be attributed to a particular class of people, while the other is randomly distributed. Perhaps there is after all a hint of this in our own associations: the 'witch' is not merely feminine and old but also poor, the 'sorcerer' has less precise social associations.

Evans-Pritchard refers to the Zande empire, an immense area extending some 750 miles west and about 500 north from the north-western border of modern Uganda. This empire was composed of a number of kingdoms which were created as the younger brothers and sons of a particular chief split off from him to establish their own areas of power. At any one time the king of a particular area would have under him people whom Evans-Pritchard refers to as 'provincial governors', who might be his own kinsmen or wealthy commoners whom he had appointed. These kingdoms were discrete areas, separated the one from the other by a wide fringe of unpopulated countryside. The king himself would invariably be a member of the aristocratic clan. Although the entire population was divided into exogamous groups which we could call clans, these had no territorial association and their members did not meet together for any particular activities. It is only the aristocratic clan which could be said to have had a function in the society, and the commoner clans were scattered and subordinated to this one aristocratic family.

Nevertheless, given this limitation, the emphasis on patrilineal descent was strong among the Azande; descent, inheritance and succession were in the male line both among the aristocrats and among the commoners, and residence was always determined by the same principle. Women occupied a markedly inferior position. Evans-Pritchard characterises family life among the Azande by this emphasis on the inferiority of the female and the authority of elders. In the past women could be used in compensation payments and could expect very little in the way of protection or support from their natal families. Young men also suffered from the predominance of the elders, who had a monopoly of wives such that it was difficult for a young man to marry without the favour of his father. Evans-Pritchard characterises the father–son relationship as marked by deep respect.

The prevalence of tsetse fly in the area made the cultivation of cattle impossible for the Azande and they lived by agriculture, hunting and fishing. The Azande also had a distinctive technological ability and a reputation as smiths, potters, wood-carvers and basket-makers.

Although, as I have said, Evans-Pritchard uses the terms 'witch' and 'sorcerer' in senses inverse to those which I have employed, his usage is rigorously consistent with Zande usage. 'My aim', he writes, 'has been to make a number of English words stand for Zande notions and to use the same term only and always when the same notion is being discussed.' To this end he sets out very early in his book to give a list of Zande terms with their English explanation. As I shall be using some of these terms and abandoning for the time being the use of inverted commas, I shall now give an abbreviated version of this vocabulary.

| Zande | English explanation |
|-------|---------------------|
| *mangu* | The Azande believe that certain people have a material substance in their bodies and that a psychic emanation from this substance can cause injury to people and to property. Both the substance itself and the emanation from it are called *mangu*. |
| *boro (ira) mangu* | A person whose body contains *mangu* or who has been diagnosed as containing *mangu* by a diviner or an oracle. |
| *ngua* | A technique which operates by the use of materials or medicines. The operation of these medicines may be accompanied by a spell. *Ngua* also refers to the medicines themselves or to any object in which a spiritual power exists. Finally, *ngua* is also used in the general English sense of medicine, that is to say both the application of surgery and the internal or external application of medicaments. |
| *boro ngua (ira ngua)* | This term is used for anybody who possesses *ngua* and also for anybody who operates as a doctor in our sense. |
| *gbegbere (gbigbita) ngua, kitikiti ngua* | The use of *ngua* in an illicit or immoral way, and the *ngua* itself thus used. |
| *wene ngua* | *Ngua* that is used in a socially approved way and the *ngua* itself when it is so used. |
| *ira gbegbere kitikiti (ngua)* | Anybody who uses *ngua* in an immoral way to harm other persons or property. |

| | |
|---|---|
| *soroka* | These are techniques for the discovery of causes which cannot otherwise be discovered and Evans-Pritchard translates the term 'oracles'. There are four principal oracles, which are: *benge*, which operates by the administration of strychnine to fowls; *iwa*, a kind of wooden rubbing board; *dakpa*, which uses termites; *mapingo*, which uses a pile of three small sticks. |
| *pa ngua (pa atoro)* | This is a human oracle: a person who, inspired by *ngua* or by ghosts, tries to discover what would otherwise remain hidden. |
| *abinza (avule)* | A corporation of people who practise *pa ngua*. Evans-Pritchard translates these two terms as divination and diviners. |

The Azande believe that *mangu* is a physical substance which is inherited. Sons but not daughters inherit it from their fathers, and daughters but not sons inherit it from their mothers. This belief immediately brings us up against an apparent contradiction which is by no means uncommon. It might seem obvious to us that if a man has been convicted of having *mangu* then, because he must have inherited it from his father, grandfather and so on, everybody who is related to him in the male line must equally have this property. Equally, if a man has been declared free of *mangu*, then one would think that his entire lineage would be free of any future suspicion. But the Azande do not draw any such logical inference and limit the application of this general principle to a man's immediate kin. In this they reason rather as we do when we attribute moral qualities or vices to a particular group, class, nation or race and make an exception for every single individual member of that group whom we happen to know and like or dislike.

The Azande have also more precise rationalisations with which to avoid the general application of the inheritance principle. First of all, the kinsmen of a man who has been proved to have *mangu* can claim that he was illegitimate and that his mother must have committed adultery with some man who carried *mangu* in his body. Or they can point to previous occasions on which relatives of theirs were accused and found innocent. Finally, they have a supplementary belief that a man may have *mangu* in his body but, to use their terminology, it remains cool during his lifetime, that is to say inoperative.

Evans-Pritchard is at pains to emphasise that the Azande are not interested in elaborating a 'theory' of *mangu*; they are only interested in understanding particular events and seeking out the motives of particular people in relation to an illness, accident or other misfortune. We can perhaps understand this better when we appreciate how pervasive is the belief in *mangu* and its operation in Zande society. *Mangu* is ubiquitous and thoroughly commonplace; it is associated with all misfortunes, both trivial and grave. The Azande do not think of *mangu* as something eerie or weird but rather as an aggressive and offensive interference in their affairs. *Mangu* is so pervasive that were an Azande to seek out its source on every occasion that he notes its operation, let alone take retaliatory action, he would have little time for anything else.

In order to get some idea of the ways in which the Azande think about the operations of *mangu* I can only ask the reader to ponder the use of the words 'luck' or 'chance' in the English language. All of us have experience of 'one of those days' in which everything seems to go wrong, when one is faced with accident, irritation and frustration on apparently every side. On such days we appear to be accident prone, omit our routine precautions about switching things on or off, for example, which we normally perform almost instinctively. Apart from such days, none of us goes through life without having small or grave accidents which are not easily accounted for, and were we to be asked why we broke that cup or did not see that other car coming we should, I suppose, have no other answer than 'bad luck' or 'chance'. Where we would use such terms the Azande use *mangu*. But *mangu* is wider in its application: we would only speak of chance, normally, when we could not attribute an accident to some other cause, such as the fact that our hands were soapy when we handled the cup or that someone distracted our attention when we were driving. The Azande, like ourselves, can fully appreciate the material causes of events; it is simply the case that these alone do not satisfy their curiosity. They go on to ask the question why *me* and why *now*? Evans-Pritchard cites among many cases one of a man who went to inspect the beer that he was brewing. It was at night and, as is the custom, he carried a torch of burning grass. Holding the torch above his head he set fire to the thatch of his hut and it was destroyed. He and his neighbours knew fully well that fire burns and that thatch is combustible. Nevertheless they pointed out that this man, and many others, had adopted exactly the same routine when they were moving about inside a hut at night but it by no means inevitably followed that they set fire to their thatch. The question remained why should this particular man suffer this particular accident at this particular moment. The answer was *mangu*.

Perhaps the difference between ourselves and the Azande is not so great after all, and resides simply in the fact that they ask questions which we do not normally bother to ask. Nevertheless, if any one of us were forced by a persistent anthropologist to answer the question 'Why?', we should find ourselves close to the Azande. We have had, shall we say, an attack of influenza. In answer to the question we presume that we have been attacked by a virus. But why should we be attacked by a virus when other people are not attacked, or have been attacked less severely? The answer could be that we let ourselves get run down, undernourished or tired, and we could adduce reasons for these conditions. Finally, however, if indeed our patience with this imaginary anthropologist has not run out, we are driven to some such word as 'chance'. The Azande simply take a short cut to the position.

*Mangu* is activated when a man feels hatred or envy in relation to another. When therefore a Zande falls sick or suffers some accident he will naturally cast around in his mind to consider who might bear him such a grudge. He may know, for example, that he has wronged a certain person and that this person may be trying to seek revenge. Equally, anything which he values himself must appear desirable in the eyes of others and therefore there is perhaps no limit to the people whom he may suspect. For example, if a man is inordinately vain of his own good looks, his very vanity will make him fear the envy of others. In addition, it is impossible for any man to get through life without coming into some sort of conflict with others, great or small, intended or not. Thus in a variety of ways and because *mangu* is believed to operate so widely, it is likely that all Zande men and women will at some time in their lives be accused of having *mangu* and of deliberately activating it against someone.

Here we come up against another apparent contradiction in the way Azande talk about these things. Carriers of *mangu* have no external physical attributes such that anybody could recognise them; this is a necessary belief because if a man suspects spiritual malpractice he will not look around among people who do not know him and his affairs. Only those with whom he is associated locally, those with whom he has quarrelled in the past, or those who know the condition of his crops or his valuables are likely to be suspected. To his way of looking at things his misfortune may come from some friendly neighbour, who is all the more friendly in his manner because he intends harm.

By the same token a man may himself be accused by his neighbour, and when we hear an account of *mangu* from the accused's point of view a somewhat different picture emerges. When a Zande is making an accusation he has in mind a conscious and deliberate attempt on the part of somebody else to harm him; when he himself is accused he is willing to accept that the possession of *mangu* may be an unconscious matter. Living in the ethos in which he does live, riddled with the suspicion of hatred and envy, he would have to be very unknowing of his own nature not to admit, at least to himself, that he has harboured bad feelings against another person. Such bad feelings together with the possession of *mangu* could have created the harm alleged. When a man has been accused of possessing *mangu* by the *benge* oracle (see p. 197) his accusers bring him a wing of the fowl which has died. When presented with this the accused will not repudiate the charge directly but rather make a conditional act of reparation. He fills his mouth with water and blows the water out on the chicken wing saying, 'If I possess *mangu* in my belly I am unaware of it; may it cool. It is thus that I blow out water.'

The situation is still by no means clear. Let us imagine that a man has blown water onto the chicken's wing in this way and the sickness which he was accused of causing clears up. This could be prime evidence of the fact that he did indeed have *mangu* in him. Again, the sick man might deteriorate and perhaps die. We might think that the accusation was a faulty one and that somebody else should have been accused. But if the accusers are convinced that the accused has *mangu*, then they can say that the man did not perform this action with his heart but allowed his *mangu* to continue at its work.

Evans-Pritchard makes it quite clear that some people are plagued throughout their lives by such accusations from angry neighbours, and he makes it equally clear that these accusations are met with a somewhat ambiguous response. On the one hand, the accused, his kinsmen and friends will privately attribute the accusations to envy and spite. At the same time, however, there seems to be a lingering doubt, arising from the possibility that *mangu* may be unconsciously present. Evans-Pritchard tells us that sometimes he would ask a man, whom he knew well, directly whether or not he had *mangu* in him. He contrasts the humility of the reply 'If there is *mangu* in my belly I know nothing of it' with the anger with which the same person would have reacted to the question 'Are you a thief?'

We can then understand how Azande can believe in the unconscious possession of *mangu*. Nevertheless, when they themselves are not being accused, they believe not only that *mangu* is consciously possessed and deliberately exercised but even that the possessors of *mangu* get together in secret meetings to plot evil. This attribution of consciousness is in accordance with Zande beliefs about human nature. As we have seen, they may not believe in the sincerity of an accused man when he blows water on the chicken's wing.

We can understand how these apparently contradictory beliefs are related. The belief in *mangu* is a necessary part of what we can call the Zande theory of causation; to think other than they do would be to become other than they are. If the belief in *mangu* and its effects is so prevalent that anyone could possess it, and most are likely to be accused of possessing it, life would become impossible if people believed that everyone believed to possess *mangu* was deliberately operating it all the time. But, equally, the beliefs about *mangu* possessors—not only that they plot together but also that they travel in spirit form, and sometimes as animals —is a comforting belief for anyone who is accused. He can accept that he may unconsciously have *mangu*, but he knows for sure that he never behaved in the way that a conscious possessor of *mangu* is alleged to behave. The situation is no different from that amongst ourselves when somebody 'accuses' us of having passed on our cold to them. We accept that this is quite possible but not necessarily absolutely true and we are, of course, conscious that we had no intention of so doing. On the other hand, somebody who knew himself to be infected with a highly contagious disease would be regarded as some kind of monster were he not to take precautions for the sake of other people.

This reference to monsters brings us to more mysterious figures in Azande society, the evil men who use *ngua* medicines. On this matter Evans-Pritchard's material is not as full as the material about *mangu*. Whereas *mangu* only makes the Azande angry, they can be said to fear the evil use of *ngua*, and Evans-Pritchard found that his informants were reluctant to appear too knowledgeable about such matters. Evil medicines were said to exist, but anybody who could put a name to them would obviously run the risk of being thought just such an evil person. Again, whereas the Azande are quite willing to make open accusations about *mangu*, they do not like to point the finger at a man who is said to possess evil medicines; indeed, Evans-Pritchard found the Azande very vague when it came down to giving precise details of cases in which such accusations had been made. *Mangu* is an open and an understandable matter. If a man suspects its effects upon him he can, from his own history of his relations with other people, name one or several suspects; the fact that he possesses something which they do not have, or the fact that he has quarrelled with one or several people, is for him an understandable reason why they might be employing *mangu* against him. But when it comes to bad medicines there is no such understandable motive other than pure, motiveless malice. Again, whereas the operations of *mangu* are slow and can be remedied by the use of oracles and the ritual of blowing water, the effects of bad medicines are swift and very often fatal; there is little that can be done to assuage or cancel their effects. One final important difference is that the most evil and powerful medicines are believed to come from outside Zande society and we shall see that this has a general significance.

For the present we can understand the belief in evil medicines as a kind of long-stop in the pattern of Zande theories of causation. We have seen that they seek a cause for every misfortune, from the most trivial to the most grave. We see also that they have a set of institutionalised practices for explaining and dealing with the vast majority of such misfortunes—*mangu* and the associated beliefs. However, there are occasions when the gravity of the misfortune is such that the conventional remedies do not work and, indeed, the Azande, like many people in the world, regard death itself as a terrible accident which can only be attributed to some evil source. Thus if a man falls ill and has used the oracle to find out possible *mangu* carriers who may be harming him, and if these people have purged themselves by blowing water, and still the man's health deteriorates and he dies, then the work of evil medicines explains why the man has died and, indeed, why the oracle itself failed to identify this source of evil in the first place.

We can present the differences between *mangu* and the use of *ngua* for evil purposes as follows:

| *Mangu* | *Ngua* |
|---|---|
| Understandable | Not understandable |
| Within Zande society | Comes from outside Azande society |
| Unconscious | Conscious |
| Spiritual | Material |

This must be regarded as a very provisional set of opposed associations, but we shall see that material from other parts of Africa tends to confirm and amplify it.

One of the best studies for comparative purposes is *Witchcraft and Sorcery in East Africa* edited by John Middleton and E. H. Winter. In this volume are collected ten studies of the beliefs and practices associated with sources of spiritual harm. In the majority of these studies we find a verbal distinction between broad categories of such spiritual malpractice, although the features associated with them are not necessarily those of the Azande. We find, for example, that among the Amba of Western Uganda the people who buy medicines to protect themselves or hurt others are, although undoubtedly bad, not *evil* because their motives are understandable. They are therefore not unlike the unconscious possessors of *mangu* among the Azande. On the other hand, among the Amba the truly evil creatures are those who operate solely by inherited spiritual powers. A feature of the utterly evil, which emerges more strongly from these studies than from the work of Evans-Pritchard, is what the editors call the symbolism of inversion. Time after time we note that those spiritual malpractitioners who fall into the category of the gratuitously evil are said to behave in ways which are contradictory to those of ordinary social norms: they work alone and at night when normal people work in groups and by day; they are said to walk upside down; sometimes they are said to be white or grey when normal people are dark brown or black; most strikingly and commonly they are supposed to practise abnormalities such as homosexuality and bestiality, incest and cannibalism. Sometimes this cannibalism is said to take the form of eating the bodies of corpses.

One of the editors, John Middleton, is the only contributor to relate the beliefs about spiritual malpractice to the general cosmology of the people whom he discusses—the Lugbara of north-western Uganda. He tells us that the Lugbara maintain that if everybody did as they should do their social system would work perfectly and there would be no reason for envy, hatred and spiritual evil. He reports an informant:

> 'God the Creator made the world. He made men here also. He kills men when they are old. He is good (*onyiru*). But we men are not all good. Many of us are evil (*onzi*). We hate others in our hearts because we are envious (*ole ber*) and we do them harm and destroy them and their wives and their children and their compounds . . . Some men are "slow", but others like fighting and quarrelling; these men destroy the words of Divinity.' (*Op. cit*, p. 261).

He goes on to show that, although in Lugbara thought all men are capable of evil, those who are most responsible for the sorrows of this world are the spiritual malpractitioners who, in this case, fall broadly into two categories: three different types who operate by innate evil powers and three others who use medicines of different sorts. The Lugbara, it should be noted, lay considerable stress on the greater power of the evil which comes from outside; this is also found in some of the other studies.

The second editor, E. H. Winter, makes a similar point about the Amba when he says that they are capable of envisaging a perfect world in which they would not be plagued by evil of this order. Clearly they are more perturbed by the presence of spiritual evil, as anybody who reads Winter's account will readily understand. However, the important point for us is the editors' discussion of the significance of inverted symbolism and its relation to morality and general ideas of the good society.

Amba society is composed of a number of small villages, each one of which constitutes, in a sense, an autonomous moral universe. It is only within the village that moral obligations of all sorts are recognised: people in other villages can be treated as strangers and exploited. What the Amba find peculiarly horrifying is the fact that the cannibalistic and evil creatures which afflict them (Winter does not give us the indigenous term but uses the English word 'witch') operate exclusively *within* the community of the village and do not attack outsiders. People who traffic in medicines, on the other hand, use them to attack people in the village as well as outsiders.

Winter explains the inverted symbolism of the 'witches' by reference to this rather fragmented political system. He lists the popular characteristics of 'witches':

(i) Witches sometimes stand on their heads or rest hanging upside down from the limbs of trees.
(ii) Witches are active at night.
(iii) When they are thirsty they eat salt.
(iv) They go about naked.
(v) They can transform themselves into leopards, or they may have leopards which will attack people at their command, as their familiars.
(vi) They eat people.
(vii) Their victims are invariably members of their own village.
(viii) The witches in various villages are bound together in a system of reciprocity. Thus if the witches in a particular village kill a person they invite the witches from another village to share the ensuing feast. At a later date, the witches of the second village must reciprocate by inviting their previous hosts to a feast at which they will serve the corpse of a victim from their own village.

Winter shows that all these characteristics are inversions of normal Amba behaviour. Concentrating on item (viii) he shows that, because the village is the only moral community that the Amba know, this reciprocity with people in other villages who are strangers, normally to be regarded as potential enemies, marks out witches not merely as the sources of misfortune but as the incarnations of evil itself. Between the members of different villages there can and should be no sense of obligation, no shared morality; strangers are there to be exploited. If therefore the Amba are to have any notion of evil, this notion can only be operative within the confines of their own society, the village.

But why should the Amba and so many other peoples upset themselves by such beliefs? The passage which I have quoted earlier from John Middleton's article gives us a clue. He tells us that *onyiru*, which in the passage quoted he translates as 'good', can also be understood to mean 'stable'; the traditional society as created by God with its institutions, customs and laws is the divine recipe for harmonious life. It follows from this that all change which either prevents that realisation of an ideal or threatens the existence of institutions is evil—*onzi*. I venture to suggest that this can be generalised not, certainly, as a general truth but as a hypothesis for the understanding of these phenomena.

There is a proverb found in widely scattered parts of the world in different forms, of which one version is 'no man calls his mother a witch'. The significance of this proverb is that, however strongly a man may believe that spiritual evil exists, he will strenuously deny that he himself practises it; we have seen that this is so among the Azande and wider reading would amply confirm it. Even in our own society we know that each one of us identifies himself or herself with the sensible, decent, law-abiding, or if not law-abiding then right, way of life. Even the professional thief has ideas of normality and decency in the pursuit of his profession, and these for him draw the line between himself and real villains. But less dramatically we know people who deplore drunken driving and the incidence of road accidents but who at the same time either imagine that alcohol happens not to affect them or believe that they drive all the better for a few drinks, being more relaxed: in short, we all have a natural tendency to regard the point of view from which we judge the world as the right one.

Unfortunately, we cannot close our eyes to the fact that the world according to our notions is not perfect, and this is exactly the position of the Azande, the Lugbara and many others. Like ourselves, these peoples have ideas of what the good life might be, although no doubt their ideas are more coherent, explicit and widely shared than ours. It is as though they were saying that if all husbands worked hard, all wives were faithful and all children obeyed their parents, if the rain fell when it was required and not when it was not required, if people did not fall sick or have accidents and so on, the world would according to their institutions be an entirely satisfactory place. They see, however, that these things do not happen: wives are unfaithful and run away from their husbands, children are undutiful, etc. Life itself tells them that it is not perfect, and this experience conflicts with that natural self-righteousness to which I have alluded. The only way out of the problem is to say that if everybody behaved as I do things would be better and, conversely, because they do not the world is an unhappy place.

Although we do not think that our own activities contribute to inflation, are dishonest, are profiteering, or that the paper bag which *we* throw away is 'litter', we do not at the same time regard other people who behave in this way as out and out villains. I recognise that the people who do these things are human beings like myself and that their motives are human motives like mine. I may even go so far as to admit that *some* of my behaviour is not unlike theirs, to the extent that I am occasionally less than perfect. We treat the day-to-day unpleasantness much as we do the common cold; something to be suffered and about which there is little that can be done. Our behaviour when faced with an epidemic, or the moral equivalent of one, is different.

Winter, describing the Amba definitions of what he calls 'sorcery' and 'witchcraft', writes as follows:

'Sorcery is set in motion by ordinary motives of envy, jealousy, and hatred. It is activated by the events of daily life, by social situations which give rise to feelings of ill will. Thus the resort to sorcery, however much it may be condemned, is intelligible

to the Amba; it makes sense to them. By contrast the activities
of witches are ultimately inexplicable. Witches, although they
may harm people in all sorts of ways, for instance by causing a
man to trip over a fallen branch, are concerned basically with
the satisfaction of their abnormal desire for human flesh, a
craving which is utterly repugnant to the normal Amba, who
cannot understand ... how anyone could have such a per-
verted taste. Although the analogy is not exact, the contrast
between sorcerer and witch is similar to the one made in our
own society between a man who murders a relative in order to
gain an inheritance and the pathological killer. One kills for
reasons which are understandable even if they do not provide
an excuse for the murder, while the other kills senselessly.'

Winters puts the point well: there are crimes and misfortunes
which are within the range of our experience or potential experience, but there are others which go beyond the reach of our
sympathy in the literal sense. The epidemic provides a good
example. We live with the common cold in winter and expect a
certain incidence of influenza. Individual and public reaction to
these phenomena is on an altogether lower scale than the reaction
to a serious epidemic. Let us note that, if the disease is a very
serious one and normally relatively rare, an epidemic will drive
us to employ diviners to find out the carriers and the channels
by which the disease has come amongst us. In the same class of
phenomena, and even further perhaps from the stretch of our
imagination, are activities of all sorts which we believe to be consciously directed towards evil as we define it. It is a notorious
fact that in times of acute national crisis there is a strong tendency
to identify a certain group, class or race with evil forces seeking to
undermine our society. It is even the case that we go so far as to
dehumanise the people who are alleged to be engaged in these
activities; they become bestial, like animals, inhuman, savage, etc.

What I am suggesting here is a very general structure of the
way in which man reconciles his identification of himself with an
ideal state of society and his recognition that this is never
achieved.

We do not believe in witchcraft and sorcery, but have the moral categories to which they refer vanished? My own view is that they must survive for as long as man cherishes the moral ideals which give shape to his universe, recognises the gulf between ideal and actuality, and blames this on others. There is a game which plays on the difference between the way I describe one and the same behaviour accordingly as it is 'mine', 'yours' or 'his'. Thus: 'I *like* my food, you're a *bon viveur*, he's a glutton'; 'I'm merry, you're tight, he's drunk'. We could extend this to 'I drive better for a couple of drinks, you want to go steady, he's a drunken driver'; 'I believe in law and order, you're a bit of a Tory, he's a fascist' or 'I'm asserting my rights, you're being unreasonable, he's a trouble-maker'. The human foible on which the joke rests is the tendency we have, given the inevitable gap between the ideal and real, to mitigate the shortcomings of the category 'we', which is composed of 'I' and 'you', and to throw the onus of offence upon the outsider 'he'. Crime, poverty, social discrimination, violence, greed, snobbery and the simple lack of consideration for other people are blatant in the world, but *I* am not guilty of any of these, although it is possible that I could be; *you* could be and sometimes are; *he* certainly is. The Azande version would be '*I* might have *mangu*, *you* do have mangu, *he*'s a sorcerer'.

## Summary

This chapter was about the ways in which man tries to resolve the conflict between his desire to live in a perfect world and the inevitable recognition that he does not; our ideas of the good or of the ideal determine our ideas of the bad or the evil and we are responsible for both. We began by looking at our own images of the 'witch' and the 'sorcerer' and we saw that, vague as the images were, we can in our imagination distinguish the two. Next we looked at Mair's definition of the terms and saw that she defined 'sorcery' as a sort of legitimate evil, a harmful spiritual activity which might be objectionable but was at least understandable in so far as it was related to social values. 'Witchcraft' she defined as really evil, incomprehensible, gratuitous malice. Then we looked at the classic study of these matters, Evans-Pritchard's *Witchcraft, Oracles and Magic among the Azande*. We were immediately alerted to the fact that this author inverts Mair's definitions and we resolved to worry not so much about the words used as about the kinds of behaviour they described: we would almost invariably find a distinction between comprehensible and non-comprehensible spiritual malpractice, and this distinction was the important thing.

We then looked at Evans-Pritchard's material in some detail; in particular we examined the concept *mangu*, and we saw that it referred to a physical property which is hereditary, but the Azande had all sorts of ways of rationalising the application of this belief. The operations of *mangu*, whether conscious or unconscious, were held to cause all misfortunes, whether grave or trivial. The Azande were not ignorant of what we would call the physical causes of accidents and misfortunes, but unlike ourselves they went on to ask 'Why me and why now?' *Mangu* is motivated by hatred and envy, so that when a man feels sick he asks himself who, for whatever reason, might harbour such feelings against him. Anyone could have *mangu* in him and even be unconscious of it. When therefore a man is accused of having caused an illness he makes a conditional reparation along the lines: 'If I did, *then* I withdraw it.' We saw that the Azande have contradictory beliefs about *mangu*: on the one hand, it is unconsciously activated and, on the other, it is quite consciously exercised by evil-minded people who plot evil together. We saw that this contradiction was necessary to the Azande world view because it enabled any individual to feel relatively innocent and still to maintain his belief that *mangu* existed. However, the Azande had a separate concept for conscious and motiveless malice, *boro ngua*, people who used medicines to work harm. The distinction between these two categories of spiritual malpractice was clear—*mangu* was a bad thing but understandable; it was in the hearts of men and operated within Azande society; it was (by contrast with *ngua*) unconscious; it was a spiritual power; and finally, its effects could be cured. *Ngua* was an incomprehensible evil; its most virulent forms came from foreigners; it was consciously applied; and there was little hope of remedy against it.

We next tested the generality of this set of distinctions on other African material and saw that, with variations, it held up well enough. The social anthropologists whose work we examined enabled us to go further and to ask why human beings should distress themselves with such beliefs. Middleton's observations on the Lugbara led us to set the problem in the wider context of the relation between good and evil; in this context we looked at the way in which we assess our own imperfections and the offences of others. We concluded that we, less systematically perhaps than people of other cultures but no less firmly, are inclined to identify ourselves sometimes with the good and often with the normal, to identify those who are like us as forgivable offenders, and to pin the blame for our misfortunes upon outsiders who, in extreme circumstances, we characterise as monsters.

## Reading notes

Burridge, K. O. L., *Mambu—a Melanesian millennium*, London, 1960. This book does not focus on witchcraft or sorcery. It is mentioned here because it relates these matters to a whole range of discussion, too vast for the present work—the pursuit of perfection. All over the world and at different times we find people's sense of this world's misfortunes becomes so oppressive that they look for a final solution to the problem of evil. Where evil is believed to be caused by witches or their equivalent it is not surprising that the witch-hunter or diviner tends to emerge, at least initially, as the leader of the movement. Unfortunately Burridge has not included a good bibliography.

Evans-Pritchard, E. E., *Witchcraft, Oracles and Magic among the Azande*, Oxford, 1937. This is the formative classic on this subject for all subsequent writers. It is a large book, nevertheless I cannot suggest selective reading. The reader should pay particular attention to Part IV, Chapter iv, in connection with the considerations raised in the note on Burridge (above).

Macfarlane, A., *Witchcraft in Tudor and Stuart England—a regional and comparative study*, London, 1970.

Mair, L., *Witchcraft*, London, 1969. A very useful introductory book.

Mair, L., 'New Religions', Chapter 6 of her *New Nations*, London, 1963. A general discussion of religion in small societies, of witchcraft, of the effects of missions, and the pursuit of perfection.

Marwick, M. G., *Sorcery in its Social Setting—a study of the Northern Rhodesian Cewa*, Manchester and New York, 1965.

Middleton, J., and Winter, E. (eds.), *Witchcraft and Sorcery in East Africa*, London, 1963.

Peel, E., and Southern, P., *The Trials of the Lancashire Witches—a study of 17th Century Witchcraft*, Newton Abbot, 1969. An excellent readable piece of work by two local historians.

Pocock, D., *Mind, Body and Wealth—a study of belief and practice in an Indian village*, Oxford, 1973. See Chapter 1, 'Introductory', and Chapter 2, 'The Evil Eye—envy and greed'.

Thomas, K., *Religion and the Decline of Magic—studies in popular beliefs in sixteenth and seventeenth century England*, London, 1971.

Tippett, A., *Solomon Islands Christianity*, London, 1967. The Christian missions as the vehicles of Western thought have played their part in sparking off the pursuit of perfection. Sometimes these take the form of schismatic or sectarian movements within the Christian churches. Tippett discusses such a schism in Part Five of his book.

Trevor-Roper, H., *The European Witch-craze of the 16th and 17th Centuries*, Penguin, 1969.

# 8

# 'We' and 'They'

'All the world's daft save thee and me, and thou'rt a bit queer.' This well-known saying reflects the kind of thinking that we have just been talking about, and we can use it to relate ideas about the sources of misfortune to the ways in which, more generally, we define our position in the world.

Early on in this book I attached importance to the theme 'Myself and My Society' on the grounds that you should become as conscious as possible of the various judgments you make about the nature of society and your relation to it. Another way of approaching this would have been to ask for an essay on your reference group. This is a term coined by sociologists to refer to the group with which someone identifies and from which he or she derives standards and values of all sorts—dress, amusement, morality, politics, etc. My reference group is composed of the people whom I think of as being 'like me', whose approval and disapproval I respect.

The reason why I did not open the discussion with this concept is that, without qualification, it can be misleading and even dangerous. It is misleading when it suggests that we all have just one reference group – the family, friends, work-mates or whatever. It is dangerous when it feeds a human tendency to identify what I and people like me do as 'natural', and encourages the consequent tendency to classify what other people do according to a scale which ranges from simply different through odd and funny to scarcely human and inhuman.

At various points in this book there have been examples of the recurring distinction we/they, which appears in extreme form in the Bedouin Arab saying 'Myself against my brother; my brother and I against my cousin; my cousin and my brother and I against the outsider'. This saying well illustrates the relativity of reference groups and the way in which my opposition to the outsider of today is qualified by the awareness that he may be the insider of tomorrow. The distinction between we and they is prevented by this relativity from splitting society apart. The individual person defines himself by reference to several groups, for example the lineage, the affinal kinsmen, the members of the age set and so on. These groups may, as groups, have conflicting interests and no doubt the individual person experiences, and perhaps even suffers, a certain degree of tension and internal conflict; nevertheless the fact that all individuals in a society have these multiple reference groups makes for the cross-cutting ties which prevent the emergence of a monolithic 'we' opposed to a monolithic 'they', a 'they', let us remember, which also defines itself as 'we'.

Nevertheless there are situations in which the relativities seem to break down or cease to operate. This is exemplified by the fact frequently reported in the ethnographies that the members of a culture have no other name for themselves other than the equivalent of human being. The Nuer are called Nuer in European literature, but they call themselves *nath*, people. Those who are unlike themselves fall into various categories: their close neighbours the Dinka, with whom they share many cultural traits, are *jaang*, and beyond them are the even more despised *jur*, everyone else. The Dinka for their part do not exclude the Nuer from their own definition of humanity, *jieng*, but everyone else falls into the category *jur*, foreigner. Dr R. G. Leinhardt tells us that 'there are also opprobrious terms for the Azande and other Sudanic-speaking peoples, whom the Dinka seem scarcely to regard as "people" '. The Nuer and the Dinka exemplify in their different ways a common situation that is also expressed in an anthropological joke about a mysterious East African tribe called the Washenzi. As European missionaries and travellers moved inland they constantly heard of these Washenzi, who were said to live a little further on. As they travelled further the Washenzi were said to be still a little further to the west. Finally, realisation dawned as the meaning of *washenzi* came clear; *shenzi* is a Swahili adjective meaning dirty, hopeless and uncouth; the Washenzi were simply savages, and this general term of abuse was used by each tribe visited to describe its neighbours.

When we say that the people of a certain culture classify others as barely human or not human at all, we must be careful not to project our own ideas upon them. It does not seem that 'humanity' in these contexts is identified with the physical species *homo sapiens* but rather with certain cultural traits. The Nuer may regard the Dinka as inferior humans, but they intermarry with them and, indeed, many Dinka lineages are incorporated into Nuer society. To take a striking example from the rain forests of Brazil, the Mundurucu of that area enjoy hunting their neighbours and value the shrunken heads of their captives. They call themselves simply 'We—the People' and associate outsiders with wild pig. Nevertheless they adopt the prepubescent children of their captives and raise them as members of Mundurucu society. In traditional Hindu society the four classical divisions— priests, warriors, traders and farmers, servants—established a hierarchy of moral worth; nevertheless the common humanity of the four orders is expressed in the myth of their common origin —they sprang respectively from the head, arms, loins and feet of Purusha, the primal spirit of manhood. In our own Middle Ages and later, what today we would call antisemitism was not directed against a 'race' but against a religion.

With this caveat in mind we can see that, nevertheless, there are interesting variations in the intensity or the clarity with which different peoples maintain one or several categories of 'they', for example the Nuer and the Dinka. Even if we cannot here explore the reasons for these differences, the topic is a central one for comparative analysis because it bears upon some of the major problems of our contemporary society—the so-called 'generation gap', the adjustment to immigrant populations, the resistance that ideas about 'national sovereignty' and the like set up to the development of supra-national organisations. We shall not pretend to solve these problems, but it is possible that we shall discover some new angles from which to consider them.

Let us look at the Nuer and the Dinka from this point of view. The Dinka are first of all some five times more numerous than the Nuer. Dinka territory is, as one might expect, much larger but also more varied than that of the Nuer; although the Dinka are affected by seasonal changes, these are less abrupt, less dramatic in a sense, than they are among the Nuer. Both peoples set considerable store by the principle of agnatic descent, but this is significantly modified among the Dinka in that they are also disposed to think of their own political system in terms of the *affinal* relationships between the lineages that make up a tribe. The Nuer, it will be remembered, think of their tribes as being formed around the local representatives of one clan, which in this context is said to be dominant.

> 'Social obligations among the Nuer are expressed chiefly in kinship idiom and the interrelations of local communities within a tribe are defined in terms of agnatic relationships.'

The implications of this difference are considerable. Every Nuer tribe is composed of two categories of unequal size and quality—the *diel*, original settlers and hence in this context the true Nuer of that tribe, and the *rul*, the second-comers who are consequently somewhat inferior (p.40). For the Nuer the typical *rul* are Dinka, and often enough some of these *rul* lineages are indeed of Dinka origin. The rules of clan exogamy require the *diel* of any tribal territory to marry with the *rul* of that territory. Of course, whatever their origin, the *rul* are not *treated* as inferior or discriminated against as immigrants; nevertheless at a certain level of thought they are associated with the archetypal outsiders, the Dinka, who are *jaang*, not *nath*, not true men.

The existence of these two categories *diel* and *rul* poses a problem. On the one hand we have the Nuer pride in agnatic descent and in being *nath*, and on the other the absolute necessity of marrying people who are in this context less than *nath*. In other words, the continuance of the lineage and of the Nuer sense of being truly Nuer depends upon the existence of non-Nuer. The greater the insistence upon agnatic descent and the political importance of the solidarity of agnates, the more must this distasteful aspect of dependence assert itself.

Among the Dinka, on the other hand, although the beliefs surrounding agnation and agnatic descent are strong, they do not manifest themselves with such political force as among the Nuer. The Dinka have relatively more descent groups than the Nuer and also recognise that they lack the Nuer capacity to unite on a wide scale. In other words, the ties of agnatic loyalty are not so strong that they make for an expanding area of conflict involving successively larger groups. The value of agnatic descent is important but not so intense, and as a consequence the relations between affines are more equal and reciprocal than among the Nuer. Dr Lienhardt tells us:

> 'The maternal uncle is regarded as the guardian of his sister, and in Dinka thought it is to his maternal uncle that a boy is grateful for the provision of his mother. The Dinka remark frequently that the maternal uncle also has married with his nephews' father's cattle. Hence, in the Dinka way of thinking, when two families have a marriage between them, each has provided the means for the continuation of the other. Each is in this respect the source of the life and growth of the other.'

It is in accordance with this that the sub-clans which provide the core of the Dinka tribes are spoken of primarily as 'mother's brothers' and that among the Dinka we do not find a distinction equivalent to that between *diel* and *rul*. For the Dinka the relationship between the mother's brother and his sister's son is regarded as a model of friendship, whereas among the Nuer certain restraints, such as the fear of the mother's brother's curse, mark the relationship.

The hypothesis here sketched out is that it is the Nuer insistence upon the unifying value of agnatic descent and upon the lineage as 'we' group that gives birth to the category distinction *diel/rul*, and that because they see descent, not descent *and* marriage, as the unifying force that welds them into a people in opposition to all others the same distinction, in the form *nath/jaang*, is operated when they think of themselves as a united people. The Dinka certainly regard some peoples as scarcely 'people' at all, but they are able to tolerate a wider category of the human precisely because their 'we' groups are less precise and simple than those of the Nuer. Significantly Lienhardt tells us:

'When we speak of "the Dinka", we represent the people as a totality, known from the outside, so to speak, and, to the extent that they are all Dinka, all equally differentiated from those who are not Dinka. No Dinka knows his whole people in this way, unless he has received education and been given opportunity to travel. A Dinka knows, not *the* Dinka, but "Dinka"—"some" Dinka; not *the* Nuer, but "Nuer", and so on. So, when the Dinka speak of "Dinka", *jieng*, they cannot have in mind all Dinka, as we know them to be . . . they know only that their land is vast, and their people innumerable.'

Is it possible that a sharp categorical distinction between first- and second-class humans is associated with a rigorous identification of the 'we' group and an insistence upon internal loyalty ? To return to the Mundurucu, we are told:

'Despite the diversity of their local and lineal origins, the men of the village and ultimately the whole tribe were expected to maintain harmonious and co-operative relationships. Co-operation in economic activities transcended the minimal necessities of their ecological adaptation and any show of aggression between men was strictly forbidden . . . tribal feeling was highly developed and conflict between villages was totally absent.'

And again:

'Open arguments are rare among Mundurucu males . . . physical violence is almost unheard of. The Mundurucu look on such behaviour as a white man's trait and consider it to be repulsive among "people".'

It is possible that the new emphasis created by Shaka upon a *national* unity by identification of all his conquered peoples with the original Zulu clan is perhaps to be associated with his repudiation of Nguni ethics of warfare. The Sioux were not peculiar among the Plains Indians in that they regarded themselves as superior to everyone else in the world; nevertheless the evidence suggests that their sense of cultural identity was rather more intense than that of others. They were notorious for their scalp raiding outside the circle of related Dakota tribes and did not hesitate to take the scalps of women.

The reference to Shaka draws our attention to another factor enforcing a strong sense of group identity making for a devaluation of 'they'. We saw how Dingiswayo and later Shaka recruited their regiments on the basis of age and established them in barracks up and down what came to be called Zulu land (p. 140 seq.). By this device all men under forty were cut off from their tribal affiliations and simultaneously divided from each other both by the separation of barracks and by distinctive insignia—dress and colours. Each regiment became therefore a strong 'we' group and all were united solely by their dependence upon Shaka. Deprived of localised tribal customs and rites, the separate age-regiments united in terms of the idiom provided by Shaka and identified themselves as 'We—the Zulu'.

One possible lesson to be learned from Zulu history is that, either by manipulation or as a result of unforeseen circumstances, powerful 'we' groups can emerge in society such that the sense of identity is unmitigated, or only slightly mitigated, by cross-cutting ties. Whether spontaneous or contrived, this emergence can produce a state of internecine conflict, more or less severe, or be manipulated by any force which is able to play upon the organising principles of such groups. In our own society rapid technological change combined with a belief in 'progress' in almost every area—athletics, aesthetics, morality, intelligence, politics—has produced generation phenomena such that each generation and sub-generation tends to its own view of what is 'normal' in these various fields and others. Other ties—kinship, class, political affiliation—prevent a major fission in society; yet who could deny that the emergence of generations as social categories has modified the tactics of commercialists, politicians, religious leaders and the like? In societies tending towards totalitarianism the heightening of generational conflict seems an almost necessary phase of evolution. Generations are, of course, not the only social categories which can become the exclusive, or almost exclusive, reference groups: what used to be called the. 'old school tie' or 'old boy' network is another, as indeed are all 'we' groups that tend to eliminate, weaken or systematically devalue the cross-cutting demands of other possible reference groups.

The most potent 'we' group in the modern world is the nation. It is safe to say that for the vast majority the nation is regarded as the largest social and political unit. Even though great enter-prises are undertaken in the name of the United Nations these are, nevertheless, still dependent upon the goodwill of the nations that participate in them who can, if they wish, withdraw their support from any particular enterprise. Many people would go further and argue not only that the nation is the largest poli-tical unit of the modern world but also that it is the *natural* one. This is understandable, because the history of the twentieth century is largely the history of the growth of nationalism. All shades of liberal opinion agree in approving the development of national independence movements, and a yet wider range of political opinion would regard national sovereignty as an un-questionable right. Disputes may no doubt occur as to the interpretation of national sovereignty, but the claim that such a right exists is seldom questioned.

From the point of view of practical politics these ideas probably work well enough. Despite much rhetoric about the 'brotherhood of man', international law and justice, it remains the case that the largest units capable of actually enforcing law by the application of sanctions are the independent nations into which the world is divided. The word 'law' in the phrase 'international law' cannot have the same significance as it does in day-to-day usage, to the extent that we cannot speak of international police and international courts maintained and supported by supra-national power.

But what is a nation? The *Oxford English Dictionary* tells us that it is 'An extensive aggregate of persons, so closely associated with each other by common descent, language, or history, as to form a distinct race or people, usually organised as a separate political state and occupying a definite territory.' It adds 'In early examples the racial idea is usually stronger than the political; in recent use the notion of political unity and independence is more prominent.' This, in fact, is a very careful summary of the various meanings that the word 'nation' has had through the centuries rather than a definition. The word derives from the Latin *natio*, meaning a being born, a birth. By extension it came to mean a race, tribe or stock. Roman writers on political matters such as Caesar, Cicero and Tacitus often tended to use the word in this extended sense in a somewhat derogatory manner to refer to people who were either unorganised or uncivilised according to Roman standards—in our terms, 'they'. With this connotation of inferiority the word 'nation' was easily equated with the word 'tribe', which had suffered a similar degradation; from meaning originally a third part of the Roman people it came to be synonymous with the common people or the masses. Thus from the earliest times we find that the terms 'nation' and 'tribe' are almost interchangeable, and both imply inferiority and some idea of common origin or descent. Writing of the British and German peoples, Tacitus tends to use the word 'nation' in a racial sense, as when, for example, he is describing the various racial types that were to be found in Britain; he tends to use the word 'tribe' to refer to more discrete political and military sections of the population having their own customs, although he sometimes also refers to these peoples as 'nations'. What is striking about these early historians is that, although they refer to the 'nations' or 'tribes' as living in particular territories, these words do not themselves connote a distinct territory having its own boundaries as, I think, the modern word 'nation' does.

I have given these brief notes on the history of the word because I think it would be correct to say that, despite the *OED* reference to a later emphasis on political rather than racial unity, popular usage still confuses the two. I can only suggest that the reader check my opinion by examining the way in which the word is used, mostly by politicians. Such an analysis is not easy, but it is revealing because you will find that there is seldom a clear distinction between those who think of the nation as essentially a racial unity and those who think of it as a political construct: one and the same speaker will shift the emphasis according to the context without, I suggest, being conscious of the shift. A typical example would be the following: 'In the current atmosphere of world economic crisis there is a greater need than ever before for national unity, and I am confident that the character of the British people will respond readily to this challenge as it has always done.'

Although politicians are wonderfully vague in their failure to define the unit that they aim to govern, there is a certain degree of consistency in this vagueness. You will find that, regardless of political complexion, those who most frequently lay their emphasis upon the *racial* identity of the nation will also tend to regard the nation as the largest *natural* political unit possible. For such people a problem also emerges about the definition of 'citizenship' or 'nationality' when foreigners wish to settle in the country. This is all quite understandable because at the heart of the racial definition lies an unexpressed assumption that the members of a nation constitute a family in the modern Western sense—a biological unit. Thus we speak of the White and the Black nations and tend to think that the distinction is meaningful.

The association of nation with race is as much an historical product, though more recent, as the association of nation with a defined territory. It could be argued that the former is potential in the development of the latter. Older polities were based on marriage alliances between descent groups, and the claim to territory was based on the membership of the kin group in this broad sense. Even after the establishment of monarchies, and even constitutional monarchies, the idea lingered on that marriages between the royal families of Europe had political implications. However, the idea of the nation as essentially a territory had been growing stronger over the centuries and in the twentieth century became pragmatically the dominant defining principle.

Nevertheless it looks as though European man could not completely satisfy his basic need for a 'we' group by identification with territory alone; the principle of descent in the form of racialism emerged to give an apparently 'natural' basis for the occupation of territory. Racialism—the belief that distinct races exist and that cultural and personality traits are physiologically determined—has grown slowly from the late sixteenth century in Europe and gathered strength as the theological belief in the common descent of man from Adam and Eve weakened. Even Christian theorists were able to tolerate racialist inquiries by taking refuge, if not literally in Noah's Ark, then in the story of what occurred after the Flood had subsided. Noah cursed his son Ham and made him the servant of his brothers Shem and Japhet. By identifying any races as the descendants of Ham, theological grounds could be found for discrimination and subordination.

As the belief that the Bible represented true history was discredited, science, the new authority, moved to offer a firm base for racialism. In 1735 the influential botanist Linnaeus divided the genus man into two species, *homo sapiens* and *homo monstrosus*, the former being divided into five varieties and the latter into six. Both Europeans and Africans were dignified by inclusion in the species *sapiens*, but the Europeans were described as fair and sanguine, covered with close vestments and governed by laws, whereas the African was black and phlegmatic, anointed himself with grease and was governed by caprice. In the nineteenth century the relation between race and nationality was more firmly established. In 1832, for example, the future secretary of the Ethnological Society of Paris, Victor Courtet, proposed the following panacea for peace in Europe:

'I say that the crisis in Europe will not cease until its different societies are re-composed so as to display natural inequalities, or racial differences more or less marked. I am not putting forward an opinion which will offend feelings of human dignity; I am proclaiming a fact which has been verified in the annals of all the peoples of the world.'

In 1842 Thomas Arnold of Rugby maintained that Germany was

'the land of our Saxon and Teutonic forefathers; the land un- corrupted by any Roman or other mixture; the birth place of the most moral races of men that the world has yet seen—of the soundest laws—the least violent passions and the fairest domestic and other virtues.'

Between 1853 and 1857 Arthur de Gobineau published his *Essay on the Inequality of Human Races*, which provided a racial- ist theory of the character of nations:

'The white race originally possessed the monopoly of beauty, intelligence, and strength, by its union with other varieties hybrids were created, which were beautiful without strength, strong without intelligence, or if intelligent, both weak and ugly.'

Gobineau's theories became notorious in the twentieth century when they were distorted and used in Nazi Germany. In his own time, however, he was only representative of a general line of thought. He himself never maintained, for example, that any race could be pure, and he argued that his ruling race, the whites, had been diluted by 'inferior' blood for over 2000 years. The pervasiveness of racialist thinking is illustrated by the reaction of some French academics to the bombardment of Paris by the Prussians in 1870. As a later scholar was to point out, both the Germans and the French at that time regarded themselves as the descendants of the 'pure noble race of Aryan conquerors' and each maintained that they had Aryanised the other. The shelling of the Paris Museum and other scientific institutions seemed to the French academics clear evidence that the perpetrators could not be the representatives of the 'Teutonic family', and sug- gested rather that the Prussians must be not true Germans but descendants of a mixture of Fins and Slavs: 'the jealous hatred of the semi-barbarians for a superior civilisation' was manifest in the manner in which they conducted warfare. German newspapers and German academics reacted with opposing theories and an academic row developed across Europe that rumbled on to the end of the century.

The high tide of *academic* racialism is over but, like any flood, it has changed the landscape and left pools and puddles behind it. Many people in our own society continue to believe in a rather vague sort of way that cultural differences are somehow related to physical differences, and this the reader can amply confirm by keeping his ears and eyes open. While I was writing the early chapters of this book I was astounded one evening when the usually benign landlord of my 'local' exploded in anger against the Maltese on the grounds that they were 'a bastard race'. He had, it emerged, been to school with several Maltese children. In other societies racialist theories inform government policies in various ways, even though the racialist element is concealed with cover theories about educational or property qualifications.

Racialism has been absorbed in a variety of ways into Western belief systems and simultaneously vulgarised by reduction to a simple discrimination based on skin colour. It is obvious that the simple perception of physical difference can, when all moral and cultural considerations are set aside, become a powerful symbol for rallying together people, otherwise very different, into a 'we' group which is easily identified over against an equally recognisable 'they'. It is possible, indeed, that the more mobile and internally differentiated an industrial society becomes, the more it is capable of uniting itself on the simple criterion of skin colour. This capability may be strengthened in times of crisis when the need for an unambiguous 'we' is associated with the need to identify the sources of misfortune, the sorcerers in our midst. This is what occurred in Germany in the 1930s, and post-war events in the United States of America have established the phrase 'witch-hunt' in the vocabulary of politicians and journalists.

Racialism feeds a xenophobic tendency which flows inevitably from man's nature as a social being. The outsiders, 'they', people other than us, are everywhere, according to social circumstances the butt for jokes, the object of criticism or the focus of hate. And yet, as the history of the growth of nations teaches us, this tendency is opposed by the countervailing drive towards co-operation. As a result of population growth and movement, the expansion of systems of communication and the development of common needs, the sense of being 'we' can expand to embrace others hitherto thought of as constituting an exclusive 'they'.

But there is nothing inevitable in this process: the more entrenched, ramified and monolithic the 'we' group, the more it is conceived of as 'natural', the less amenable will it be to this kind of modification by expansion. The saying quoted at the beginning of this chapter recognises in the form of a joke a mildly paranoid proclivity in individualism. Carried to an extreme, such an attitude would indeed be pathological. Do you think that circumstances have emerged or could in which the concept of a national identity might be so described?

# Appendix

## Essay A

1 One of the most features of my society is the complex division of labour which it has evolved. This division of labour binds each group to the others because they are interdependent. The essential requirements for survival—food and shelter—are looked upon as something to be provided by specialised groups in exchange for money. We have evolved a system where it is necessary for only certain groups to possess the necessary skills and resources. The education of most people in the society does not include the learning of these skills but a bond of dependence is created between those who do not have them and those that do. I am not prevented from acquiring such skills but like many others, I have chosen to be educated in a different way and to fulfil a different role in society to that of builder or farmer. Improvements in technique and technological advancements create the need for a new category of people to master them and transmit them to others. Usually those possessing certain skills or who are educated in a particular field are made responsible for the practice and transmission of their own special knowledge or skills. By selling our own talents and labour, we are able to buy the special skills and labours of others. We fulfil a certain need in society, and rely on other people to fulfil the rest.

2 In the field of education, children are taught by a series of educational specialists and only in very early childhood are children left in the complete care of their parents. However,

educational specialists are encouraging parents to send young children (three years old) to nurseries and organised play groups as an 'essential' part of their education. From the age of five the main part of one's education is left to trained specialists. My education was gained mainly through books and the formal learning at school. My mother having left school at fourteen was soon inadequate to help me in any academic way. Domestic skills, not taught in schools, were learnt from her but haphazardly by watching her rather than instruction. My mother's fourth child was born when I was twelve years old. This gave both me and my elder brother an opportunity to learn about the rearing of a young child through observation and practical experience. This opportunity was exceptional amongst our friends who mostly belonged to smaller families in which the children had been born within two or three years of each other and had no real experience of bringing up young children. Formal education does not deal with this aspect of life and few middle-class children have the opportunity to observe closely for themselves. Contact with my father has always been so restricted it has been difficult to learn very much from him. His employment kept him from the house for as many as eleven hours a day and when at home he tended to watch television. This gathered us together in one room but by its nature prevented much conversation.

3 The formal education I received was at northern single-sex grammar school. Here middle-class values were stressed and praised. Loyalty, honesty, obedience and endeavour were strongly recommended to the pupils. The staff demanded a high standard of conformity to middle-class values and culture. Any show of nonconformity was punished by a general harshening of staff attitudes, less interest in a child's academic achievements and subjecting her to such ridicule as wearing a beret in school throughout the day. The school was an institution for education in middle-class culture. It tried to restrict all intrusions of popular sub-cultures by

controlling such manifestations as hairstyles, clothes and books. They commended only those creative works classed by the middle class as works of art. It is reasonable to suggest that works of art have no single common characteristic other than being called a work of art. But our category of works of art only contains those works preferred by the dominant class. To exercise its social superiority it evolves a vocabulary which suggests that the works that they prefer have objective value and they pay enormous sums of money for works of art. Their vocabulary is very pervasive and schools commend it and its category of works of art rather than popular music or comics. The school serves as institution for conserving this middle-class culture.

4 My circle of friends has to large extent been determined by educational establishments. At infant and primary schools I formed friendships with children of widely varying ability and, within the district, of wide social background except for those who attended private schools. When we were split into ability groups to go to secondary school, I soon ceased to know or speak to the friends who had not gone to the same school. I associated with those that had, for another two years especially those who lived near me. However, streaming at the end of the first year made contact with old friends more difficult as new friends were made in the new group. In the sixth form, when division was by subject not ability, old friends reappeared and new friends made within the subject group. Now I know no one who attended infant school with me, one who attended primary school with me but was also in my sixth form. The rest of friends from school are those who took one of the same 'A' level subjects. Contact with them is becoming increasingly difficult as most of them are scattered over the country at educational institutions or in employment.

5 As I mentioned above, those educated in a particular field are made responsible for transmission of their special skills or

knowledge. The skills are learnt by participation in the work in apprenticeships or trainee schemes or by attending an educational establishment on day release or more permanently. Some institutions teach people to fill certain roles for example Sandhurst or a Police College. Others are created to educate people in certain fields—universities, colleges or polytechnics. People attend such institutions for the education it provides or sometimes to attain a degree or diploma which will act as 'ticket' to another sphere or higher level.

6 A larger proportion of young people are leaving the home environment for purposes of education and employment. Long periods spent some distance away can cause the weakening of family ties. When one sees relations for only short periods after long intervals, interests become widely diverged and there are few common binding experiences. Whereas those living closely together find it much easier to maintain close contact.

7 The Welfare State in which we live makes it less necessary to maintain large family groups with close emotional and economic ties. The family is not expected to support or even care for its old and infirm. Contributions are made by working people to the State system which provides homes or financial assistance to those who are too old, too ill or unable for other reasons to work. The parent–child contract has become weakened. The child is no longer expected to support its parents when they are no longer able to work. The parent is no longer expected to provide his child with an education, and if he refuses to bring up the child the state will take care of it. The eventuality of old age is provided for by contributions to the national pension scheme, insurance policies, investment and savings. Independence in old age is regarded as very desirable. Living in the house of one's child is thought to cause friction and to be detrimental to the young family. I do not, therefore, expect to provide for my parents' old age even though they have supported me for nearly twenty years

of my life. It is not necessary to make provision for them in my plans for the future. This does prevent the possibility of parents becoming a burden or liability to their children but can cause many single old people to feel isolated and lonely especially when the family has left the district and they are not incorporated into any group.

8 The feeling of mutual responsibility between employer and employee is disappearing as relations in industrial and business organisations become increasingly impersonal. This development must be due, to a large extent, to the size of such institutions which are created in preference to smaller less efficient ones. Mass production by such specialised industries is thought to be the cheapest and most efficient way to provide society with the commodities it needs. Efficiency and cheapness are the goals of most producers. Small local shops are becoming increasingly more rare as they are replaced by large supermarkets with few assistants. The reduction in personal service and the benefit gained by bulk buying make prices slightly lower and thus for some people the supermarkets are more attracted. In such shops, the large and constantly changing body of customers are not recognised or known by the staff and in large firms the large numbers of workers are often little more than working parts in a massive system, who are not treated as individual human beings. The personal contact between individuals in such places is automatic and superficial.

9 But economic growth is the goal of many of the politicians who govern in our society. Increased productivity and increased buying power can raise the standard of living. That the standard of living should be constantly improving is the desire of most people in this society. This means to them a larger and improved set of material goods—houses each having a fridge, television set and a central heating system. However these improved material standards do not always guarantee a qualitative improvement in life. People do not

always enjoy living in a brand new house if other needs are not satisfied. The increase in delinquency, and depression in housewives on new housing estates tend to suggest that material well-being is not the complete solution.

10 The people who make the decisions in the governing of the society are chosen in elections by the people. Amongst themselves they form a power hierarchy. They rule in the name of the people not for themselves. The system of our government rests on the assumption that they make decisions which benefit the majority of people and not in any way for their own personal ends. One chooses the representative whose ideas correspond most closely to one's own, if any do. Their success is judged by the amount of things they do which please the majority of people.

11 Offenders against the laws made by the government for society are caught, judged and punished by groups of people who represent society. Society takes responsibility for the actions taken, not any person or groups of people. The actual people who carry it out are seen merely as representatives of the impersonal body and their actions when they are fulfilling the representational role, are expressed as the actions of society not as the actions of them as individual human beings. It is the will of society not theirs personally that a certain punishment should be carried out.

12 Such specialists as judges are made necessary by the size of our society and made possible by high degree of social organisation which has evolved and in which we all play a part.

## Essay B

1 In every society the individual has a specific role or roles,

which he must perform to an accepted standard to become a member of his society. As Goffman suggests, in his book *Presentation of Self in Everyday Life*, the performance of these roles often becomes an act for the individual, and his true self is not displayed to his audiences. These roles can be considered in two parts: the personal role which involves the individual's 'style' associated with the individual's 'name label'; and the societal role such as acting as a citizen of a town which involves conforming to local customs etc. We can witness that the personal role is altered to fit different audiences, and the 'name label' can be altered to fit differing performances, by the use of full titles or nick-names.

2 The social structure of the British Isles is greatly orientated around advanced technology and urban life, although in more remote areas folk-like cultural characteristics can be observed. The crafting community of the Shetland Island studied by Goffman shows a folk-like culture: a traditional way of life associated with specific occupations, but even here the urban culture has had some effect, for example many young men now work for higher wages in factories, although they still wear traditional crofter's clothes to show they are still part of the community. The presence of this sub-cultural variability must always be borne in mind when viewing the society of Britain as a whole.

3 In most areas of our society we can find the horizontal division of society into social classes, arising from members having different access to resources and positions of power. This division has been observed by Goffman in the Shetland Island, and anyone living in an urban community can notice it for themselves. This division can lead to much stress if an individual is not satisfied with the societal role he is playing as a member of a certain class, and wishes to change his position. He will have to change from one group of people to another, and must first go through the process of proving himself acceptable to the group he wishes to join.

4 There are many kinds of social groups of which the individual may be a member: residential, kinship, peer groups, social groups and institutions, all of which can vary in formality and permanence. The members of a group will often maintain a team performance to present the desired image to their audience, they will also act differently with members of the group and outsiders. An example of such team performance is found by Goffman in Holcombe's *The Real Chinaman* who discusses price setting by appearance of the customer. 'One particular result of this study of a customer is seen in the fact that if a person enters a store in China, and, after examining several articles, asks the price of any one of them, unless it is positively known that he has spoken to but one clerk, no answer will be made by him to whom the question is put until every other clerk has been asked if he has named a price for the article in question to the gentleman. If, as very rarely happens, this important precaution is neglected, the sum named by different clerks will almost invariably be unlike, thus showing that they fail to agree in their estimates of a customer.'

5 The team performance can be guided in many ways, from glances exchanged between members, portraying encouragement or disapproval, to a complete pre-planned course of action. If the performer is concerned with presenting a certain image, for example parents entertaining guests, he will pick team mates who are reliable, and such members as children or those with little tact or intelligence will be excluded.

6 Although we are not always conscious of the fact, most people are members of some sort of group or team. The society itself can be considered as a large group, with sub-cultural variabilities. Even those individuals who consider themselves to have 'dropped out' of society, in fact only go to make up the group of people who do not wish to conform to the

society's standards, but who are, nevertheless, still part of society.

7 One of the most common groups in the British society is that of the family, and most members of the society, myself included, are associated with such a group. The family group can vary in size and 'closeness'; a whole family of three generations may live in the same house or district and form a close-knit group, or alternatively an individual may live in relative isolation with only his spouse and children. My own family group extends to close-knit ties between grandparents, parents and siblings, and to a lesser degree aunts, uncles and cousins. The behaviour in such a group obviously varies with the strength of the kinship bonds between individuals, temperaments and so on. There is usually a strong urge to protect this family group from outside intrusion and criticism, although open criticism is often allowed between group members. The family group will also act as a team to present an unreal image for visitors and outsiders, for example parents will not argue, children will behave, or meals will be served in formal surroundings instead of in the kitchen.

8 For a member of society, such as myself, a student, membership of many different groups or teams is involved. For many students the membership of two residential groups is unavoidable, one being the family 'home', the other being created by the environment of the university or college accommodation. The latter may take many forms, but often comprises of a number of colleagues forming a team, permanent or otherwise, which varies in the degree of cohesive interplay. From this division between 'home' and 'away' two social groups will develop possibly providing at least two or more teams of which the individual is a member. Further team membership may arise from religious or political affiliations.

9 Much common social interaction can be viewed as a dialogue betweén two such teams and their members, and many disruptions such as anger or embarrassment can occur if the situation ceases to be clearly defined, previously stated positions appear less tenable or the participants find themselves without a clearly defined course of action. Such disruptions can be more far reaching, and a team or member may find his 'real self' showing through the performance he is presenting for his audience.

10 From the observation of such teams functioning, class structures, communications and other aspects of the society as a whole, much can be learned of oneself in relation to this whole: aspects of behaviour which are easily recognised in others are less easily identified in oneself. In some cases the emphasis laid on team performance and social grouping can tend to reduce and obscure the role of the individual in society. In the British society the rights of the individual to 'act his own part' is still respected to some extent, but even an individual performing the supposedly uninhibited role of a student is expected to conform to social conventions to some extent, and this can tend to obliterate the 'real self' in favour of the social front.

# Essay C

1 I think the task of writing about myself and my society is a rather difficult one and I have doubts as to whether I will be able to do justice to the subject. My difficulty occurs because I see elements of society, especially if one has lived for a considerable time in a large cosmopolitan city, as complex and multidirectional and as a result quite frequently not very well defined. However I still consider that the basis of my society is the class system and that these structures are correspondingly perpetuated by the type of educational

system in operation in this country. In terms of job opportunity educational qualifications are a definite advantage and equally so one's job tends to determine one's place in the social system.

2 The introduction of the comprehensive system of education is still in its infancy in Britain and one cannot yet see the advantages (or in some people's eyes the disadvantages) of this type of training. Society is still affected by the public, grammar and secondary modern type system. The attitudes and values expressed in schools are essentially middle-class ones—Michael Carter in his book *Into Work* demonstrates that the working-class child experiences conflict during school life because of the values experienced in their own lives as against those they are expected to assume within the school system and it is a similar conflict I have experienced although from a slightly different point of view. My initial schooling up to the age of eleven was in a convent in this country and then my family emigrated to Canada where I went to an undenominational High School. I was now associating with other children from varying backgrounds and for the first time for me from varying religions. I was to experience a widening of my attitudes and thinking which I believe is reflected in how I see my social environment today.

3 The increasing complexity of life created by industrialisation and technology is also manifested in the greater mobility of people within the class system. A change in a person's life style generally assures that the children, having benefited from a higher education than the parents, will assume a different role in the system. Referring back however to the beginning of my essay I consider that this new identification is more difficult to see in large cities than it would be in smaller and more compact communities. In my own case my circle of friends ranges across many groups of race, religion and class and I think this diversity makes it difficult for me to identify solely with one group. I believe that this is a

desirable situation and that greater convergence of groups is an ideal that society should aim for in its endeavour towards a greater process of humanisation.

4 Within my society changes are occurring with the meeting of various groups from other countries and the British people. Fears are expressed that the 'British way of life' is in danger of being overtaken by 'foreign' influences emanating from the various nationalities now living here. However the 'British way of life' is not always seen in similar lights—winter in the Caribbean and skiing in St Moritz is an entirely different way of life to a family of eight in two rooms without sanitary facilities. British people have generally accepted, often without realising or questioning, that there are already many ways of life in this country.

5 Which way of life, one asks, is going to be changed by these 'foreign' influences? Preferably one would hope that people will come to accept that instead of taking away from life here the various groups of new citizens will be adding to it and thereby making it richer. British people now have to face the realisation that they are becoming a multi-racial society—for the majority they are facing for the first time an experience of different cultures. The possibility that a new class group called 'immigrant' could arise, if in fact it has not already embedded itself, is a cause for great concern and one that any society should guard against. People do now have greater opportunities to experience other cultures and this can lead towards breaking down the barriers of fear and ignorance. Mostly for the British people the cultures previously experienced have been on a similar pattern to their own—however the increasing opportunities for people to travel within other countries and experience customs different to their own could lead towards a greater respect of other people's attitudes and values resulting from those customs.

6 Further changes have occurred within the last ten years or so affecting my social environment caused by 'pop' culture. I think for young people unable to find a group identity within the traditional class system 'pop' has become the new life style. Dress and language have taken on a different appearance causing friction on the one hand from the older generation group who find it difficult to understand these changes and on the other from the younger generation group who feel a greater identity with their peers than their parents. However the kinship system in my society does not hold the same prominence as it does in a small-scale communities and as a result the social relationships established take on a different form. This possibly explains why younger people do not feel bound to adhere to the patterns of life established by their parents.

7 Education in any society plays a crucial role today and is of no less importance in my own. Alexander King writing in an article in the *Listener* 1.9.1966 so aptly sums up the present situation in a way that I could not that I'm taking the liberty of quoting what he says—'Until recently the process of education, with its mixture of cultural and vocational aims, has been conceived mainly as transmitting accumulated experience to the young in order to provide them with a knowledge of the nature and history of their society, together with sufficient background information to enable them to acquire later the skills, both intellectual and manipulative, that they will need throughout a productive career. Within the slowly evolving societies of the past this approach has provided continuity and made progress possible. But since the end of the War all this has altered. Social, economic and indeed political evolution have been rapid, spurred on by an explosive rate of technological change. And this is just the beginning of a process of change that will last at least to the end of the century when those now entering school will be at the peak of their careers. In such changed circumstances the assimilation of new concepts and information has become too slow and, in

fact, traditional education tends more and more to transmit the ideas of the past rather than of the present to prepare young people for life in a rapidly vanishing world and not for the future.' Five years later this point of view is even more valid. How are people to adjust to increasing change in their lives brought on by highly advanced technology. In a conference I attended last autumn on Cybernetics and its effects on society, one of the speakers stated that in the next fifty years we will acquire more knowledge than we have since time began. As a result of this knowledge explosion people are going to need to be trained and retrained at least two or three times in their industrial lives. My own view is that not enough resources are being allocated to these needs. The difficulties experienced by a man in his forties coping with new ideas and methods are self-evident and the retraining programmes quite frequently do not meet this type of need. Fear of the changes brought on by advances in methods is a real problem that I do not believe we have started to cope with. Increasingly the worker feels an even greater alienation from his work and as a result can find no identity within his industrial set up. Education could play an important role in alleviating this problem of fear of the future. Training programmes in industry, if well run, can open up for many people aspects of their own talents that hitherto have not been cultivated because of educational deprivation at an earlier age.

8 My own situation is part of this educational dynamic. As part of my work at London Airport I witnessed the problems associated with those peoples attempting to gain access to this country on a semi-permanent or permanent basis. My initial incredulity at the desire of whole families or individual members of a family—thus breaking up family units—wishing to enter and make their home here changed from pity to elements of respect and admiration. Why should an apparently happy Indian family, for example, tear itself from a presumably deep-rooted supportive friendly environment

to jump into a totality of meaningless cultural contradictions where everything but everything shrieked hostility. Economists and personnel directors propound the dogma of 'human inertia' as being the planners' greatest problem in terms of innovation and change. Implicit in this notion of human inertia is the reluctance of geographic migration as exemplified by such groups as the ship builders of the North East of the country; the coal miners of South Wales; the dock-workers of the North West or the families of say East London. If this is a particular human phenomenon, reluctance to move away from house, friends, etc., why are so many Indian, Pakistanis, and West Indian families disregarding this 'human' dynamic? It would be arrogant to attempt to explain the insistence of other peoples to remain in this country as indicative of cultural superiority. Yet, again, to look for one particular cause of this apparent cultural suicide would indicate a purely superficial understanding of the frightening powerful forces at work.

9 As stated above I feel a part of this potent force that uproots people from their known environments into totally alien environments. I don't pretend to be able to provide one set of answers to the reasons behind this international migration but I perceive what I think are similar desires on both sides to attain, for want of a more suitable phrase, a 'better' way of life. Better in this case, not to be thought of in terms of superiority but as an advancing and widening of one's horizons.

## Essay D

1 My present position in my society is one which depends upon both my past and my upbringing, and the future as I see it in terms of my hopes and projections.

2 An essay of this type must to some extent be an historical essay since my childhood is, as I am aware, extremely important and any interpretation of my relationship with society today would be futile without any knowledge of my inculturation.

3 The first fifteen years of my life was spent with my parents in a council flat in south-east London. Looking back on these years the principal feeling that comes to mind is one of security. Our flat was one of some two thousand that constituted the estate on which we lived. Even the design of the estate was such that one felt enclosed by the blocks of flats which formed a square enclosing a lawn (albeit a decimated one scattered with air-raid shelters), and a large concrete area which was a playing area, parking area and contained many posts between which lines were strung for the drying of washing. It was a very close-knit community, everybody being at least on nodding terms with everybody else, and usually everyone knew everyone else's business. As a child I had among my neighbours a number of aunts and uncles; that is these were adult friends of the family who were very close to my parents. These people formed a distinct category, as it seems in retrospect, of whom and towards whom distinctive types of behaviour were expected. For instance one always ran errands for them without expecting or accepting if proffered any reward; one always received Christmas and birthday presents from them; also one could always rely on them for shelter and supervision in the absence of one's parents.

4 The other main feature of my childhood which contributes to the impression of security that I have is the 'gang'. The gang was really quite simply all the children in the estate between the ages of seven and the age when one's interest in girls passes from the realm of masturbatory fantasy to a desire for actual contact—usually about fourteen years of age. The gang fulfilled the needs of the children in three

ways: firstly it gave one a sense of belonging, each member knowing his place in the hierarchy based on guile and fighting ability; secondly it provided recreation for its members, the year being divided into distinct 'seasons'—the cart season, the football season, the fag-card and the conker seasons; thirdly and most importantly the gang was the source of one's attitudes and ideas, for instance I was smoking two or three cigarettes daily at the age of ten and knew the rudiments of sex at the age of about eight, I even remember announcing to my parents that I would be refraining from attending Sunday School on the grounds that I had become an atheist at the age of eight. The gang had few rules but those that it did have were strictly enforced, the supreme crime being to 'split' on someone, i.e. if you were caught for some offence to give the name of your accomplices; although we were not above even stealing lead from church roofs and selling it to scrap-metal merchants if the need for pea-shooters or fireworks was pressing enough.

5 The first change in my life which affected me to no small extent was my passing of the 11 plus and my admission to a (locally at least) highly esteemed grammar school. The reaction to this on the estate was quite astounding, my peers in the gang treated me with a mixture of admiration and contempt whilst my mother was given advice as to how I was in danger of finding my home 'not good enough for me any more', and becoming a snob. Indeed with the pressure of homework and other commitments the style of my life did change, but not my outlook and for some time I was very sorry for myself. However at school there were some five or six people in the same position as myself, that is they were working class children in a school which catered for mainly middle-class children, most of the pupils commuted from the suburbs to the school in Southwark whereas we walked to school.

6 This small group constituted my peer group now, and as was
   pointed out on several occasions we had 'chips on our
   shoulders'. We never quite fitted into the school properly, we
   scorned book-work but all did well in games, we despised the
   suburban kids but secretly wished we lived in the suburbs.
   This period was extremely important and it affected us in
   different ways; for although now I lived under the same
   conditions and was subject to the same kind of influences as
   middle-class teenagers at school, I still maintained the
   expectations as my former friends in the gang. These
   expectations were as follows: from sixteen to eighteen or
   nineteen one sowed as many wild oats as possible, drinking,
   sexual promiscuity were to be indulged in as often as possible
   and there was a great deal of influence attached to how one
   appeared, i.e. in terms of dress, particularly appearing 'clean-
   cut and smart' (an attitude still to be found among 'skin-
   heads' who in the main come from backgrounds similar to
   mine); after this period of seeing the world one found a girl
   with a view to becoming engaged and then married. It was
   essential that this girl was a virgin and that she at least
   was seen to remain so until you were married. Engagement
   was essential and so was a church wedding followed by a 'good
   do', which in practice meant saving for several years in order
   that one's relatives and friends could first fill themselves with
   food and then with free drink. This pattern is or was accepted without question by us and our contemporaries of the
   opposite sex and sure enough it fulfilled itself or at least in
   some cases—almost.

7 I was engaged two months after leaving school, my fiancée
   who was older than me paying for the ring. This also
   happened to my friends most of whom went on to get
   married. However after leaving school I discovered George
   Orwell and began to 'think'. My interests widened immediately and my desire to just get married and find a 'good' job
   waned. Within a year of being engaged and after many more
   stimulating books, we broke up. I decided to try to go to

university and the girl—nothing daunted—found another fiancée and within a year was married.

8 Having been completely uninterested at school my 'A' level grades were hopelessly inadequate to equip me for the University entrance race. I took H.N.C. in Biology and obtained a place at Aberystwyth but badly broke my leg and could not go. At this stage my mind was in a turmoil and I was completely disorientated, my old expectations and values were no longer adequate. A brief excursion into Marxism faded and even my passion for Science could not quell the storm in my head. Taking advantage of the time at my disposal (as I had now been offered a place at Sussex, my first choice), I took a job as a lorry-driver, not as a regular driver but as a spare on holiday. This job gave me plenty of spare time and I read avidly, trying to find a justification in *a priori* terms for the socialism that at the moment was based on emotional grounds. After reading many writers from Plato to Russell I learnt two things, that the safest position was one of Huxleyan agnosticism, and that Man was a paradox which seemed to be beyond the comprehension of any particular member of the species.

9 All of which brings to me the present. I now conceive of my society, in the sense of what is important to me, as being all of mankind and believe that there is a fundamental unity in Man which is capable of rationalising his affairs, but also believe that the likelihood of these potentialities being realised is almost non-existent. I see a society doomed to conflict because of the contradictions within it, contradictions which are exacerbated by the lack of shared expectations, and conflicting belief systems. One part of the world is disproportionately consuming the earth's resources and ensuring that there will be rapidly decreasing capability on the part of the earth to support life in the future, whilst the majority of the world still find it impossible to secure enough of the basic necessities today. In the face of mass starvation the right to

irresponsible conception still enjoys priority over the right to a full belly in which it laughingly called the list of basic human rights.

10 In my more immediate society i.e. 'Western Civilisation' I find even more grounds for fear and frustration. Consumption has become the objective in life, or rather to be seen to be consuming. The profit motive drives us to extremes of lunacy which to an impartial observer must be scarcely credible. Pragmatism is the ruling philosophy; 'what should be' is condemned by virtue of the fact that it is what we should be and not what is. The problem seems to be that changes in the environment which call for modifications in behavioural patterns are left unanswered. The result is that our society is becoming less and less integrated. The categories and plans, although not all of them, that we use today lead very often to hopelessly inappropriate responses. For instance when we think of a large corporation we expect it to maximise profit and/or growth and to do this at the expense of its rivals, and indeed they do this, now quite apart from the moral question this also leads to an even more controversial position. This is the question of pollution; each company will do as little as is legally possible (and, very often even less) to cut down on pollution because such measures are expensive and therefore cut down on return, and also because all the other corporations (abroad if not at home) will be trying to do the same; consequently the decimation of our land, sea and air carries on inexorably, a menace which will affect us all in a very great way in the not too-distant future.

11 Because of our attitudes to sex which still is greatly regarded as taboo, education on the subject is little more than laughable. The population increases in an alarming fashion despite the widespread malnutrition in the world. Volumes have been written on the biological effects on individuals of population excess, yet they remain in the specialist journals unread except by specialists. Because of the attitudes to sex which are

culturally inherited which condemn sex before marriage but in no way prevent it from occurring, serious attempts to educate children about pregnancy and VD, and ways of preventing conception are piecemeal if they are not thwarted entirely. The net result is not the prevention of sex before marriage, but the rendering of the sex that does take place, ill-equipped and irresponsible.

12 Other examples of inappropriate responses to situations in our society could have been quoted. It can be argued that what I have been attacking is not so much intransigence as a lag, since practice does in the end affect our beliefs. However this seems to me to be an academic argument since the danger is here waiting to be dealt with now, and time is getting short. The way in which lemmings control population may be effective but it is hardly rational, or at least it would be irrational, if the lemming had more effective and less painful ways of achieving the same ends at its disposal and yet did not use them. Man's plight is even more perilous since not all the lemming species jumps into the sea, a fate which is a distinct possibility for *Homo sapiens*.

13 A culture must be judged, if we are not going to remain too aloof or too pusillanimous to judge it, by the stability it exhibits and the scope and security it offers its members. Using these criteria it seems to me that the society in which I find myself is certainly found to be sadly, if not dangerously lacking.

# INDEX

*)*

# SOCIOLOGY

## J. H. Abraham

This book has been written to provide both the student and the general reader with a basic but comprehensive account of the principles and practice of sociology. Beginning with an historical narrative of the science from Plato to Comte and the modern theorists, the book goes on to outline the scope and methods of sociology. The author then discusses the basic sociological concepts such as social stratification, the family, the state, and social control and mobility, and examines their significance and interrelationship.

A clear, vivid, and frequently personal picture of both the development and the contemporary role of sociology, particularly useful for those approaching the subject for the first time, which does not avoid the problems inevitably raised by an investigation of social institutions. Now in a newly revised and extended edition.

# PSYCHOLOGY TODAY

## Contributing editor: W. E. C. Gillham

This book is a joint enterprise, having been written by members of a large and diverse university department of psychology. Each section covers a defined area of modern psychology, contributed by a specialist in that particular field, and presents a comprehensive survey in language no more technical than the subject-matter warrants. The areas themselves have been defined on arguable but conventional grounds which for a work of this introductory nature may constitute an advantage for the student. Designed as a basis for further study, the text incorporates lists of further reading throughout.

In this multi-level text, the material is presented so as to make it accessible to the general reader, to the student in secondary education whose course includes a psychology component, and to the student commencing a degree course in psychology. Above all, this book demonstrates that psychology today is a relevant and critical discipline, characterised by the broadening of its base as a science and by a radical extension of its practical applications in contemporary society.

# ANALYTICAL PSYCHOLOGY

## David Cox

There is no doubt of the immense value to be gained from an understanding of Jung, but it is a formidable task to begin a study of analytical psychology from his original works. The aim of this book is to make his ideas accessible at an introductory level and to establish the essential concepts of Jungian psychology.

The many conflicting views on psychology can often appear confusing to the student. This book meets this problem by outlining other contemporary theories before going on to discuss the principal concepts of Jungian psychology. But the central theme is the same as that which ran through Jung's life and work, a concern for the spiritual nature of man and his need for self-knowledge.

# PRINCIPLES AND PRACTICE IN MODERN ARCHAEOLOGY

## David Browne

This book is based on the belief that there is a certain body of data that is traditionally the concern of the archaeologist and that this can only be discovered and studied by archaeological means – and that therefore archaeology is as much a subject in its own right as history.

The book begins by establishing the framework within which archaeologists work, the concepts on which their activity is based, and then goes on to examine the ideas and methods current in modern archaeology. The techniques of finding and excavating an archaeological site are described, and separate chapters are devoted to the methodology of conservation of finds, on and off the site, and to the analysis of both organic and inorganic remains. The emphasis throughout is on the constantly advancing techniques of modern archaeology and on the necessity of developing expertise and professionalism in the field.

Anyone involved in archaeology, whether as a student or as an assistant at a 'dig', will find this book both relevant and informative. Above all it presents the major techniques of modern archaeology in such a way that can only increase archaeologists' understanding and enjoyment of their subject.